TAKING FIRE

TAKING FIRE

Saving Captain Aikman: A Story of the Vietnam Air War

KEVIN O'ROURKE AND JOE PETERS

CASEMATE
Philadelphia & Oxford

Published in the United States of America and Great Britain in 2013 by
CASEMATE PUBLISHERS
908 Darby Road, Havertown, PA 19083
and
10 Hythe Bridge Street, Oxford, OX1 2EW

ISBN 978-1-61200-126-5
Digital Edition: ISBN 978-1-61200-138-8

Cataloging-in-publication data is available from the Library of Congress and the British Library.

10 9 8 7 6 5 4 3 2 1

Printed and bound in the United States of America.

For a complete list of Casemate titles please contact:

CASEMATE PUBLISHERS (US)
Telephone (610) 853-9131, Fax (610) 853-9146
E-mail: casemate@casematepublishing.com

CASEMATE PUBLISHERS (UK)
Telephone (01865) 241249, Fax (01865) 794449
E-mail: casemate-uk@casematepublishing.co.uk

CONTENTS

DEDICATION

For the children and grandchildren of June 27, 1972.

FOREWORD

"I had to decide whether we should risk the loss of maybe a dozen airplanes and crews to get just one man out," General John W. Vogt, Jr. explained, as he reflected on the Oyster 01 Bravo SAR. "Goddamn it, the one thing that keeps our boys motivated is the certain belief that if they go down, we will do absolutely everything we can to get them out," he continued, "I just said, 'Go do it!'"

This quote from General Vogt, the 7th Air Force commander in 1972, shows the U.S. Air Force's commitment to rescuing its service members who are downed in combat. Even though I was the pilot of the helicopter that rescued Oyster 01 Bravo, I wasn't aware of the General's statement until I saw it in *Taking Fire.* Reading it made me cry.

Having been involved in several of the search and rescue missions (SARs) in this book, I thought I knew exactly what happened with each one. I was amazed to discover so much more about these missions by reading *Taking Fire.* The authors' research has been comprehensive and extensive. They spent years tracking down and getting interviews from the key players and even accessed archived information about the airplanes and helicopters involved in the SARs.

I first heard from Kevin O'Rourke in 1983 when he was working on his undergraduate degree at Framingham State University. I got a call from this inquisitive college student asking me questions about the 1972 rescue of Capt. Lynn Aikman, known as the Valent 04 Alpha mission. I gave him the short version of my role in the SAR. Kevin also contacted two other

Jolly Green crew members, copilot Rufus Hutchinson and PJ Chuck McGrath, as well as the survivor, Lynn Aikman. Since Kevin had conducted telephone interviews with all of us, we thought he had enough background for his project. But Kevin wasn't finished. Soon the four of us found ourselves on commercial airplanes to Boston, where a studio was set up to film interviews with us. Kevin told us he hoped that this project would lead to a larger product, such as a full-length documentary, movie or book. We were a bit skeptical.

But back then I didn't know about Kevin O'Rourke's determination and commitment. In 2012, I had been retired from the Air Force for nineteen years and living in Montana, when I got a call from Kevin telling me that he had revived this project. I was pleasantly surprised to learn that after three decades, a book was nearly finished and that other prospects were still cooking.

The importance of a book such as this and the manner in which it has been written is illustrated within the story itself. I had exchanged Christmas cards over the years with Lynn Aikman, the downed F-4E pilot, but I never had a chance to actually talk to him, even on the day we rescued him. I got that opportunity in 1982. Contained in *Taking Fire* is the story of when Lynn invited to his house the three Jolly Greens, Rufus Hutchinson, Chuck McGrath, and me, all stationed at the Pentagon at the time. It was ten years to the day that we had pulled Aikman out of a ravine in North Vietnam. That gathering was a chance for us to tell our stories to each other . . . for the first time. It was a seminal event that I'll never forget.

Now, through *Taking Fire*, readers will have a chance to share in this story. The authors have been able to responsibly weave the details of other missions with this SAR, giving the readers insight into the men involved in this rescue.

Chuck McGrath and Lynn Aikman maintained a close relationship over the years. That bond began with McGrath dragging the seriously injured Aikman down a steep slope through the jungle to the awaiting helicopter's rescue hoist. McGrath and Aikman endured eighteen minutes under fire on the ground, only to see the rescue-hoist cable sever and the helicopter fly away. My helicopter arrived four minutes later to make the second rescue attempt. As Lynn entered the hovering aircraft, his ankle was shattered by a bullet. After another ten minutes of taking fire, we got the hell out of there. To make matters worse, our two HH-53C helicopters, each carrying a wounded crew member and receiving battle damage, encountered a MiG that made a run on us on the way home. The full account of the SAR is pretty scary reading. It may be hard to believe. Even I had forgotten about the danger our two helicopters were in until I was reacquainted with the events through reading this book.

Keep in mind that the Jolly Green crews are not alone. They are led by the A-1H Sandy pilots who pinpoint the survivor's location and risk their lives "trolling" for ground fire, and then "beat back" or kill the enemy to allow the helicopters to pick up the survivor. Squadron commander Major Jim Harding, the A-1H pilot, was my idol and a legend within the A-1H community. He was the on-scene commander for many of the tough SARs. When anything endangered "his Jollies," he attacked them like a pit bull. You can bet that we Jolly Green pilots wanted him on our SARs.

All of the Jolly Green crew members describe their combat experience the day of the rescue. Major Leo Thacker and his crew weathered eighteen minutes of small arms fire at their hovering helicopter. Also featured is Captain Ben Orrell, who recovered Valent 03 Alpha earlier in the day. He had a total of thirteen rescues during his tour. Cool under fire, Ben was the finest Jolly Green pilot that I encountered during my tour. Known as "Gentle Ben," he had a lion's heart.

This particular SAR was a gathering of highly decorated and experienced crew members. Sergeant Chuck McGrath received the Air Force Cross, second only to the Medal of Honor, for his bravery in the rescue of Captain Aikman. The Jolly Green crew members and the A-1H pilots who flew on the two Valent SARs received four Air Force Crosses and over twenty-five Silver Stars, the nation's third highest medal for valor, during their combat tours.

Many SAR articles don't cover the "rest of the story;" however, *Taking Fire* does. The book describes the shoot-down of each aircraft and what happened to the crew members who got captured. Due to authors' persistence and attention to detail, there is a complete picture of what transpired on the various SARs and why.

"That Others May Live," is the fitting motto of Combat Air Rescue. General Vogt's statement of the U.S. Air Force's resolve and determination to save just one man, while risking both aircrews and aircraft, still holds true in today's rescue community. *Taking Fire* is one of the most comprehensive accounts ever written about a search and rescue mission.

DALE E. STOVALL, Brigadier General, USAF (Ret.)
July 2013

INTRODUCTION

On October 31, 1968, five days before the elections, President Lyndon Johnson announced a halt to America's bombing of North Vietnam. When newly elected President Richard Nixon takes office the following year, he continues the bombing moratorium. Three years later on March 30, 1972, the North invades South Vietnam in a massive attack that becomes known as the Easter Offensive. With American troops strength in Vietnam on the decline—from a peak of over 500 thousand in 1969 it will fall to under 25 thousand by the end of 1972 under Nixon's policy of Vietnamization—the president is loath to reinforce ARVN (Army of the Republic of Vietnam) with American ground combat forces. Airpower is a different story, however, and on April 4 the president authorizes bombing of the North up to the 18th parallel, a limit that will be extended over the coming days to include virtually the entire country.

As the air war heats up in the spring of 1972, so does the risk for Air Force aviators who are discovering that Hanoi has used the years of the bombing moratorium to greatly strengthen its formidable and sophisticated air defenses. In the two-week stretch from June 21 to July 5, the Air Force will lose more than twenty planes while only taking out four enemy MiGs.

The worst of these worst days for the Air Force may have been June 27, 1972, when four USAF F-4 Phantoms with eight crewmen, four pilots and four weapons systems officers (WSOs or backseaters, as they were called) were shot down.

What follows is the account of the rescue of one of these shot-down crewmen, a seriously injured pilot, by the Air Force's guardian angels: crews assigned to the 40th Air Rescue and Recovery Squadron. It is through this mission that we meet many of the significant characters and events of air rescues in Vietnam. In what seems to be a conspiracy of fate, a highly decorated cadre of airmen came together to bring one of their own back to safety. This singular day and this singular rescue link together a litany of aspects of the war, the rescue service, and the remarkable men and women who served in Southeast Asia.

In this story, which includes a pair of newlyweds serving their country, we learn about the willingness of members of America's armed forces to put their lives at risk because, as they emphasize to this day, it was their mission. But it is also clear that as their homeland churned with protest and their politicians engaged in bickering about how to achieve President Nixon's goal of peace with honor, there was a bond among these professionals that was very personal. From the most heralded fighter pilot down to the most junior enlistee, duty was not just to the mission but to each other.

CHAPTER ONE

THE LONG RIDE IN

United States Air Force Sgt. Chuck McGrath awoke on June 27, 1972, much the same way he had throughout his tour of Southeast Asia. As a member the 40th Aerospace Rescue and Recovery Squadron (40th ARRS), the twenty-three-year-old McGrath knew that the only guarantee of the forthcoming day was that it would not be the same as the previous one.

The Sikorsky HH-53C helicopter was the workhorse of rescue operations in Southeast Asia. During such a mission the aircraft's flight engineer would have to lean out the door of the aircraft to guide the hoist line and forest penetrator, a device for lowering pararescuemen and retrieving survivors. During these moments the flight engineer would be in constant contact with the pilot, giving positioning updates.—*National Archives*

By rank, McGrath is a sergeant, an enlisted airman. In the hierarchy of the military, he's a commoner, someone who had walked off the street into a recruiter's office. At the other end of that hierarchy are the officers. They're college graduates from the respective academies or ROTC programs. And in the Air Force, the elite of this elite are the fighter pilots. These are the men entrusted with multimillion-dollar aircraft, rocketing at twice the speed of sound, dogfighting the enemy and executing maneuvers so physically awesome that they require specialized G-suits.

Yet, McGrath is no ordinary sergeant. He is a member of a select, highly-trained fraternity that could turn military protocol on its head. On the rare occasion when he and his colleagues might cross paths with their aviator brethren, they'd rarely have to pay for a drink. And while salutes and "sirs" are respected, it isn't unusual for some pilot to do a favor for this class of enlistees of common rank but uncommon training and duty. McGrath is part of a human safety net in Southeast Asia. He is a pararescueman, a weaponized guardian angel whose job it is to leap into peril and bring some unfortunate brother in arms back to safety.

Somewhere in McGrath's mind this June morning he knows his tour is coming to an end. The previous month, he had passed-by his first date to rotate home after a year of combat duty—DEROS, Date Eligible for Return from Overseas in the parlance of the military. He chose to extend his stay for one very good reason. Unlike some of his colleagues, McGrath hadn't left a wife or sweetheart at home in the States. She had come to Southeast Asia too, and he wasn't leaving without her.

The six-foot tall, brown-haired Maryland resident had graduated high school in 1966. "So I went to college. In those days everyone was going to college," McGrath explains, alluding to the draft deferment men would receive if they were working toward a degree. "I was taking classes, but I was also working and eventually lost my deferment."

Then on December, 1, 1969, the Selective Service System implemented a lottery for the first time since 1942. The United States was in the midst of the Vietnam Conflict. For a decade, rebels backed by communist North Vietnam had been trying to topple the government of South Vietnam. President Richard Nixon and his military advisors believed a surge of American troops would be necessary before the South's military could stand on its own and enforce a forthcoming treaty with the North.

Nixon's plan actually was to reduce U.S. presence in the area, handing all the fighting over to the South Vietnamese. However, 1968 had been the peak of U.S. involvement in Southeast Asia with more than 500 thousand troops in the region. In order to gradually step down the American presence and also rotate troops home when their tours were up, Nixon needed more manpower.

Hence, Selective Service developed the lottery as an attempt at a fair way to augment the draft. The lottery featured 366 blue capsules, each with a birth date inside. The televised drawing involved randomly pulling the capsules from a bin to determine the order in which men would be conscripted into the military. The first capsule drawn was September 14. The ninety-sixth capsule was December 16, Chuck McGrath's birthday. With those odds, the twenty-year-old figured he would rather enlist than be told where to go. "I didn't mind going," McGrath says of serving in the wartime military, "but I wanted to have some kind of control over what I was doing. I didn't want to be just a number. I wanted something technical, something I could use when I got out."

Chuck's assessment of his draft odds proved correct. In 1970 alone, Selective Service reached all the way to number 195 on the lottery. The following year, Selective Service modified the lottery slightly after some noted a seemingly not-random correlation between late birthdays—say those in December—and being drawn early in the draft. The assertion was that the capsules were put into the bin in order, January first, December last, and hadn't been mixed well enough.

While that may have helped explain how Chuck ended up with a low number and his buddy at the time ended up in the 360s, it didn't change the fact that at some point, likely early in the forthcoming year, he would be drafted. Chuck made the decision that many potential draftees did. He chose to enlist, and he already had some thoughts about the different branches of the military given that both his father and step-father had served in the Navy.

"And so I pretty much knew I didn't want the Navy," he deadpans. Growing up, Chuck moved around, as military families do, and in addition to spending his high school years in Maryland, he also lived in Hawaii and California. "And so from six or seven years old, I was always in the water," he says, "whether in a pool or the ocean. I was a water rat."

During high school he would visit his aunt and uncle on the Delaware coast. Enthralled with idea of being a lifeguard, he took lifesaving classes and spent the summer before his senior year of high school and the next two summers as an ocean-beach lifeguard at the shore in Delaware. In between college semesters he would lifeguard at the beach. In the winter he worked at other jobs and eventually worked at a pharmacy and swimming pools in Columbia, Maryland. One of the regular pharmacy customers, a man named Jim Davis, ran a timber operation and must have thought that the large-framed McGrath had what it took to join his small crew.

In 1969, he signed on with Davis, who would serve as a bit of a father figure for McGrath. In the fall of '69, he was again taking college courses but continued to work cutting timber on days when he had no classes. That was his routine up until December 1, when a random draw of a blue capsule set in motion the events that led him to this June morning in 1972.

Seeking to join the burgeoning world of computers, he sought out an Air Force recruiter. "At that point when you entered the Air Force you had four fields you could select for: electrical, mechanical, administrative and general. And under general was where the data processing came in," he says. And so that became his goal when he completed basic training and reported to Lackland Air Force Base in San Antonio, Texas. However, when they displayed the list of available positions, none in data processing were open to the new enlistee.

There he was on base, wondering if he might be relegated to serving out his enlistment in some terribly boring way when in walked—actually he more limped than walked—a staff sergeant.

"Here comes this big guy, and he had jump wings, flight wings, a whole mess of ribbons, walking with a cane," explains Chuck. "His face is kind of lopsided, and he says 'I want to talk to you about pararescue.'"

Staff Sergeant Tommy Miles proceeded to give an overview of being a pararescueman, a PJ[1] as he called it, and he was there recruiting for the next class. About nine months earlier Miles had been the sole survivor of a harrowing rescue attempt gone wrong. While as a member of the 38th ARRS, Miles was on board an HH-43 helicopter that had been assigned to check for crew trapped inside a B-52 that had skid off the runway at U-Tapao air base in Thailand. The bomber was fully loaded with ordnance as it burned from the minor crash. As the helicopter circled lower, Miles saw a bright flash. His next memory was twenty-two weeks later, waking up in an Air Force hospital.[2]

In addition to sustaining serious burns, Miles broke virtually every bone in his body and had a crushed skull that had to be repaired with a titanium plate. As McGrath came to understand the story, Miles apparently died and was resuscitated three times in the immediate aftermath of the crash, his fellow pararescuemen at his side the entire way, ushering him from death's door.

If this tougher-than-death recruiter wasn't enough to entice interest in pararescue, he also offered another attraction: Any man interested in hearing about PJs could sign up and get an opportunity to watch a movie about the pararescue service. For McGrath, who moments earlier saw looming boredom on the horizon, both pararescue and the opportunity to be distracted from barracks life had unavoidable appeal.

As Chuck went to the sign-up sheet for the movie, Miles stopped him, "Are you a good swimmer?"

"I've been a lifeguard for four years." McGrath answered.

The HH-43 "Pedro" was a predecessor to the HH-53 for rescue operations in Southeast Asia. Compared to the larger HH-53, it lacked speed, range and load-carrying capability. It was an HH-43 very much like this one that PJ Tom Miles had flown in on July 19, 1969, when he and the crew of Pedro 70 were blown out of the sky from the exploding ordnance of a crashed B-52. Staff Sergeant Miles, the lone survivor, like other PJs, went recruiting for the pararescue service while recovering from his injuries. In the spring of 1970, a fresh enlistee named Chuck McGrath, after hearing Miles's pitch for pararescue at basic training, decided to enter the rigorous qualification and training that many refer to as "Superman School."—*R. Hutchinson*

"I didn't ask you that," shot back Miles. "I asked you if you were a good swimmer."

"Yes sir," said McGrath.

"Don't sir me," responded Miles. "I'm a sergeant."

McGrath realized the mistake as the words left his mouth. He was just finishing basic training where everyone was "sir" to the new enlistees. Thus began Chuck's baptism to the world of pararescue. The movie consisted of showing the day-to-day tasks of PJs, going down helicopter hoist lines, parachuting into water, and other high-adventure but high-risk duties. Miles also discouraged any interest from married men as PJs had a high rate of divorce.

At the end, he told the group of about sixty or so that if they had lost interest, they could leave. About half the room stood up and walked out. McGrath was fascinated, however, and Miles continued with a second movie.

"They were talking about jumping into water, climbing, parachuting, just all sorts of neat stuff," Chuck recalls about this introduction to pararescue. "These were just all things that sounded as though they would interest me."

The next step for McGrath and the others was to sign up for a physical training (PT) test. The test required running a mile and doing a specified number of pushups, sit-ups and other exercises within set time limits. At each step, PJ hopefuls would drop out or not make the cut. Then came the swim test at a pool on the base of the nearby Brooks Air Force Base. The test was to swim one mile in under an hour, an easy task for a water rat like McGrath.

As Chuck and the other recruits were in the water, Miles, whose legs were held together with pins, seemingly had had enough of watching and not doing. He threw down his cane, dove into water with full jungle fatigues. The veteran PJ came up from the water and snarled at the pararescue hopefuls. This was a long way from lifeguarding.

Miles wasn't just recruiting. He was working his body back into shape. While he did go back on active duty, he never did serve in combat again. But, he made an impression on McGrath, who was quickly proving he had the basic physical tools for the program. Next, Chuck had to be cleared for airborne assignments with a flight physical.

Between his birth date being pulled on December 1 and when he reported for basic training the following March, Chuck took advantage of what was left of his freedom from military structure and discipline. "I partied a bit," he says. Also, while cutting timber, his upper body had bulked up from carrying logs and heavy chain saws. McGrath had reported to basic training weighing 212 lbs. In just the week since, which included his PT test, he had dropped down to 204. But for the flight test, McGrath, whom the Air Force measured as 5-foot, 11-and-3/4-inches tall, he had to be 194 lbs to meet the height-to-weight ratio. At six feet, 205 lbs would have been the mark Chuck had to hit.

As much as the inflexible rules reminded him what he didn't like about the military, the sergeant in charge of the flight test had worked with a number of PJs and must have seen McGrath was right for the specialized service; he gave McGrath seven days to drop the 10 lbs. to qualify. McGrath made the weight in three.

With all the testing complete, of the sixty-or-so men that had packed into the room for Staff Sergeant Miles's initial presentation, Chuck was the last man standing, the only man of the original group to receive orders to report to the pararescue training program.

The history of pararescue traces back to World War II. In August 1943, a C-46 transport went down near the China-Burma border with twenty-one people aboard, including a young, relatively unknown, war correspondent named Eric Severeid. Long before the age of high-altitude reconnaissance, never mind any kind of satellite-assisted surveillance or navigation, the only way to get the men out was to parachute in, aide the injured, and then somehow guide the entire party to a more accessible location.

A lieutenant colonel and two medical corpsmen volunteered for the job. Over the course of a month, while caring for the injured, they led the entire group toward safety. Severeid, who went on to become one of the early and great broadcast journalists in America, later wrote of his rescuers, "Gallant is a precious word; they deserve it."

The American military didn't need such praise or publicity to recognize the evolving nature of war, particularly where the battlefield was shifting toward the skies. There was a need for an elite type of rescuer, a soldier-doctor-superhero that could go anywhere to save the injured. Before the end of World War II, the military began practicing early pararescue operations. But the future of this fledgling function was unclear.

At some point during his initial recruitment, McGrath noticed Miles wearing a maroon beret. He perhaps didn't even think twice about the distinctive headgear, which also featured a silver badge, a "flash" in the vernacular of the military. Little did he know at the time that it was that beret and flash he would be working toward over the next sixteen months.

The beret was a symbol of military elite. During World War II, British paratroopers wore a red beret, and in a display of Allied respect, they gave a version to their comrades in the U.S. Army's 509th Parachute Infantry Regiment. Thus berets were introduced to American military dress, for the most part being reserved for elite units. To this day, U.S. airborne units wear a red beret as a nod to the origins of the tradition. As an airborne unit, the PJs were given their own red berets. However, in 1966 then Air Force Chief of Staff General John McConnell authorized a maroon-colored beret for the pararescuemen, the word-of-mouth reasoning being that maroon symbolized the blood sacrificed by this special brand of rescuer.

The complement to the beret was the flash. Engraved on it was a winged guardian angel embracing a globe. Inscribed beneath in capital letters was a simple, direct message: THAT OTHERS MAY LIVE.

The words form the conclusion of the Pararescue Creed, authored by the first commander of what was then called the Air Rescue Service (ARS), Richard T. Kight. In 1946, Lieutenant Colonel Kight was handed command of the of infant ARS. His orders were simple: build up the ARS or shut it down. He became an avid supporter of air rescue operations, lobbying for more resources while also formalizing the pararescue training. His indelible mark on the program was the creed:

> It is my duty as a Pararescueman to save life and to aid the injured. I will be prepared at all times to perform my assigned duties quickly and efficiently, placing these duties before personal desires and comforts. These things I do, That Others May Live.

With the formation of the Air Force in 1947, the Air Rescue Service was transferred to this new branch of the military with its aviation expertise. By the time the Korean Conflict came, practices had been refined with a formal training program that resulted in nearly a thousand rescues during the war. But it was the Vietnam Conflict that cemented the role of PJs in the military.

That role reflected both the nature of the Vietnam war and war in general. During these Cold War years, the military futurists were predicting war fought from a distance. The focus was a nuclear conflict, not the skirmishes to be fought in the remote locations of the third world. As a matter of fact, military air-rescue operations had been rolled into the space race, serving as the recovery units for astronauts splashing down in the Pacific on their return to earth.

However, what Vietnam established was that the sophisticated weapons and airborne strategies meant that no matter your role as a warrior, you could at any moment, find yourself isolated. Whether you were a pilot ejecting from a damaged craft or a group of infantry on patrol and suddenly ambushed, cut off from your comrades by difficult terrain, battle-line warfare was a thing of the past.

But even as the role of pararescue took clearer shape during Vietnam, it was still a young service, searching for an identity, a paradigm for the creed Kight authored. That identity would come in the form of William Pitsenbarger.

A little more than six years before this June morning in Southeast Asia, when McGrath was still in high school, Airman 1st Class Pitsenbarger was part of an operation to rescue part of a group of about 130 infantry that had been ambushed by what was estimated to be 500 Viet Cong rebels just east of South Vietnam's capital, Saigon. The twenty-one-year-old had already taken part in more than 250 rescue missions in Southeast Asia.

On April 11, 1966, as a member of the 38th ARRS, Pitsenbarger flew into the site of the ambush on board an HH-43B, call sign Pedro 73. The original plan was that Pedro 73, alternating with a second HH-43B, would hover over the location and lower a litter via the hoist so that the infantry could load their injured comrades, and the crew of the HH-43B would pull them up to the cabin where the PJs could begin care for them. However, the Southeast Asian triple canopy jungle—dense undergrowth, a middle layer of thick trees, and then another layer of trees as tall as 150 feet—and the infantry's lack of familiarity with the rescue litter hindered the first attempts. Pitsenbarger volunteered to descend to the jungle floor in the midst of the intense fighting to facilitate the extraction of the wounded soldiers.

By most accounts, Pitsenbarger had several opportunities to return to his helicopter after showing the infantrymen how to use the rescue litter, but he chose to stay even as the fighting intensified, treating the remaining wounded as the helicopters flew to a nearby aid station. After a few trips, the helicopters hovered as Pitsenbarger loaded more wounded into the litter. Suddenly, small-arms fire erupted from the ground, striking Pedro 73. Momentarily, the pilot could not control the aircraft, and it lurched away from its hover, dragging its hoist line with the attached litter, which snagged on a tree in the canopy. Anchored now by the ensnared litter, the crew had to sever the hoist line.

With daylight fading, the fighting intensifying, and forthcoming air strikes to beat back the Viet Cong, it was clear the helicopters would not be back until morning. Pitsenbarger continued to treat the injured, improvising splints from the surrounding trees and vines. He rounded up ammunition from the dead, and distributed it to the other infantry.

When the helicopters returned the next day, they found Pitsenbarger lying on the jungle floor, shot dead by Viet Cong fire. As the story is told,

Airman First Class William Pitsenbarger epitomized the Pararescueman's Creed of foregoing any personal comfort or concern "so that others may live." On April 11, 1966, Pitsenbarger was on the ground assisting in the rescue of several injured infantrymen when the rescue helicopters were chased away by enemy small arms fire. Pitsenbarger chose to stay with the wounded on the ground and the American soldiers engaged in an intense firefight throughout the night. Shot dead by the Viet Cong sometime during the night, Pitsenbarger was found with his medical kit in one hand and rifle in the other. Initially awarded the Air Force Cross, Congress raised Pitsenbarger's recognition to the Medal of Honor on October 30, 2000.—*U.S. Air Force*

locked in his grasp were his rifle in one hand and medical kit in the other. The men Pitsenbarger extracted the day before, along with the others who fought through the night, survived that battle thanks in large part to Airman Pitsenbarger and the heroic actions he took so that they might live. For his sacrifice, Pitsenbarger was posthumously awarded the Air Force Cross, which is second only to the Medal of Honor. The Air Force Sergeants Association also created the Pitsenbarger Award in his memory. On October 30, 2000, Pitsenbarger's Air Force Cross was elevated to the Medal of Honor.[3]

This was the culture into which McGrath was jumping, a far cry from studying computers. But before he would get a chance to don the maroon beret, he would face a year of training. What he didn't know is that not only would the training lead to a distinguished military career, but it would also bring him together with the love of his life.

Today, the pararescue training program is referred to as the Pipeline, signifying the ordered series of military schools that PJ candidates must attend. Back in 1970, the process wasn't so ordered. As spaces opened up in the different schools, the Air Force would send the PJ hopefuls in an effort to get them trained.

Various segments of the military run specialized schools for their elite forces. As a PJ hopeful, Chuck would be sent to programs such the Army's airborne school and the Navy's dive school. For the PJs, while they carried the designation of special forces, their training and mission was to be wide ranging, to have such a broad schooling in all these specialties to prepare them for any combat terrain or situation. Today, many refer to the pararescue pipeline simply as "Superman School."

Surprisingly for the former lifeguard, for Chuck the hardest part of the training came in the water. "SCUBA school was definitely the most difficult," he recalls. "Physically, it was just very hard. You would be doing pushups with 70 pounds of gear on your back."

The longest school in the program in 1971, and still today, was the Air Force's rescue medical school at Sheppard Air Force Base in Wichita Falls, Texas. The school was attended by personnel from the Air Force whose assignments required the medical training. As intense as it was, there were moments of downtime during the program. As McGrath neared the end of his medic training, he decided to attend a dance at the airman's club on base. He looked across the room and his eyes fell on a pretty, auburn-haired girl sitting on the side.

To say that Chuck McGrath had proven himself to be one of only a relative handful of elite men is no exaggeration. His pararescue training had established that, but his sweaty palms and lump in his throat also confirmed that the twenty-two-year-old hadn't quite figured out how to approach an attractive woman.

For her part, Candy Driggers wanted little to do with distractions such as love-struck airmen. The tomboy daughter of a Coast Guard chief warrant officer (CWO4), her family moved all over the United States and Hawaii, before it was a state, in her youth. After a year of classes at the University of Florida, she had a yearning to see more of the world but also a sense of duty. "I wasn't part of the burn the bra crowd," Candy recalls about herself as a nineteen-year-old. "I wasn't part of the ranting and raving. I had a strong sense of Americanism. I wanted to serve my country, not tear it apart."

She had also experienced a painful breakup back home in Florida. Falling in love was the last thing on her mind. So when the good-looking, brown-haired airman stepped up and asked her to dance, she politely agreed with little thought of it leading to anything more.

"Actually, my first impression was he was a little shorter than the guys I usually danced with," says the 5-foot-9 former Air Force medic. "I was tall, and usually the guys I danced with were at least 6-3."

But she waived that guideline for 5-11-and-3/4s. The two danced, and afterwards they sat together and talked. Chuck explained he was there as part of his training as a PJ. Candy offered that she was at the base receiving her training to be a medic. She had no idea what a PJ was, but had made note while dancing that this young airman seemed well built. His description of pararescue was fascinating, but still, it was just a dance. After all, being a female in the military in the early 1970s subjected you to a certain numerological attention that the pretty but shy, at least in her own assessment, medic-to-be had become accustomed to.

"But he kept following me around," Candy says with a laugh. Especially in the high-testosterone world of the Air Force, Candy had seen plenty of machismo and bravado. That made Chuck a bit different. He wasn't the slick-talking, guns-blazing type. Still he was persistent, incessantly trying to get information about Candy from her friend, "Shorty." "He was very protective of me," Candy says of her friend at Sheppard. "I wore my heart on my sleeve, and Shorty knew I didn't want to be hurt."

Somewhere along the way, Chuck, must have won endorsement from Shorty because Candy did finally agree to go on a few dates, one of them concluding with a goodnight kiss.

"It was that night that I went back and told my roommate that he was the man I was going to marry," Candy says.

With rescue medical school behind him, Chuck moved onto the PJ transitional training program at Eglin Air Force Base in Florida, the final stage of his training. Still, he did manage to grab a trip or two back to Sheppard to see Candy. Then, as Candy was finishing her training, her father in Florida took ill. She requested an assignment to Tyndall Air Force Base in Panama City, near her parents. This assignment also placed her within a hundred miles of Chuck on the Florida pan handle. With the two so close, Chuck invited Candy to watch some of his training, and she obliged. It was at this point, seeing the PJs conduct their daring exercises and parachuting out of HC-130s that her eyes were opened to the extraordinary man she was dating.

"It was all very exciting. I would sit on the hood of my car and watch them," Candy says. Thus, also began her entry into the tight-knit pararescue fraternity. For all the seriousness of their training and eventual assignment, the PJs, perhaps because of the near daredevil nature of their duty, also knew how to have fun. Candy was Chuck's guest at pararescue parties then and to this day when the couple attends PJ reunions.

McGrath had nearly completed his training, which would culminate in his award of a maroon beret. As many as half the men in Chuck's class would receive orders for a much sought-after assignment to Southeast Asia. Candy had already begun her assignment at Tyndall, and it wasn't lost on the young lovebirds that they might end up a world apart.

Given the prospect of being separated, each assigned to duty thousands of miles away from each other, Chuck and Candy gave serious thought to a prospect they had already entertained for after Chuck's return from Southeast Asia: marriage. At the time, the military had a policy of trying to assign married couples to the same regions. They would not necessarily end up at the same base or deploy at the same time, but the prospect of their both being in Southeast Asia seemed far better than some of the alternatives.

In the spring of 1971, Chuck McGrath completed his pararescue training, receiving the distinct maroon beret of PJs, and drawing a coveted assignment to Southeast Asia. Knowing that if they were married, they could be assigned to the same region, Chuck and Candy, his Air Force medic sweetheart, married on May 1, not long before Chuck went overseas. Candy followed a few weeks later, assigned to a base about three hundred miles away from Chuck. While the two had arrived in Southeast Asia separately, Chuck wasn't going home without his wife. By June 27, 1972, Chuck had already extended past his first DEROS (date eligible return from overseas) and continued to fly rescue missions while waiting for Candy to finish her tour.—*C. McGrath*

Candy's parents were none too keen on the idea, however. In Florida at this time, a woman needed to be twenty-one to marry without consent of her parents. As Candy explains, her parents concern wasn't so much about Chuck but about the high-risk nature of his profession and the hole that it could leave in Candy's heart if the unthinkable happened. "They thought he was a nice young man," Candy says of her parents objections. "But they didn't want us getting married. There was the chance Chuck would be killed. They didn't want to see me hurt like that."

Without the expressed permission of her parents, Candy and Chuck were left with the prospect of marrying in a state where the age of consent was only eighteen. Chuck's home state of Maryland was just such a place. They were to be married in Chuck's church, a Lutheran one. However, the PJ didn't want to completely sever a relationship with his soon-to-be in-laws. He insisted that Candy, a Catholic, go through the process of receiving a dispensation from her church so as to maintain her standing in her family's religion. "He didn't want me to have any regrets," says Candy.

On May 1, 1971, the couple held their sparse wedding. Candy had only two friends attend and none of her family. They spent the next week honeymooning at Chuck's aunt and uncle's beach house, where years earlier he had first dreamed of being a lifeguard, and then another week with Chuck's mother before he shipped off to Thailand. Candy then returned to Tyndall, awaiting her orders.

Chuck was assigned to the 40th ARRS, which was then based at Udorn, Thailand. In June, Candy received her orders. She would be assigned to Korat air base about three hundred miles southwest of Udorn in central Thailand. When she flew into Bangkok, there was Chuck at the airport, ready to greet her. He exercised what pull and logistics he could to get much of the in-processing protocol waived for Candy. Rather than her being tied up for three hours in the military's indoctrination, the two newlyweds left the airport and headed for a hotel Chuck had booked.

It's hard to imagine any other couple embarking on such a whirlwind experience, being newlyweds while serving a year of combat duty, but for them it worked.

As a PJ, Chuck served as one of a crew of five (sometimes six) on a Sikorsky HH-53 Super Jolly Green Giant helicopter. These Greyhound-bus sized helicopters had become the workhorses of the Air Force's rescue and recovery squadrons. Often these aircraft would be referred to simply as Jolly Greens and even their designation in operations would be abbreviated JG.

Today, June 27, 1972, Chuck was stepping aboard JG 73 with his roommate, Chuck Morrow. Morrow was on the fourth of a daunting five combat tours in Southeast Asia. On December 2, 1969, the day after McGrath's birth date had been drawn as the 96th number in the lottery, Morrow played the key role in one of the few night rescues in Southeast Asia by recovering a downed Air Force pilot. For his efforts, Morrow was awarded the first of five Distinguished Flying Crosses, along with three Silver Stars, during his tenure as a pararescueman.

In PJ lore Morrow was also known for helping initiate what became a long-standing tradition for the rescue services. In 1971, Morrow bumped into a fellow PJ at the end of three tours in Southeast Asia. This fellow PJ was contemplating some souvenir of his time in the war, and the two airmen eventually dreamed up the notion of a commemorative icon from the local tattoo parlor.

The symbol was a simple pair of green footprints as though a miniature Jolly Green Giant had stomped on their behind.

McGrath never took part in the tradition. "Honestly, I think I was afraid of catching some infection," he says half jokingly. But the message the PJs annunciated with the tattoo was the indelible connection between the lumbering helicopters and their mission.

This particular HH-53, JG 73, was part of the pair of Super Jolly Greens that were the first helicopters to make a trans-Pacific flight in August 1970. For its search and rescue operations, each helicopter would be commanded by a pilot who flew with a copilot up front. In the main section of the helicopter, there would be a flight engineer responsible for operations in the main cabin such as running the hydraulic hoist lines. Accompanying him would be a pair of pararescuemen. All three crew—the engineer and the two PJs—would also be responsible for manning the aircraft's three miniguns. Two of the guns were located on the left and right sides of the craft. However, to operate the hoist, as would happen during a rescue attempt, the minigun on the right side would be inoperable as it would be slid out of the way with the helicopter's door. The third minigun was in the rear of the helicopter. The rear of the HH-53 sloped up toward the tail. Built into this part of the fuselage was ramp to permit quick egress of troops. In flight, it could also be lowered to horizontal and a crewmember could fire the minigun from this rear perch.

The two PJs on the crew were numbered. The PJ1 typically manned the left side minigun, and PJ2 would be assigned to the rear ramp gun. The determination of positions on any flight would follow a set protocol.

"We flipped a coin," explains McGrath. Whoever, won the 50-50 toss would have their choice of being PJ1 or PJ2. Should there be need, it would always be PJ1 who would be the first to go down the hoist line and tend to any injured on the ground. For the pararescuemen, PJ1 was the desired position. Only if a fellow PJ hadn't seen much action lately, might a coin-flip winner defer to being PJ2 on a mission. Hence, when Chuck McGrath won the coin flip this June morning, and with little time before he would leave Southeast Asia, he took the PJ1 position.

Occasionally, an aircraft would also have a photographer assigned who could also take on the combat duties of firing the miniguns or small arms. As was the protocol on all Air Force aircraft, each crewman was assigned a letter. In the case of an HH-53, the pilot was A (Alpha), the copilot B

(Bravo), flight engineer C (Charlie), 1PJ D (Delta), and 2PJ E (Echo).

Nearly every rescue operation involved a pair of HH-53s. One would serve as the low bird, whose duty it was to swoop down and extract a downed pilot. The other would fly as the high bird, serving as backup for the low bird.

During a rescue mission, the PJs would flip a coin to determine who would be PJ1 and who would be PJ2. If a survivor needed assistance, it would be PJ1 who would descend to the jungle via the hoist and assist the survivor while the helicopter (an HH-53C in this photo) maintained a hover overhead. On the morning of June 27, 1972, Chuck McGrath would win the coin flip with his roommate Chuck Morrow.—*National Archives*

Often preceding the helicopters into a rescue would be a flight of two to six Douglas A-1 Skyraiders, well-armored, prop-driven airplanes that could clear enemy forces away from a downed pilot with a number of different weapons. The Skyraiders were often referred to as Sandys, the call sign they took whenever performing search-and-rescue (SAR) missions.

Ahead of the Sandys would often be some form of a forward air controller (FAC). At this juncture in the war, the Air Force had begun using F-4 jets as "FastFACs" but also still relied on prop-driven FACs such as OV-10 Broncos and O-2 Skymasters. No matter the craft used, the mission of the FAC was to scout for downed pilots and enemy defenses in the area.

On occasion the entire airspace over a downed airman would be patrolled by a group of F-4s on guard for enemy MiG fighters. Orbiting just outside the North Vietnamese border, typically over the mountainous, uninhabited regions of Laos would be HC-130 refueling tankers that would replenish the helicopters by means of the HH-53's refueling probe. In contrast, the F-4s used different tankers, KC-135s, for their refueling. The Sandys had no midair refueling capability.

Also maintaining watch of the operations would be a Disco, the call

A significant feature of an HH-53 was its refueling capability. Here is a pilot's eye view of an HH-53 hooking up to HC-130 tanker for a fill up.—*C. McGrath*

sign of an Lockheed EC-121 Warning Star, which was equipped with the latest radar and early warning technology. Somewhere out in the South China Sea there would also be a Navy cruiser[4] serving as Red Crown, the call sign for the ship using its radar and state-of-the-art early-warning tools to detect enemy jets launching from bases in the North in addition to tracking all friendly aircraft.

The spring of 1972 had seen a spike in SARs as the U.S. air war heated up. At the end of March, the North had launched a massive offensive that in turn called for a massive response from the Air Force, the primary fighting element in Southeast Asia at the time.

The enemy surge had been coined the Easter Offensive because it had begun at noon on Friday, March 30, Good Friday that year on the Christian calendar. As the enemy punched with this offensive, the U.S. counterpunched with resumed bombing in North Vietnam. For those in search and rescue it readily became clear the stakes had been heightened with this new offensive.

For those in search and rescue, the rules of the game were changing. No longer could they count on friendly ground troops in the area. Moreover, the enemy was continuing to prove resourceful, if not devious, in adapting their tactics to the American air war.

In early April, shortly after the start of the Easter Offensive, an EB-66 with the call sign Bat 21 was shot down by North Vietnam. There was a sole survivor from the five man crew. Over the course of eleven days the Air Force would lose as many as five aircraft, including the entire crew of a Jolly Green Giant trying to rescue the survivor, as well as a forward air controller who had been shot down during the initial rescue efforts. For the Air Force command the massive effort and loss of craft and life gave it pause.

However, for members of the 40th ARRS there was no hesitation. While they were keenly aware of the intensity of the offensive and the fact that survivors were often treated as bait by the enemy, their role as a safety net didn't change. If anything, during the spring and early summer of 1972 their role became more critical as the Air Force and Navy became the last U.S. military resources still in Southeast Asia.

With the routine of Air Force bomb strikes from bases in Thailand in the morning and from Navy aircraft carriers on Yankee Station in the afternoon, the need for the 40th's safety net only increased. Still, Chuck had passed on his first date to rotate home to the United States. As a matter of fact, when the war had turned more dangerous Chuck was trying to fly as often as he could, knowing he was short on his combat time. That was the makeup of the PJ culture as it had been introduced to him by men like Tommy Miles.

But for Chuck McGrath, on June 27, 1972, he had two reasons for being on that Jolly Green even though he could have been far away from combat. First, he taken an oath and subscribed to a creed, to do all that he could so that others might live. Second, although he came to Southeast Asia ahead of Candy, he wasn't leaving without her.

NOTES

1. In truth, PJ is not an acronym but a sort of nickname adopted by those in the specialized pararescue service. In the early days of the Air Force, flight logs would identify anyone on board qualified to jump, but did not have a specific assignment (e.g. pilot, navigator, etc.), by the designation "PJ" for para jumper. When those in the pararescue service began flying on aircraft, their role was recorded as the generic PJ. The nickname stuck. While many, even those within the Air Force, will assign the term

"pararescue jumper" to the initials PJ, the men who have served in pararescue typically refer to their role, formally, as being a pararescueman.

2. This account is compiled from *Vietnam Air Losses*, Hobson, Midland Publishing, pp 185, 186 and "Pedro News: Ring of Fire" (http://users.acninc.net/padipaul/pnl016_10_06/ROF.htm), Steve Mock
3. This account of April 11, 1966, is based on *Leave No Man Behind* by George Galdorisi and Thomas Phillips (pp 265–266), Zenith Press, and the National Museum of the Air Force fact sheet on Airman 1st Class William Pitsenbarger. There are several accounts of this mission that provide varying specific details. The authors' intent in providing this version of Pitsenbarger's last mission is to focus on the unifying fact: A1C William Pitsenbarger chose to stay in the midst of heavy fighting in order to aid other service men, exemplifying the selfless mindset and creed of the pararescue service.
4. In order to accommodate the hardware for the Navy's PIRAZ (Positive Identification Radar Advisory Zone) technology, the ship serving as Red Crown typically had to be a cruiser. However, there were a few large destroyers (such USS *Mahan* and USS *King*) that functioned as Red Crown as well. These destroyers were often referred to as to destroyer leaders or frigates.

CHAPTER TWO

THE MISSION

It's near dawn on June 27, 1972, at Takhli Royal Thai Air Force Base (RTAFB) in central Thailand. Captain Lynn Aikman is a half a world away from his home, where two months earlier he kissed his wife, Sandy, and newborn daughter, Stephanie, goodbye before shipping out for a second combat tour in Southeast Asia. The twenty-seven-year-old Oregon native is among the heralded echelon of the U.S. Air Force; he is a fighter pilot. This morning he had just heard the briefing for the day's mission: another flight into heavily defended North Vietnam.

While the defenses in the North, especially those around its capital of Hanoi, may be the most sophisticated of any ever faced by the Air Force, the timid did not find their way to the cockpit of multimillion-dollar

Lieutenant Lynn Aikman poses in front his F-105 at Takhli Royal Thai Air Force Base in 1968. In the spring of 1972, now Captain Aikman returned to Southeast Asia as an F-4 Phantom pilot with the 4th Tactical Fighter Squadron based at Da Nang, South Vietnam. In late June, the 4th relocated seven hundred miles west to Takhli, and June 27 was the 4th's first mission from its new base.—*L. Aikman*

jet fighters. Aikman and his brethren were warriors. They were cut from a mold and trained not too differently from the men rocketing to the moon as part of the Apollo space program. Seven years later, author Tom Wolfe would famously describe such astronauts as having the "Right Stuff," and with little doubt, the aviators in Southeast Asia were motivated by very similar "stuff."

For the past two months, Aikman has been flying the MacDonnell Douglas F-4 Phantom II, a two-seat, twin-engine jet capable of reaching twice the speed of sound. The F-4 represents the latest evolution of fighter-jet technology. Not only is it powerful, but it is ubiquitous. It can be outfitted in any number of ways to execute any number of missions. Whether bombing, protecting bombers, searching out ground-based targets, or providing reconnaissance, the F-4 could do it all. Its multi-function nature made it an ideal fighter for both the Navy and the Air Force. However, for Aikman, who had flown mostly the single-seat F-105 and F-106 and had less than a hundred hours in the F-4, his two-month courtship with the jet was ongoing and hadn't yet blossomed into a romance.

"The F-106 was like a sports car. It was very fast and comfortable to sit in," Aikman says, recalling his early impressions of transitioning to the F-4. "With the F-4, the cockpit felt a little cramped and the stick was short."

At this point in the war experienced jet-fighter pilots would go through an abbreviated training program when transitioning from one jet to another. While on paper this was a sensible program because these pilots were already well versed in Air Force basics such as flying in formation and combat maneuvering, it shortchanged pilots getting accustomed to a new aircraft.

"For the F-4, I went through a modified or short check-out program," says Aikman. "It was only about 30 or 40 hours. The check-out in the 105 was 120 hours, and I felt comfortable going into combat with that amount of training. With a new airplane, in order to get really comfortable with all the switches, performance and maneuverability of it, it probably takes 100 hours or so."

The building blocks of the Air Force are elements, which are comprised of two or more aircraft, and two or more elements make up a flight. A squadron will have two or more flights. Several squadrons then comprise an operations group (as opposed to maintenance or medical groups), and the groups are all housed under a wing. For the most part, each wing has

The McDonnell Douglas F-4 Phantom II was a multifaceted fighter with two powerful jet engines. It had a two-man crew sitting tandem with the pilot up front and a weapons systems officer (WSO) in the backseat. This photo shows an F-4E version, which featured an integrated cannon in the nose, a weapon originally absent from the F-4 as its designers believed that air-to-air dogfighting was a thing of the past. *—M. Cavato*

a specific assignment, reflective of the aircraft its squadrons fly. And in Southeast Asia during the Vietnam Conflict virtually all Air Force personnel and resources involved in the war reported to the 7th Air Force.

Aikman was no stranger to Takhli. During his first combat tour in 1967, he flew F-105s out of the base. At the time, the Air Force and Navy were conducting sustained bombing of targets in North Vietnam under the umbrella of Operation Rolling Thunder. In January 1968, however, the North Vietnamese and Viet Cong initiated a surprise, multi-prong attack during Tet, the lunar New Year. Although the Tet Offensive caught U.S. and South Vietnamese military off guard, over the ensuing months they were able to decisively defeat the Viet Cong and North Vietnamese Army forces.

However, despite this military victory sentiment in the United States turned markedly antiwar. The body-count centric media, in part a product of the Department of Defense inclination for statistics, focused on the number of Americans killed combating the Tet Offensive. President Lyndon Johnson had challengers within his own party as the 1968 election season got under way, and the president's advisors were torn over the effectiveness of the Rolling Thunder bombing and the general prognosis for the war.

Up until Tet, the public face of the administration claimed that the enemy was growing weaker under the bombing; the Viet Cong and North

Vietnamese would soon lose the capacity to fight; American commander in Vietnam General William Westmoreland had proclaimed that he saw "light at the end of the tunnel." However, the highly coordinated and initially effective Communist offensive seemed to contradict such proclamations. On March 31, 1968, a despondent Johnson announced that he wouldn't run for reelection. Then, seven months later, he ordered a halt to all bombing of North Vietnam, citing progress in peace talks.

At the same time Aikman's first tour was up, and he was given a domestic assignment in 1969, flying the F-106 for the Strategic Air Command. However, as a career-minded and duty-aware Air Force officer, he wanted to get back to Southeast Asia and flying combat missions.

Captain Aikman got his wish. A couple of months before this day in June he received orders sending him to the 4th Tactical Fighter Squadron, part of the 366th Tactical Fighter Wing, which flew the latest model of the F-4, the F-4E. The 366th had a long history in Vietnam, a history that had just come to a close, or nearly so, on June 27, 1972. In October 1966, the 366th was the first Air Force wing to take up residence in the Republic of Vietnam in the South, in this case at the massive Da Nang base that was within 150 miles of the North Vietnam border. With the withdrawal of American combat forces from the country under President Nixon's Vietnamization policy, however, over the past month the 366th had been steadily moving its resources seven hundred miles west, leapfrogging over Laos, to Takhli in Thailand.

"We were the last wing to leave South Vietnam as part of Nixon's overall policy of getting out and turning everything over to the South Vietnamese," Aikman explains. "In June, we started moving out. On the 25th, we flew out of Da Nang, up into the North, and recovered to Takhli. On the 26th, our squadron didn't fly that day. We were getting equipment squared away, setting up our barracks and all that. So the 27th was the first day our squadron was flying out of Takhli."

Another factor in 366th's departure from Da Nang was that three months earlier, during their Easter Offensive the North Vietnamese Army (NVA) had rolled across the Demilitarized Zone (DMZ), a 10-kilometer-wide buffer between North and South Vietnam that was only about 135 miles north of Da Nang. In actuality, the NVA didn't roll just across the DMZ, but also around it from Laos and under it from Cambodia.

Over the course of the North's offensive as many as 120 thousand enemy troops poured into the South. In addition, those troops came with an array of weaponry including mobile surface-to-air missiles, tanks, and field artillery. Prior to the offensive, the United States had significantly reduced its ground forces in the country. In 1968, there had been well more than 500,000 thousand U.S. military stationed in South Vietnam. In 1972, that figured had dropped to only about 25 thousand.[5]

While a spring ground offensive during the monsoon season, when the Air Force couldn't always fly, was part of the cycle of the nearly decade-old war, this push south appeared to catch U.S. and South Vietnamese military leaders off guard, perhaps a consequence of the U.S. political posture that peace was at hand. That March, there had been ongoing peace negotiations, but they seemed to have stalled, and the frustrated U.S. diplomats walked away. On March 30, the North launched the massive offensive.[6]

Da Nang had long been a target of the Viet Cong, the Communist rebels operating in the South. The U.S. military, both Marines and Air Force, at the base had taken to calling Da Nang "Rocket City" due to the frequent attacks using mostly Soviet-made surface-to-surface missiles. Now, with the regular NVA pushing into the south with more advanced weaponry at their disposal, it was a good time for the wing to be relocating to Takhli.

However, it wasn't just a relocation for the 366th. Even though U.S. and South Vietnam forces were in the midst of countering a massive offensive, the U.S. stuck to a timeline for sending troops home. As the 366th vacated Da Nang, it also shut down its 390th Tactical Fighter Squadron rolling any members who still had time left on their tours into Aikman's squadron, the 4th TFS.

The immediate response to the North's Easter Offensive was Operation Freedom Train. The Nixon administration lifted the three-and-half-year halt on bombing targets in North Vietnam. This counterpunch to the North's offensive evolved into Operation Linebacker. Named for the defensive position in football that can thwart a running back trying to cross the line of scrimmage, Linebacker looked to bomb critical targets in the North in order to force the invaders back across the DMZ.

While the Air Force had experimented with new laser and optically guided bombs during last stages of the Rolling Thunder campaign, Linebacker would signal the first real use of these new "smart" bombs. The ability of these weapons to precisely attack their targets gave the Air Force the ability to destroy different lines of transport and communication in the North that had previously been resistant to aerial interdiction. By decimating the enemy infrastructure—bridges, roads, ports—the Air Force, bombing in the morning, and the Navy, bombing from the carriers in the afternoon, would kill the Easter Offensive by cutting off its supply.[7]

As Aikman had heard this morning, today's target was a truck repair facility just north of Hanoi. Linebacker was proving effective in stopping the major routes in and out of North Vietnam. Now, by going after the next level of infrastructure, the ability to transport supplies over roadways, the U.S. military leadership hoped to further choke the offensive.[8]

A typical Linebacker bombing mission for the Air Force would directly involve several dozen jets in the attack force and several dozen more indirectly in support roles, such as, refueling tankers, airborne command craft, and rescue HH-53 helicopters and A-1 airplanes. Leading the attack would be a group of jets whose job it was to seek out surface-to-air missile (SAM) sites. Next would be a group of typically eight or twelve chaff bombers. Chaff, metallic foil much like Christmas tree tinsel, would interfere with enemy radar. These bombers would set up a "chaff corridor" that would protect the two dozen or so bombers following a few minutes behind.

The notion of such interference wasn't to hide the attack—the presence of chaff was enough of an indicator that a strike was on its way—but to prevent the enemy's advanced targeting technology, particularly that related to ground-based SAMs and antiaircraft artillery, from being able to lock on to the oncoming bombers. As effective as the new laser-guided bombs were, the Air Force had only a limited number of F-4s outfitted with the special laser-guiding pods, code named Pave Knife. For this reason, Linebacker strikes were a bit more beefy on the perimeter, protecting the high-tech resources of these bombers.[9]

This would be Aikman's role this morning, being part of a four-jet escort flight to protect the chaff-dropping F-4s from another base that would be flying ahead of the bombers. In order to lay the chaff corridor, the F-4s had to fly level at a constant speed. These parameters would make an F-4 a sitting duck for the North's Vietnamese Peoples Air Force (VPAF), which flew variants of the Soviet-made, and Chinese-copied, MiGs. This kind of escort was a form of combat air patrol, CAP as the Air Force abbreviated, and identified as MiGCAP to distinguish the role from other assignments such as RESCAP (combat air patrol covering rescue attempts) or BARCAP (barrier combat air patrol intended to protect the air space between strike package and likely hostile territory).

F-4 crews would be paired into elements, a lead and wingman, and typically a four-aircraft flight of two elements, one lead and the other the second, supporting element.—*M. Cavato*

For the June 27 morning mission the chaff bombers would be coming from a squadron of F-4s from Udorn RTAFB, some three hundred miles north of Takhli. Aikman's 4th TFS was responsible for supplying a flight of F-4Es to escort the chaff, and that is why Aikman awoke well before dawn this June morning. He had been scheduled to fly on what was the 4th TFS's first mission out of its new home at Takhli.

"We were up early," Aikman recalls about June 27. "No one really knew how long it would take from wake-up to wheels in the well," he says, referring to pilot slang for having the landing gear retracted after take off.

During the Vietnam Conflict, the military divided North Vietnam into segments known as Route Packs. This was a way of splitting the aerial attacks between the Air Force and the Navy. There were six designated Route Packs. Route Pack VI covered the North's capital of Hanoi and its critical harbor of Haiphong. As such, even before the bombing halt, Route Pack VI was heavily defended and considered one of the most hazardous assignments. And, during the three-and-a-half-year bombing hiatus, it only became more so as the North continuously improved its defenses.

Heading toward Route Pack VI was nothing unexpected for Aikman and the 4th TFS that morning. The mission briefing, for the most part, was uneventful. The intelligence officers summarized the target and known threats in the area. "We found out we were going up North, and there would be antiaircraft, SAMs and MiGs, all expected to be up there at the same time," recalls Aikman.

Of all the defenses posed by the North, the MiGs were the most significant adversary. The antiaircraft artillery, triple A as the pilots abbreviated, wouldn't be an issue for the F-4s at their typical altitude. The SAMs were a dangerous weapon, but a combination of technology and tactics reduced their effectiveness against U.S. aircraft. At about 30 feet long and 20 inches in diameter, the SAMs were often described as a rocket-propelled telephone pole by U.S. aviators. Electronic jamming tools reduced their effectiveness and as long as an F-4 pilot had fair warning and enough altitude, he could engage in a maneuver such as a SAM break, a quick dive that the SAM's guidance systems couldn't follow. SAMs were still knocking down aircraft, but As Captain Rick McDow, one of the air crew who would be joining Aikman this morning, observed, they had become common during Linebacker. "To give you an idea," explains McDow, "we once had a flight up North, and at the debrief, the intelligence officers asked us to estimate how many SAMs we saw. It turns out that among the four guys in my element, I had the lowest estimate, and I said one hundred."

The MiGs, by far, were the greater concern. Technologically they were different from the F-4, smaller and more maneuverable. This didn't necessarily make them better, but the Air Force never trained against such dissimilar aircraft. For the F-4 crews it was on-the-job training when it came to fighting a MiG.

In contrast to the U.S. Air Force, where pilots routinely rotated to other assignments, many of the North Vietnamese pilots had several years experience. During the bombing halt, the North's air force continued to fly not only in their own country, but many had gone to the Soviet Union for training.

Also, the bombing halt permitted the construction of a sophisticated radar and warning system. This ground controlled intercept (GCI) system, as the U.S. termed it, contributed to a North Vietnamese strategy where its pilots took orders from ground-based commanders. This brought forth a very calculating approach to the North's aerial defense. The MiGs would only engage when VPAF officers on the ground had data indicating conditions were favorable for them to engage their U.S. counterparts.

The U.S. had its own, somewhat disjointed, version of GCI, too. The Air Force used an airborne Lockheed EC-121 aircraft with two radomes, bubble-shaped radar coverings on the top and underside of the fuselage. With the call sign Disco, the aircraft relied on its technology and on-board intelligence operators to detect airborne threats.

The Air Force also relied on a Navy cruiser[10] serving as a PIRAZ station about thirty miles off the coast of North Vietnam. With the call sign Red Crown, a PIRAZ cruiser had various resources aboard to detect the whereabouts of the VPAF's MiGs and was able to track U.S. aircraft. It was air traffic control for the war, and for many aviators in Southeast Asia the prevalent feeling was that Red Crown had better tools, and thus better information than Disco.[11]

The American GCI system, as well as a few F-4s, were equipped with a new technological asset code named Combat Tree. Military aircraft carry an identification friend or foe (IFF) transponder that can identify them to their own forces. The North Vietnamese held their pilots on a tight leash, directing them from ground-based control centers. To be able to do this the VPAF pilots had to have their transponders on all the time so that the controllers could know precisely where their air resources were.

With some engineering and cooperation from its allies, the United States was able to use this system against the North. During the Arab-Israeli Six Day War in June of 1967, Israelis shot down an Arab MiG with a Soviet transponder. From this technology the U.S. was able to crack the Soviet transponder system and engineer Combat Tree, which could identify a MiG from as far as sixty miles away by either receiving its IFF transponder signal or actively interrogating it.[12] For the F-4s outfitted with Combat Tree there were still rules on how close a pilot should be before firing on the enemy. In a head-on attack the rules of engagement required the MiG to be within about five miles. If an F-4 with Combat Tree was attacking from the rear, the minimum distance was about fifteen miles.[13]

Although Combat Tree and its variants used by Red Crown and Disco were still in limited use by 1972, none of the Valent F-4Es had the secret technology. Further, Disco had various limitations due to the nature of orbiting, having all that moving equipment in what could be unpredictable and electronically unfriendly weather. While Red Crown, was relatively stationary and had more resources, perhaps making it a better tool than Disco, it was limited by distance. Especially the northwest, farther-inland section of Southeast Asia, comprising North Vietnam and Laos, could be beyond Red Crown's capability.

This was a further compromise in the political objective of moving U.S. military out of Vietnam. Whereas up until two days ago the 366th had been flying out of the coastal base of Da Nang, they were now starting from Takhli, some seven hundred miles inland. A further factor in the use of Red Crown was that it was a Navy asset. While Red Crown often was available during the morning Air Force strikes, its resources would be refocused on the afternoon Navy strike starting around noon local time on typical Linebacker mission days.[14]

By June of 1972 a common scenario was that the VPAF would wait until after the strike package hit its target and look to catch the F-4s as they were leaving North Vietnamese airspace, usually to the west toward northern Laos where refueling tankers were waiting. Low on fuel, an F-4 became a much more palatable target for the North's MiGs. As U.S. pilots headed for the refueling tankers they would have to drop air speed and altitude for the rendezvous, putting themselves in an arena that called for low-altitude, tight-turning, guns-firing dogfighting—exactly the place that the F-4, and perhaps the U.S. Air Force, was not built for.

At the conclusion of the mission briefing, Aikman joined the flight briefing. The four F-4s in their flight would use the call sign Valent for the day. Throughout the Vietnam Conflict the Air Force flew variations of four-jet formations; the most basic of them was known as the fluid-four or finger-four formation. If someone were to look at their right hand, palm down, the tips of each finger would represent the location of the four jets. The middle finger would be the location for the flight lead, the number 1 plane. Adjacent and left to 1, at the tip of the index finger, would be his wingman, the 2 plane. The ring finger would represent the location of the 3 plane, the lead of the second element. Lastly, the pinkie finger would be the 4 plane.

The overall design was a bit of follow the leader. The 1 plane would lead the flight with the number 2 being slightly behind and on the outside. The second element, led by the 3 plane would position itself according to whatever the lead element was doing but be behind it. The number 4 plane, like the other wingman, the number 2, would be behind and outside of its lead, the number 3.

Overall, the staggered nature of the formation permitted the wings to cover the rear, the ever-vulnerable six o'clock position, of their leads. In the same way, the trailing second element could cover the lead element's six o'clock. To provide further coverage, the two elements of a Fluid Four could weave. Each time the two pairs would cross, the pilots could roll the jets up on a banking turn so that the backseaters—the two-man Phantom crew sat tandem in the cockpit with the pilot in front and the weapons systems officer (WSO), the backseater, in the rear—could get a decent view behind.

A major vulnerability to this four-plane formation was that the 4 plane had no one covering it from behind as it was the rearmost jet. Further, the wings, the 2 and the 4 planes, being on the outside, typically used more fuel as their turns were invariably wider. Especially in a weaving formation where the two elements would cross in front of each other, the wingman was always to be on the outside. For example, the 4 plane might be the rightmost jet, but as the two elements crossed, the 4 would cut across not only its lead but the lead element of the 1 and the 2 plane so that it would have flipped positions entirely—moving from the rightmost plane to now being the leftmost.

Also, the nature of the second element following the lead, made the 4 plane one of the more difficult positions to fly; its pilot would be reacting to the reaction of the 3 plane's pilot to the lead element's movements. To add to the dynamic, the Air Force typically identified the 1 plane, the flight lead, as the shooter in an engagement, that is, the lead would focus on attacking an enemy aircraft. The alternate shooter in the fluid-four/finger-four formation was the 3 plane. As such, typically the most experienced crews (pilot and WSO) were placed in the 1 and 3 planes. Less-experienced pilots would be assigned to the more difficult flying positions on the wings of the formation, the 2 and the 4 planes.

All these factors conspired to create a situation where statistically the most likely F-4 to be shot down was the 4 plane, exactly where Aikman was scheduled to fly on this morning's mission.

The pilots and the WSOs would be distinguished in their call sign by an A for the pilot and a B for the WSO. Hence, Aikman was Valent 04A. The pilot of his element lead, Valent 03A, was Robert Craig Miller. Miller, like Aikman had done an earlier combat tour flying F-105s, but this was two years before Aikman in 1965. Miller had substantially more time in the F-4 than Aikman. He had also taken part in developing some of the instructional programs for the pilots. Miller very likely was the most experienced pilot in the flight, a fact not lost on his backseater, Valent 03B, Rick McDow.

"I really thought Craig should have been the flight lead," McDow offers. "He had a lot more current experience."

McDow and Miller had both been rolled into the 4th TFS from the 390th when the entire wing moved from Da Nang. McDow had missed

The ill-fated F-4E that would be flown by Robert Craig Miller and his backseat Rick McDow sits in its improvised hangar at Da Nang, just a few days before the 4th TFS moved to Takhli RTAB. *—R. C. Miller*

out on pilot training due to his not-quite-perfect eyesight. Still he wanted to move to the front seat at some juncture and knew one way of getting there was promotion. "When I got to the 390th, I asked them to give me the worst job there was. Whatever it was, I wanted to take it on, hoping that it would help me get promoted." McDow was assigned to being the administrative officer of the 390th, an experience that confirmed his superiors had followed his wishes. "I have to say administrative officer probably is the worst job you can get in a squadron."

But while the 390th was still operating at Da Nang, he had the opportunity to fly with Miller and build a rapport. As the two of them were being moved into the 4th, McDow spent most of his time with his administrative duties, not having much opportunity to get to know his new squadron. This wasn't purely a lost social opportunity. McDow also had missed out on getting a feel for his new squadron mates, whom he would inevitably have to trust in combat.

Lynn Aikman's F4-E on the ramp at Da Nang prior to an escort mission. On June 27, 1972, for the 4th's first mission from its new base at Takhli, Aikman's regular backseater would be unavailable. Aikman, who had become a father just two months earlier, would be paired with an experienced WSO named Tom Hanton, whose wife was expecting the couple's first child back in the States.—*L. Aikman*

"What it came down to was that there were only certain people you wanted to go North with," he explains. Miller was of similar sentiment. When McDow asked Miller to request him as his regular backseater for flights North, Miller happily agreed.

As comparison, Aikman and his backseater had never met until the flight briefing that morning. "My normal backseat had flown the day before, filling in for someone else's backseat," says Aikman. "They had some sort of engine problem so they had to recover to Udorn."

Valent 04B on June 27, 1972, would be Captain Tom Hanton. The twenty-seven-year-old Hanton had been in Southeast Asia about five months and had already flown more than 130 combat missions. The son of a career Air Force officer, Hanton had more than two years experience as an F-4 WSO including time as an instructor. As a matter of fact, just weeks earlier, when the Valent flight lead had arrived back in Southeast Asia, Hanton was the pilot who had given him his check-out flight.

For Hanton, he was troubled by the squadron's scheduling. The 4th seemed to follow a policy of mixing up the flights and sending crews North that had only limited experience with each other *or* Route Pack VI. Still, Hanton wanted to fly as much as he could. He loved jets and, like many backseaters, wanted to move up front to the pilot's seat some day. For these reasons, he asked to be scheduled as much as possible, which made him the late addition to the flight that morning.

Hanton and Aikman had never met before. Unknown to both, the two shared the connection of fatherhood, or at least soon-to-be fatherhood. Aikman and his wife had just welcomed their firstborn. Back home in the States, Hanton's wife was pregnant with their first child.

While the three-and-a-half-year bombing halt gave the North the opportunity to regroup its defenses, in the eyes of Miller, it also permitted the U.S. to let some of its combat readiness atrophy. "We had very little continuity from Rolling Thunder days to the Linebacker phase," he explains. "What disturbed me the most, was the reinventing of the wheel when we started going North again for Linebacker. A lot of what went on cost a lot of aircraft and lives."

Miller's biggest concern had to do with the way the squadron liked to fly its escorts of the chaff bombers. "The 4th had some ideas about how to escort the chaff birds," he says. "They would have us just sit back and do this weave, two elements of two weaving back and forth. And the chaff birds, they would fly line abreast. So for me, you would have all these planes you would have to keep track of—the two elements weaving back and forth and the chaff birds—and you wouldn't have time look out for MiGs."

In a theme repeated by pilots in other squadrons, such as those flying the HH-53 rescue helicopters and the A-1 Skyraiders that escorted them, Miller notes that the shortcoming in experience was evident, even among the units' leadership. One aspect of the lengthy war was an increase in size of the active-duty military. For officers who wanted to make a career for themselves, combat command was a critical stepping stone. At the same time, the influx of personnel was at the junior level. There was a shortage of experienced, battle-tested officers. While the three-and-a-half-year pause in the bombing of North Vietnam far from halted the air war in Southeast Asia—the Air Force continued to fly missions into heavily defended Laos and nonbombing flights, such as reconnaissance and interdiction against enemy infiltration routes, as well as ground-support missions in the South—the game had changed. Officers cutting their teeth during the halt weren't as experienced, particularly in air-to-air combat and SAM evasion, as those who had been in Rolling Thunder. Further, not only was there the question of combat experience, but also a question of relevant experience. Officers might find themselves in leading flights of aircraft with which they only had limited experience.

While the F-4 was a jack of all trades, it was a fuel guzzler. The Phantom's twin engines could get it out of trouble in a hurry, but it could be out of the frying pan and into the fire for its crew. Hitting the afterburners could burn a thousand pounds of fuel in a minute. A pilot and his backseater could easily find themselves out of fuel—flaming out—somewhere over the inhospitable lands of Southeast Asia.

To guard against this every flight would calculate the minimum fuel necessary to return to a safe base. The calculation would vary depending upon weather and flight conditions of the particular mission and would be noted by a simple and apt code word: Bingo. When the pilot, and it had to be the pilot because, much to the disappointment of WSOs, there wasn't a fuel gauge in the backseat of an F-4, reached this fuel level, he would call out to the other members of the flight, "Bingo!"

Then the dynamics of the flight formations once again came into play. Because the wings flew on the outside of the formation and were trying keep up with their element leads, they would tend to use much more fuel than the leads. For example, when a lead turned, the wing might have to use his aircraft's gas-guzzling afterburners to maintain position.

This meant that the initial Bingo call for a flight usually came from a wing, leaving a flights' lead to evaluate whether the aircraft could stretch a little more time on mission. After all, Bingo signified the minimum amount to return to a base, and there were refueling tankers orbiting over

An F-4 pilot receives a thumbs up after refueling from a KC-135 tanker. For every mission, a flight would determine the minimum amount of fuel necessary to return to a safe base. When a crew reached that level, they would call out "Bingo" over the radio. While this alerted members of the flight to low-fuel status, the North Vietnamese would also listen to these calls because when an F-4 was low on fuel, its pilot was very limited in his ability to engage or evade the enemy.
—*National Archives*

Laos. "But you could never be sure they would be there," says Valent 03B, Rick McDow. "Maybe they had gotten chased off or there could be a queue [of other aircraft] to hook up."

With its two massive engines the F-4 could reach speeds exceeding Mach 2. Compared to the Soviet MiGs, the Phantom was larger with far more thrust. A tell-tale sign of its massive engines, however, was a trail of black smoke, which made it visible from quite a distance.

The North Vietnamese were outfitted with different versions of the Soviet MiG, the most advanced of them being the MiG-21. Compared to the Phantoms, the single-seat, single-engine MiGs were smaller, more nimble, and harder to spot. One of the major design features of the MiG-21 was a triangular delta wing that increased the jet's maneuverability at subsonic speeds.

In short, the F-4 was the big-bore V-8 American muscle car of the skies whereas the MiG-21 was the small foreign sports car. And like the muscle cars rolling off the Detroit assembly lines back home, the twin engine F-4 traded power for economy. In many circumstances that was a fair deal. Thrust was an essential resource for fighter jets. Whether attacking, evading, or just intimidating, there was little substitute for the ability to quickly climb, turn or strike. However, if an F-4 found itself low on fuel, a pilot's repertoire became much more limited and far more predictable.

To compensate for its thirstiness, the F-4 could carry up to three external fuel tanks located under the wing tips and centerline. However, these tanks interfered with the maneuverability of the aircraft. "One of the first things you wanted to do was jettison the centerline tank," explains Hanton. The center tank not only added drag to the F-4 but there were cases where in attempting to make quick turn while the tank was still attached or jettisoning, it could collide with the underside of the jet where any number of things could go wrong, from hitting the under-wing-mounted ordnance to damaging the fuselage or rear ailerons.

American airpower operated under restrictive rules of engagement in Southeast Asia. Partly this was to prevent a broader war with the Chinese or the Soviets. The North Vietnamese airspace near the Chinese border was off limits. Bombing air fields and other selected military installations was avoided out of Pentagon and White House concern that foreign advisors (Chinese or Soviet) might be present. Any threat of civilian casualties was a major concern as well; the American leadership wanted to win not just the war in South Vietnam, but also the battle of public opinion both at home and internationally.

During the early aerial operations against the North, pilots needed visual confirmation to fire on the enemy. Primarily, this was to avoid any accidental downing of civilian craft or, more importantly, other American aircraft. MiGs, however, were about half the size of Phantoms. To visually confirm them meant getting in close, and this exposed another flaw in the F-4 design: The original versions of the F-4, which was designed to be an interceptor, had no gun. The designers envisioned modern air-to-air combat in a context similar to the ballistic missile race of the Cold War; attacks would be launched from a significant distance away, eliminating any concern about fighting within close quarters. The supersonic jets were equipped with Sparrow and Sidewinder missiles, capable of taking down an enemy fighter via the infrared and radar tools of modern technology. However, these weapons were ineffective at relatively short distances, and the F-4 lacked any kind of gun or cannon essential to the dogfighting that was characteristic of earlier aerial combat.

The Phantom was originally a Navy design, but the Air Force started flying the jet in the mid-1960s when the F-4 had reached its third generation, F-4C, model. Faced with mounting air-to-air combat losses on their initial entry to the war, the pilots of the 366th took charge of the issue, campaigning for a gun on the F-4 for such close-air combat. In late 1966, crews started experimenting with a 20mm cannon mounted under the nose of the plane. While a gun pod may have been crude, it immediately proved effective. Within the first month of its introduction in May of 1967, 366th pilots recorded four MiG kills. This earned the 366th the moniker it still carries even decades later, "the Gunfighters."

While some in the Air Force were reluctant to embrace the idea of a cannon and dogfighting during the bombing hiatus, the Navy launched an aerial-combat-maneuvering program, famously known as "Top Gun." However, the Air Force waited until after the war to adopt its version of the dogfighting school, "Red Flag."

The first F-4 design that was driven entirely by the Air Force was the F-4D, which arrived in Southeast Asia in June of 1967. Not long after, the F-4E debuted with an internal cannon and advanced electronics. The entire 4th TFS flew the F-4Es, which was one of the reasons it drew escort assignments.

While bureaucrats and diplomats made distinctions forged from the comfort of viewing a map, the reality was that the Communist-led war was not limited to Vietnam. Decades later, the men and women who found themselves fighting the strategic air war against the North hardly ever refer to war's location as Vietnam. Almost without exception, they call their battlefield Southeast Asia, or just SEA, forever indulging the military proclivity for abbreviation. Vietnam, Laos and Cambodia were all involved in simultaneous efforts to shed a history of Western (particularly French) colonial rule and ruling class monarchies. The region was swept by a sense of nationalism that served as catalyst for Communist influence.

While publicly the United States tried to focus on Vietnam, the truth was that the Air Force was also heavily involved in missions in Laos and a lesser extent in Cambodia. However, for air crews, like those in the Valent flight, while all three countries were engaged in this war, not all three were equal in terms of the risk posed. North Vietnam, perhaps because it had been an established country, recognized by Western and Communist powers alike, was defended by a more professional military than its rebel counterparts in Laos, Cambodia, and South Vietnam, which were more militia based.

While North Vietnam's treatment of prisoners, by every account, fell short of the international standard for humane, the Pathet Lao in Laos, and Khmer Rouge, in Cambodia, had developed notorious reputations. Tony Marshall, a WSO in the 13th Tactical Fighter Squadron, who over the next several weeks would experience events that would connect him forever with the members of the Valent flight, says there wasn't a best option for being shot down in Southeast Asia. "If you were shot down over South Vietnam or maybe Laos, you had a good chance of being rescued," he explains. "But if you weren't going to be rescued, it was probably best to go down over North Vietnam." Marshall and other air crews came to understand that with an organized military and government with strong ties to international powers like China and the Soviet Union, the North wanted prisoners alive and accounted for. In the remote areas of Laos and Cambodia where there was no real government or professional military, however, all bets were off. To a lot of crews, parts of Laos and Cambodia were like black holes; someone lost in those places might never be heard from again.

For a pilot like Aikman, who had more than a hundred combat missions in the F-105, he was back at a familiar base, making a familiar flight into Route Pack VI, but doing so with men he had never flown with, in a jet he was only beginning to get comfortable with. For all the aspects of the F-4 that made it a versatile and powerful fighter, there was also one feature very distinct from any other jet Aikman had flown. The location of the ejection handle on the F-4 was between the legs. On the F-105 and F-106, the handle was to the side, right under the left arm. Aikman had never ejected from an aircraft, and he wasn't planning to this morning. Still, during his transition into the new jet, he made particular note of this feature because not only was the ejection handle in a new location for him, but what the F-4 designers left in its place was just as important. "In the F-4, on the left side, is where they place the release for separating the pilot from the seat and parachute," explains Aikman. This emergency release was intended so that a pilot could quickly escape the cockpit if something went wrong on the ground. For a pilot rocketing over the jungle, accidentally confusing the seat release and the ejection handle could disastrously seal his fate.

With both the mission and flight briefing behind them, Aikman and Hanton ate breakfast, and then made their way to the flight lockers. Most air personnel flew with few personal items, like wedding rings. For the most part, what they carried would be their ID card, dog tags, and Geneva Convention card. At their lockers, they would also pack up their survival gear, which included emergency radios, three cans of water, and a smoke flare. It was then out to the awaiting aircraft to perform the preflight check of their aircraft and be ready for takeoff, which was scheduled at a little before 0800. However, as they arrived at their F4-E, they became aware of a rather significant problem. "As we got out to the flight line, there were seven or eight maintenance guys running around the airplane," explains Aikman. "They had the back seat out and were checking something, the radio or the ejection seat." Aikman sent word ahead to the flight lead that he and Hanton might not get airborne. "The procedure was that if you weren't able to get airborne within thirty minutes of your flight, they had an airborne spare, and that would take your place."

Whatever the fault was, the maintenance crew seemed to get it in order quickly. They buttoned up the F-4E, and Aikman and Hanton went into their preflight check. "We managed to get off about twenty to thirty minutes after the rest of the flight, just inside the window," explains Aikman. "I took the most direct route to the rendezvous point possible, and we were able to get there and take our normal spot in line with tankers."

For the most part, the eight men who comprised the Valent flight that morning were unfamiliar with each other. The four men of the second element, Valent 03 and 04, couldn't know the day's events were about to bond them together in a harsh, unexpected way. Perhaps most telling, despite the significance of what this day would come to mean for each of the four, each of them only has a vague recollection of the members of the first element, other than of their flight lead.

Simply put, the 4th TFS was about to fly a team of eight men into the most heavily fortified area an air force has ever seen, and most of them didn't even know each other's name.

NOTES

5. "Vietnam War Almanac," John T Correll, *Air Force Magazine*, September 2004
6. "Linebacker: Overview of the First 120 Days," *Contemporary Historical Examination of Current Operations* (CHECO), September 27, 1973, p. 12
7. "Linebacker: Overview of the First 120 Days," *Contemporary Historical Examination of Current Operations* (CHECO), September 27, 1973, p. 22
8. Ibid.
9. Ibid, p 45.
10. On June 27, 1972, the USS *Sterrett*, a Belknap-class cruiser was on PIRAZ station as Red Crown. Earlier in the war, in addition to other cruisers, the Navy also used large destroyers as Red Crown.
11. *Clashes*, Marshall Michel, Naval Institute Press, p 226.
12. *USAF F-4 Phantom II MiG Killers 1972–73*, Peter Davies, Osprey Publishing, p 16
13. *Clashes*, Marshall Michel, p. 194
14. "Linebacker: Overview of the First 120 Days," *Contemporary Historical Examination of Current Operations* (CHECO), September 27, 1973, p. 72

CHAPTER THREE

MAKING THE BEST OF A TOUGH SITUATION

At NKP (Nakhon Phanom, Thailand), it was nearing dawn as Chuck McGrath assembled his gear and boarded Jolly Green 73, the Sikorsky HH-53C that would be piloted by Maj. Leo Thacker today. Rounding out the crew for Jolly Green 73 this morning would be copilot Capt. Frank Mason and a flight engineer.

This was their routine. June 27, 1972, was like most mission days. McGrath and the crew of the Jolly Green had only limited knowledge of what the rest of the Air Force was doing this morning. They knew there was a mission North. There always was a mission North. The specifics were irrelevant for the 40th ARRS. Their job was to be airborne ahead of the F-4s and other elements of mission, go into an orbit near the North Vietnam border, and wait.

The HH-53, with its twin engines, midair refueling capabilities,

On June 27, 1972, Jolly Green 73, with Chuck McGrath and Chuck Morrow in the back as PJs, was piloted by Maj. Leo Thacker. Thacker was a very experienced helicopter pilot who flew with a combination of faith and skill.–*R. Hutchinson*

and minigun positions on the sides and out the rear, was an effective tool for search and rescue. It could orbit as long as necessary, occasionally meeting up with a HC-130 tanker to take on more fuel, while the fighters were in harm's way.

As pilot, Major Thacker was in command of the aircraft. The crew's job was to meet up with another HH-53 and divide up their high-bird, low-bird assignments should a call come in. Thacker already had more than ten years with the Air Force and was on his second tour of Vietnam.

Thacker loved flying helicopters. His first tour flying a Bell UH-1F was with the 20th Special Operations Squadron, whose primary role was the conduct of unconventional warfare. With the 20th Thacker participated in several harrowing missions and also found himself affected by the high-risk lifestyle that went with the squadron's assignments. At some point the rush gave way to burnout. Decades later, Thacker openly acknowledges that his nerves were shot as a combat pilot. Then, in the midst of the hell that is war, he found a new taste for religion. Prayer services helped lead him to embrace both God and his mission.

In McGrath's opinion, Thacker was an experienced pilot who always brought the bird home safely. That's what mattered most. Whether it happened by physics, luck, or divine intervention didn't matter.

The Air Force put its faith more in operational protocol. Not long after takeoff from NKP, copilot Frank Mason noticed a warning for the utility hydraulics. For an HH-53C arriving over a survivor with no hydraulics would be like a fire engine showing up at an inferno with no hoses. The utility hydraulic system was critical to operating the hoist. During a rescue attempt, the hoist would be lowered with a forest penetrator attached, a device that when folded resembles a pregnant javelin and can push down through the canopy of jungle trees to the ground below. When unfolded, the sides of the forest penetrator, the three "paddles" as they are referred to, create impromptu seating for a PJ or a survivor. Then the hydraulics kick in again, pulling up the hoist line with whomever is attached.

With the hydraulic warning noted, Thacker was directed to divert JG 73 to Udorn, a base slightly northwest of NKP. As it turns out, the Jolly Green that was flying high bird for Thacker that morning had also developed an issue and it was being diverted as well. The 40th's alert Jolly Greens, the backups for JG 73 and 60 would be pressed into action and sent north to their orbit over Laos.

With another high bird and low bird on their way north, Jolly Green 73 might end up on the second string today. Even if the hydraulic issue was remedied quickly, only something near catastrophic, like the shoot-down of multiple planes, would call for JG 73 and its crew to be sent north. For a PJ like Chuck McGrath, who was trying to fly as much as he could on what was left of his tour, it looked like the day might turn out to be a bust.

For members of the 40th ARRS, Udorn had been their home up until July of 1971 when the squadron started to transition to NKP, which was east of Udorn, right on the border with Laos. McGrath, however, couldn't be faulted for having bad feelings about a return to his first home in Southeast Asia because, even after having relocated to NKP as a novice PJ, McGrath made another trip to Udorn on a day he could never forget.

NKP was east of Udorn, and being on the border, it was the ideal location for launching rescue missions in Southeast Asia. Just about eleven months ago the 40th ARRS was in the middle of its transition to the new base. Just a little earlier, Candy McGrath had arrived in Thailand and was settling into her post at the base in Korat, about three hundred miles southwest of Chuck's new home at NKP.

While the rest of the 40th transferred to the new base, the PJs at NKP were on six-day alerts for flight operations. On the morning of July 21,1971, the call came in for a SAR package to head north. Chuck was going to get a crack at his first operational rescue. However there was a twist to this operation: the Jolly Green wasn't being sent in to rescue a downed airman, but a remote piloted vehicle (RPV), the precursor to today's unmanned drones. The RPV had gone down in Laos just north of the Plain of Jars, and it was carrying critical reconnaissance data. While they were going in with an escort of prop-driven A-1 Skyraiders, there would be no backup high bird.

The RPV was an interesting aircraft in Vietnam and the Cold War era. In the fall of 1968, with President Johnson's ordered halt of bombing North Vietnam, the Soviets and Chinese began to pump resources into the North to build up its defenses. Ships from the Soviet Union and China's northern rail lines arrived with SA-2 surface-to-air missiles (SAMs), MiG-21s, and antiaircraft artillery (AAA). Just as important, Soviet and

Soviet-block technicians and military advisors arrived to train the North Vietnamese on how to use this technology.

As North Vietnam's air defenses grew stronger, U.S. Air Force reconnaissance flights likewise became more hazardous. The American intelligence community began to rely heavily on satellite imagery and photographs taken from high altitude SR-71 Blackbird flights. While the intelligence gathered from these sources was quite good, it didn't give as complete a picture as needed. But low-altitude passes over the heavily fortified areas of the North were too risky.

Though not widely known at the time, the CIA had been using RPVs to penetrate China's airspace. The development of these unmanned craft came in response to the May 1960 shoot down of Francis Gary Power's and his U-2 by a surface-to-air missile over the Soviet Union. The incident established two facts: One, the Soviet SAMs, successors of which were now being employed extensively in North Vietnam, were formidable weapons. Two, the political fallout of an American pilot and his spy plane being shot down over Communist soil was too much to bear.

The CIA needed an aircraft that could fly low enough to avoid SAMs, take its pictures, and then get back safely. But it was all the better to hedge this survivability with expendability; make it cheap, replaceable and unmanned, and it would be reconnaissance without the risk.

The prototype was the Firebee pilotless target drone built by Ryan Aircraft. The Ryan AQM-34 flew countless missions over North Vietnam taking pictures and probing SAM radar sites. They were carried aloft on a DC-130, a specialized Hercules optimized to carry and control drones. Once released, the RPV would fly a programmed round trip over their target, sightseeing all along the way, taking dozens of critically important aerial photos. Normally these RPVs would be recovered in midair. In addition to a main parachute to slow its descent, the RPV would deploy a drag chute, a smaller parachute with several hundred feet of cable connecting it to the body of the RPV. A helicopter equipped with a MARS midair retrieval system, a sort of trap that could be extended below the helicopter, would catch the drag chute in midair. Once secured, the attached line would be reeled in and the main parachute released. If the midair rendezvous failed the RPV initiated a signal beacon that was used to track it to its location.

This particular RPV, called Buffalo Hunter, had come down in northern Laos, not the most accessible or hospitable region of Southeast Asia. But Air Force intelligence wanted the information Buffalo Hunter had collected, and it fell on the shoulders of McGrath and the crew of the Jolly Green to get it.

This shows the crash site of the Buffalo Hunter drone and Jolly Green 54. The drone's parachute is visible near the top of the photo, indicating the drone's initial location. The crew of JG 54 used cargo straps to drag the drone downhill to a clearing on the hillside so that the HH-53C would be able to hover over it and attach a full cargo sling.—*C. McGrath*

Normally a group like the 21st Special Operations Squadron would be assigned to this kind of operation, but the 21st, which was based at NKP at the time, lacked refueling probes for their Sikorsky CH-53helicopters. While these helicopters were a close relative of the HH-53 Jolly Greens flown by the 40th ARRS, the Jolly Green's midair refueling capability was a critical advantage for search and rescue, even when it was an inanimate drone that needed rescuing.

The Air Forced tapped Jolly Green 54 for the job. It would fly out north from NKP under the command of Maj. Clyde Bennett, the pilot. His copilot was Captain Hugh "Butch" Robins. In the back TSgt. James "J. D." Adams was the flight engineer. The other pararescueman joining McGrath on this mission was TSgt. Jon Hoberg, a veteran PJ who was a bit of a mentor for McGrath and other young PJs.

The preflight briefing that day revealed the challenge facing the crew: recovering the RPV required the use of a cargo sling. However, the RPV had gone down in very hilly terrain, and a cargo sling could only reach about fifty feet below an HH-53. Given the terrain and the jungle canopy, for the helicopter to get that low would be impossible.

The plan was to use a series of cargo straps tied together. One PJ would descend from the Jolly Green and attach the cargo straps to the drone. The straps wouldn't be strong or stable enough to carry the drone all the way back to their base, but they should be sufficient for the HH-53 to drag the drone to a clearing where Major Bennett could hover lower than fifty feet so that one of the PJs could hook up the cargo sling. The helicopter could then return with the RPV hanging from its belly.

Clyde Bennett waits in the 40th ARRS alert shack, smoking one of his cigars. In July 1971, Bennett piloted JG 54 to the hilly terrain of northern Laos where Chuck McGrath would take part in his first combat mission as a PJ. Bennett had been an All American end on the University of South Carolina's football team and had played a year of professional football in the Canadian Football League prior to joining the U.S. Air Force.—*C. Bennett*

Every preflight briefing had one consistent question: What about the bad guys? A Jolly Green was a large, relatively slow-moving target. Bennett and Robbins would have their hands full holding the craft in a hover on the hillside location. With Adams, McGrath, and Hoberg in the rear manning the miniguns, they could suppress small-arms fire for awhile, but the terrain wouldn't offer much flexibility. The major tactical advantage for a helicopter is its maneuverability. Compared to a jet, it isn't fast, but it is nimble. For example, should the rescue bird start taking ground fire its pilot could readily change the helicopter's profile making it harder to hit or orient it so that the crew could return fire using the miniguns. However, the more difficult the terrain and its features, such as, rocks, steep valleys, and tall trees, the less flexibility a pilot has to use his aircraft's maneuverability. Further, the HH-53 had a significant defensive weakness in that it had no forward-facing gun.

The intelligence officers in the briefing for this mission had reasoned that given the remoteness of the area and the lack of reports of any North Vietnamese or Pathet Lao activity, Major Bennett and his crew could expect an uneventful flight. They weren't even going to have to cross the border into North Vietnam and would be out of the range of the SAM batteries and other defenses the North had built up over the years.

Just as the Viet Cong and North Vietnamese had ignored the July 1962 agreement to stay out of Laos, the United States also ignored some provisions of the pact, conducting a secret war in Laos. While the North Vietnamese partnered with the Pathet Lao in terms of using Laos as a supply route to the south, American activity was generally limited to pilots who provided air support to anticommunist Laotian fighters on the ground. This was primarily an advisory role as the pilots flew generally unarmed, slow-moving, prop-driven aircraft like Cessna's O-1 "Bird Dog" or the U-17. Completely covert, the planes carried no U.S. insignia and the pilots wore civilian clothes.

These forward air controllers were known as Ravens, and for McGrath's mission of recovering the RPV his Jolly Green would rendezvous with a Raven FAC to lead them into the area to recover the downed RPV. The mission itself didn't have to be covert as the recovery of downed personnel and aircraft, such as this RPV, in Laos was permitted by the July 1962 treaty. But, with a Raven FAC and the classified nature of Buffalo Hunter's assignment, the Jolly Green crew understood that the sooner they got in and out with the drone, the better.

Technical Sergeant Hoberg, the more experienced of the two pararescuemen won the coin flip and took the PJ1 position on the operation. Chuck would be PJ2, manning the rear minigun, which was operable when the rear ramp on the HH-53 was lowered to a level position. This would be Chuck's first combat mission even though he had been on alert several times, and as much as he felt ready for today's quasi-covert mission, he still hadn't fully gotten his feet wet.

Chuck, like anyone who had yet to see battle, was an unknown quantity to everyone in the 40th ARRS. He had all the training, but the question how would he respond to the unpredictable world of a PJ in combat was impossible to know.

For the veteran PJs, like Morrow and Hoberg, there was an incentive to mentor these newcomers. They were part of a team, part of a Jolly Green crew. As good as the experienced PJs were at their mission, war could turn the tables in a hurry, and their lives might depend on these youngsters.

Hoberg's previous tour had been with the 37th ARRS out of Da Nang, flying in the smaller Sikorsky HH-3F. Hoberg had seen his share of action with the 37th and received a Distinguished Flying Cross for his part in the rescue of an F-100 Misty FastFAC pilot in October 1969. A year later, Hoberg was assigned to the 40th ARRS and made the transition to the newer HH-53. As a member of the 40th he took part in one of the most celebrated rescue missions of the Vietnam war, the Son Tay raid of November 21, 1970.

The Son Tay POW camp was just outside Hanoi, and U.S. intelligence believed as many as eighty POWs were at the camp. To rescue these POWs they devised a daring special forces raid. As it turned out, the North Vietnamese had evacuated the camp and the POWs before the operation, but the mission proved to be a tactical success and Hoberg's selection for it, along with the Silver Star he received for his role in it, established him as a PJ that a novice like Chuck McGrath could learn a lot from.

On McGrath's first combat search and rescue, he would also be joined by decorated flight engineer J. D. Adams, who had begun his Air Force career in 1955 as a woodwind player in the Air Force Band. After nine years of service, with a wife and three kids, and frozen in pay grade, Adams volunteered to be retrained as a helicopter mechanic, deploying to Southeast Asia in 1968 where he was assigned to the 21st Special Operations Squadron. The only problem was the 21st already had plenty of mechanics. The operations officer handed Adams the flight engineer exam, which he aced. "He said 'Congratulations son, you are now a flight engineer. Good Luck,'" Adams recalls. Sergeant Adams went on to receive a Distinguished Flying Cross for his part in the rescue of two members of a long-range-reconnaissance patrol in Laos. In addition, he received Silver Star for helping to organize the ground defense after his CH-3E helicopter was shot down while trying evacuate Thai mercenaries from a Laotian air strip at Muong Soui.

PJs Gary Osborne (left) and Jon Hoberg (right) in Guam 1968. Gary Osborne was one of Chuck McGrath's roommates at NKP. During Chuck McGrath's first combat mission on July 21, 1971, Hoberg, one of Chuck's mentors in Southeast Asia, was seriously injured. Hoberg would eventually recover and served as a PJ in the Air Force Reserves for a number of years. He also had a successful career in computer programming in civilian life.—*Angela Osborne*

With veterans who both had earned a Distinguished Flying Cross and a Silver Star on either side of him, McGrath felt comfortable riding in the back of the Jolly Green.

The monsoon season had begun in Southeast Asia, and both rain and cloud cover were causing some problems for the pilots, Bennett and Robins, as they headed north, into the "barrel," a name pilots used to describe northern Laos, in part because Operation Barrel Roll was the name given to the secret U.S. air war in Laos. The HH-53 eventually rendezvoused with a Raven FAC, flying just due north of Vientiane.

For this mission there would be two Raven FACs providing support, the primary FAC, Raven 12, was a propeller-driven Cessna U-17 flown by Lt. Jim Roper. Roper had been flying FACs first in South Vietnam and now in Laos for close to a year. In fact, this was his first day back flying having just recently returned from leave in Australia. Earlier this morning he had flown out of Lima 54, an Air America airstrip at Louangprabang, with another Raven to locate the downed RPV and to determine the best route through the mountains and weather to the crash site. McGrath's Jolly Green and the accompanying Sandys would rely upon Roper's expertise to find a break in the cloud cover and get them safely through the steep karst rock formations and valleys.

During this earlier flight, Roper had directed an Air Force RF-4, a specialized reconnaissance Phantom armed only with cameras, over the site as it made several low-level passes, photographing the downed drone. The U-17 carried several tubes under its wings for holding smoke rockets, which could be used for marking targets. On one of the passes, one of the rockets appeared to fire, perhaps due to faulty electronics. The rocket narrowly missed the other Raven FAC. After finishing some notations, Roper headed back to Lima 54 to take on additional fuel and check out the electrical system on his U-17. The only other arms onboard were Roper's sidearm and a M16 he carried in order to defend himself in the event he was shot down. Upon landing at Lima 54, one of the Air America's mechanics checked out the rocket tube. The misfire had not been caused by an electrical problem at all. It had been caused by ground fire hitting the end of the tube. The mechanic pointed to several bullet holes under the fuselage.

Clearly this meant despite the assurances to the contrary, there were unfriendlies in the area. Refueled and armed with the knowledge of enemy presence in the vicinity of the RPV, Roper headed off to rendezvous with Jolly Green 54 and the accompanying Sandys. At least the weather had taken a turn for the better in that it had stopped raining, but clouds still lingered.

Before proceeding to the rescue site, Jolly Green 54 would need to refuel in flight with a HC-130 in order to complete the mission. While Pilot Bennett and Flight Engineer Adams were busy coordinating the refueling, McGrath and Hoberg tied the cargo straps together that they were going to use to drag the drone down the hillside to a more accessible location for the Jolly Green's cargo sling. After topping off the tanks, JG 54 made contact with Roper's Raven 12. Roper found a hole in the clouds and took the Sandys down into the valley where the drone was located. Its orange and white parachute draped over the tree limbs and clearly marked the RPV's position. As Roper closed on the location he wanted to make sure the Sandys had their guard up.

"Sandy lead, this is Raven 12," Roper radioed to the A-1 Skyraider, "Be advised that I took ground fire from this location this morning. There are no friendlies in this area. So, you are clear to engage if fired upon. Do you copy?"[15]

The Sandy lead acknowledged Roper's message and suggested some ground passes to troll for fire. After at least a dozen passes over the site without drawing ground fire, Roper and the Sandys figured it was safe to bring in the Jolly Green.

After orbiting over the area, Jolly Green 54 got a good look at the downed RPV. It had crashed on a heavily forested hill, which had almost a forty-degree slope. However, just below the site was an opening in the forest that was suitable for lowering a PJ to the ground. Bennett made some calculations regarding the drag that would be caused by carrying the RPV and the resultant fuel consumption. He gave the go-ahead to retrieve the RPV in one piece.

This sign at 40th ARRS' shack on the Nakhon Phanom (NKP) base says it all. The 40th was in the process of transitioning from Udorn to NKP in July 1971.—*D. Stovall*

Hoberg would ride down the hoist line on the jungle penetrator, which looked like a three-prong anchor that could be folded up. Once on the ground, Hoberg would make his way to the RPV and cut away the main parachute. The Flight Engineer Adams and PJ McGrath would open up the hatch on the bottom of JG 54 and lower the cargo straps to the ground by tying additional straps to them until they could reach Hoberg on the ground. He would then secure the string of cargo straps to the drone so that Bennett could drag it to the clearing.

After being lowered to the ground Hoberg stumbled and fell due to the steep grade, losing his rifle in the dense undergrowth. Making his way to the RPV, Hoberg cut away the parachute. Then, Adams and McGrath began to lower the cargo straps, but they were a few feet short of reaching the RPV, requiring Bennett to bring the helicopter closer to Hoberg.

Some of the surrounding trees were close to two-hundred-feet tall. This left JG 54's pilot very little room in which to maneuver. If, for whatever reason, he drifted off his position while attempting to lower the helicopter, the rotors of the Jolly Green would crash into the trees. With Adams guiding him, Bennett dropped into position. At that moment, Bennett's intercom sounded.

"PJ to pilot, I can hear gun fire," Hoberg reported. Immediately tension rose. Enemy fire was coming from somewhere in the jungle. The Jolly Green was not only hovering like a sitting duck, but it was in a precarious spot between the tall trees and steep hillside. Unlike a normal rescue operation, this covert mission had no backup bird. With the sound of gunfire increasing, Hoberg hurried to hitch up the straps to the RPV, and Bennett began to drag it down to the clearing.

Once the RPV reached its improved location, Bennett brought the helicopter into a low hover. Adams and McGrath lowered the cargo sling to Hoberg. Adams watched through the HH-53's cargo hatch as Hoberg attached the sling to the drone. Adams then began to work the hoist controls on the right side of the helicopter while watching out the open door to see Hoberg on the ground. Everything was set: The cargo sling was secure, the drag chute was on the RPV, and Hoberg was waiting to be pulled up the hoist line. As Hoberg was hitching up to the penetrator, Bennett, began to apply power to the Jolly Green's engines to pull up from its position. Suddenly the entire crew of JG 54 heard a loud bang. It was the unmistakable sound of ground fire hitting the fuselage. Bennett continued to apply power, but the aircraft didn't seem to be going anywhere. The pilot knew he was experiencing a power loss. The ground fire must have hit the engines. What was worse, the RPV was now an anchor, sliding down the hillside, pulling JG 54, its crew, and Hoberg, dangling on the hoist line, with it.

Bennett knew he had to find a way to increase power or his Jolly Green was going to crash into the jungle trees. In an effort to maintain a hover, he jettisoned the two external fuel tanks. Surmising the situation, Adams released his gunners belt and dived toward the cargo hatch with the hope of releasing the sling, freeing the Jolly Green from its anchor.

Bennett realized, however, that the HH-53 wasn't going to make it. "Jon, get out of the way. We're coming down!" he shouted to Hoberg who had his feet on the ground at this point.

All the while, McGrath was on the rear minigun and could see the trees getting dangerously close to the rotor blades. He began to warn Bennett over the intercom but before he could utter anything more than "We've got trees," the novice PJ could see the main rotor hit the trees, cutting a swath through the forest with the snapped-off rotor blade flying in all directions.

Crashing into the steep grade of the hill, the twenty-ton helicopter, tumbled over onto its side. As it did, what was left of the rotor dug into the ground, kicking up dirt and vegetation, clouding the air with debris as pieces of the six blades flew into the jungle.

The HH-53 continued to roll down the hillside. Inside the helicopter, fire extinguishers, which had been lashed down, crashed about. Ammunition cans spilled their contents while loose small arms careened across the interior of the bird. The mangled craft finally came to rest against a stand of trees on the hill. Major Bennett and his copilot, Captain Robins, both of whom had remained securely fastened to their seats, came through the crash unscathed and managed to exit the HH-53 through its forward escape hatch.

During the ordeal, Adams, who had unbelted himself when trying to release the cargo sling, had been thrown around the inside of the craft as it rolled down the hillside and hit by the loose debris in the cabin. Now, as the crumpled Jolly Green settled into place, Adams found himself laying on his back on what had been the ceiling of the cabin, soaked in fuel.

Fearing for his safety, Adams tried to make a quick exit through the helicopter's open side door. As he did so, he was struck by intense pain. Expecting the helicopter explode at any moment, Adams managed to exit the craft, passing by one of the HH-53's two massive engines that had been torn loose. Once at a safe distance, Adams collapsed, feeling pain all over his body.

McGrath was the last person out of the belly-up bird. With only his gunner's belt to restrain him, he had been tossed about the aft cabin as well. Equipment was strewn all over the interior of the wrecked helicopter. As he exited the crash, McGrath heard moaning. He turned to see Adams who was holding his side.

"What's the matter?" asked McGrath. "My ribs, my back," responded Adams. McGrath's pararescue training kicked in. He began working on Adams, and then called out to Bennett, casting aside the formality of rank and salutations. "I don't know where Jon is," the junior PJ said in regard to Hoberg.

Pilot Bennett and Copilot Robins made their way over to McGrath. Bennett looked up the hill and told McGrath he would search up the slope for Hoberg. McGrath resumed tending to Adams injuries, but it was only a moment before Bennett returned. "Hey, PJ," the pilot said starkly to McGrath, "Better get your medical kit. The man's hurt real bad."

McGrath retrieved the medical kit from the wreck and ran up the steep slope. Reaching Hoberg, he stopped instantly and looked at the prone man. Never in his life had he seen anything like it. Hoberg managed to sit up, and the extent of his injuries became even more apparent. A piece of the shattered rotor blade had torn off his helmet and had neatly sliced off half of his face from below his left eye. The cheek bone and part of his jaw were gone while the flesh hung down in one piece.

McGrath looked at Hoberg. "Jesus, Jon," was all the junior PJ managed to say as he quickly went to work on his mentor. He applied a head bandage to Hoberg's face after gently placing the flesh back into place. The massive gash had caused some loss of blood, but amazingly, Hoberg did not seem to be heavily bleeding; the bandage seemed to be controlling most of the bleeding. Hoberg looked up at McGrath and pointed to the inside of his arm. "You want an IV?" asked McGrath. Hoberg nodded his head. Injured as he was, Hoberg still retained a PJ's medical awareness. He needed intravenous fluids to keep him from going into shock.

McGrath had little problem finding one of Hoberg's large veins and began the IV. Finding nothing to hang the bottle from, he strung it around his neck. In the aftermath of the crash of JG 54, McGrath, who had been tossed around in the aft cabin, had lost his helmet. Realizing he might need a helmet with its radio headset, McGrath grabbed Hoberg's helmet that had been cut by the rotor blade.

Jim Roper in Raven 12 had been monitoring Jolly Green 54 while orbiting over the RPV site. He had been speaking with Bennett and Robins, and they had reported that they were picking up the PJ and getting ready to lift off. Everything appeared to be going quite well, and Roper made a left bank over the site, momentarily losing site of JG 54. When he came back around, he was surprised to see the Jolly Green was gone. He wondered if it could have lifted off so quickly and flown up through the cloud cover.

"Jolly Green 54, this is Raven 12. Do you copy? Over," Roper queried on the radio. Then he passed over the site and realized how quickly things had gone from fine to disaster.

"Sandy Lead, this is Raven 12," Roper said into his radio. "Jolly Green 54 has gone in and is invert on the ground." Roper pulled out so that the Sandys could swoop in. Bad guys were on the ground somewhere and the Sandys might need to take them out. Meanwhile, it was clear to Roper the crew of the Jolly Green was in trouble, and he made the call for help, which was heard by Air America aircraft operating to the south.

Overhead, McGrath could see a pair of Sandys and Roper's Raven U-17. Off in the distance was the sound of rifle fire. Pulling a radio from his pants pocket, McGrath tried to reach Bennett, "Jolly 54 Alpha," McGrath said, querying Bennett's call sign "This is 54 Delta."

Hearing McGrath on the radio, the Sandy pilot interjected before McGrath could raise Bennett. The Sandy wanted to know the status of the crew.

This baptism by fire was affirming that Chuck McGrath belonged among the enlisted elite known as pararescuemen. The year and a half of training was coming to fruition as he took charge of the situation. But this was still his first mission. For all that he knew and could do to get the five of them to safety, some of the finer, seemingly inconsequential details were lost. In his earlier transmission, he had referred to himself as "Delta," the PJ1, who in fact was Hoberg. McGrath didn't bother to correct it as he was with Hoberg. Now, needing to communicate everyone's status to the Sandy, rather than confusing the matter for the A-1 pilot, he continued, transposing his and Hoberg's call signs.

"Alpha and Bravo are OK," McGrath transmitted relaying the status of Pilot Bennett and Copilot Robins. "Charlie has back injuries and Echo has critical injuries." He needed to communicate that Flight Engineer Adams was hurt and that PJ Hoberg needed emergency care. He could clarify the call signs later, but perhaps it hadn't dawned on the twenty-two-year-old who else might be listening to the radio traffic.

"Roger, we'll orbit, help is inbound" said the Sandy pilot. "ETA of help is fifteen minutes." Hoberg heard the last response from the radio. He looked skyward and extended his middle finger toward the planes. To a seasoned veteran like him, "fifteen minutes" was military speak for "no idea." Fifteen minutes later, Hoberg managed to get McGrath's attention. He pointed to his watch. Still no rescue bird. Hoberg looked skyward and again gave his one-finger salute.

With his injuries, Hoberg was nearly choking on his own blood. His mouth would fill with blood and he would occasionally lean forward, to spit out what he could. He now started to have problems breathing. "Jon, do you want a cric, a cut?" McGrath asked referring to an emergency cricothyrotomy—an incision near the top of the trachea to create an emergency airway. Hoberg shook his head no.

Roper in Raven 12 headed out of the valley to rendezvous with two Air America helicopters, a UH-1 Huey and Sikorsky H-34 to pick up the survivors. Roper made contact with the pair of aircraft, and it was apparent the UH-1 pilot was none to happy with his mission because he was low on fuel. The two helicopters followed him through a break in the clouds down into the valley.

Off in the distance McGrath could hear the distinct sound of a Huey, and after a minute, both he and Hoberg could see the blue and silver Air America markings. The helicopter spotted the pilot, copilot, and flight engineer down the hill before he saw McGrath and Hoberg, who were in an opening above them. The steepness of the hill and the thickness of the trees made it impossible for the Huey to land.

Low on fuel, the Huey pilot planned to fly out Adams and Hoberg, but he needed to find a place to set the helicopter down and somehow manage to get the two injured men off the hill. The clearing where Hoberg and McGrath were would work, but the pilot couldn't land at Adams's location even though he was hovering right over him, Bennett, and Robins.

"Hold on to the skid of the copter," the Huey's flight engineer shouted to Adams. "We'll drag you up to the clearing." Adams did as he was told. And as the craft tried to move up the hill to the clearing, McGrath could hear Adams screaming over the noise of the helicopter engine. Jim Adams was crying out in pain as he hung from the skids of the helicopter making its way to the clearing where the two PJs were waiting.

Once in the clearing, the pilot brought the helicopter to a hover with the nose pointing in toward the hill. While bird hovered, McGrath helped the Huey's flight engineer pull Adams into the helicopter. McGrath then went back to Hoberg and helped him to the Huey. The Air America flight engineer grabbed Hoberg's IV bottle from McGrath as he climbed aboard to care for his fellow PJ. The flight engineer looked at him and pointed out of the aircraft. With Hoberg and Adams already on board, there wasn't any room for McGrath. As McGrath jumped out, the Air America pilot made a 180-degree turn before taking off. This sent McGrath scrambling to the ground to avoid the rear rotor blades of the helicopter. As the helicopter followed Raven 12 out of the valley, Jim Adams looked at Jon Hoberg and his bandaged face.

Hoberg, unable to speak, took his right index finger and began to write in a pool of his own blood on the cabin deck. Adams read the word "where" and answered. "I don't have a clue, Jon."

The pair were heading for Lima 54's airfield and then on to the Swiss Infirmary in Louangprabang for immediate medical treatment. That is, if their Huey's fuel supply would hold out.

Cleaning himself off and spitting out the dirt he had eaten getting out of the way of the helicopter's tail rotor, McGrath made his way down the hill to join Major Bennett and Captain Robins. The group waited for a second Air America helicopter to arrive.

A Sikorsky H-34 made its way through the hills to the clearing where McGrath and the group waited. It hovered above the clearing, dropping a horse collar device to pick them up. Robins was first up. Bennett looked at McGrath, "Go ahead, son, I'll stay here."

"No, sir, you go ahead. I'll secure the radios and the medical kit," said McGrath. He didn't know what kind of medical facilities might be waiting for Adams and Hoberg or how long it might take to reach proper medical care.

"Okay, get the equipment and make it back here in a hurry," said Bennett as he ascended up the hoist. McGrath made his way down the hill, grabbed the additional radios and medical equipment and headed back to the waiting helicopter. Once there the H-34's flight engineer lowered the horse collar to McGrath. McGrath attached the horse collar around his body and gave the thumbs up signal for the flight engineer to lift away. The device didn't budge. After a moment, the engineer looked down at McGrath and signaled that the hoist wasn't working. They would have to send another helicopter to get McGrath. McGrath promptly unhooked the collar and watched as the helicopter lifted up and flew out.

In the wake of the departing helicopter, there was a growing silence in the valley, broken only by the sound of the Sandys overhead and the occasional rifle fire that was undoubtedly aimed at the orbiting A-1 Skyraiders. McGrath realized that if the bad guys could shoot at the Sandys, they could shoot at him too. He looked toward the skies and called on his radio, "PJ to Sandy. When's the bird going to make it here?"

"Hang on. It'll be here in 15 minutes," replied the pilot in the Sandy. It wasn't the assurance McGrath had been seeking. Off in the distant he could hear the distinct "crack" of an AK47 rifle. McGrath looked down at his .38 revolver. He'd be seriously outgunned if it came to it. He knew someone was working on getting him out of this predicament, but he couldn't help a feeling of being alone on this hillside.

The truth was McGrath was far from being alone. His squadron mates at both NKP and Udorn had been monitoring the progress of the recovery mission on UHF radio frequencies. They were well aware of the plight of the aircraft, the drone and the crew. As a matter of fact, due to McGrath inverting the PJ alpha codes, his squadron thought that it was McGrath, not Hoberg, that was one the seriously injured.

In the midst of these radio transmissions, the telephone rang at the PJ Section of the 40th ARRS at NKP. On the other end of the line, calling from the hospital in Korat was Airman Candy McGrath looking to speak with her husband. The mission had been classified. They couldn't even tell her he was out on a search and rescue. What was worse, everyone in the shack through Chuck was the one with severe facial injuries. No one wanted to tell a newlywed that her husband of a few months had just had half his face torn off by a disintegrating rotor blade. Technical Sergeant Chuck Salome got on the phone and tried to bluff Candy, telling her that her husband was up at Udorn for the day. Candy got off the phone with Salome and called the PJ shack in Udorn only to be given the same vague treatment regarding Chuck's whereabouts.

Back on the hillside in Northern Laos, McGrath heard a helicopter in the distance heading directly toward him. As it neared, he could also hear the sounds of gunfire. As the bird came over him, McGrath could see it was another Air America H-34. Once again, as the pilot went into a hover, a flight engineer sent a hoist line down to McGrath. He hooked on, hoping the hoist would hold together long enough to get him into the helicopter. As he rode the line up, McGrath could more clearly hear the gunfire. The rounds were coming from directly in front of them. Little did he realize that this would not be the last time in Southeast Asia that he would have to ride up a hoist line among gunfire.

Once at the door, the crew chief pulled McGrath inside just in time for the pilot to execute a 180-degree turn for a high-speed exit with the orbiting Sandys bringing up the rear. It was a relatively quiet ride to Lima 54. While they hadn't taken him home to NKP, McGrath was happy for the lift to safety and wanted to make a point of thanking the crew when they landed.

McGrath was wearing Hoberg's helmet, and the boom mic had been ripped off by the disintegrating rotor. Since he couldn't talk to the crew on the intercom, he began writing a note, and recounted how they had taken fire from the twelve o'clock position as he was going up the hoist. He wondered if the crew had realized it. As he left the helicopter, he noticed the flight engineer with an Uzi machine pistol.

Something told McGrath that this probably wasn't the first the crew had taken fire. Crazy or cool, it was hard to tell which was the better description for these Air America crews, but McGrath was grateful nonetheless for the ride.

Both Hoberg and Adams were admitted to the Swiss Infirmary for treatment. The medics had managed to stitch Hoberg back together enough so that he could handle an eventual transport to an Air Force hospital in Thailand. It would be a long road to recovery for the PJ, and his time in combat service would come to an end even though he continued serving in the military for many years.

Adams had his broken ribs taped and his back X-rayed. Like Hoberg, he would spend the night at Lima 54 before being transferred to an Air Force hospital.

Chuck was alone waiting at the airfield when Bennett and Robins returned from seeing Hoberg and Adams. The word was they were to catch a flight to Thailand before night fall. In the course of communicating back with NKP, the crew was able to clarify who was serving as PJ1 and who was PJ2, or more clearly, that it had been Hoberg, not McGrath, who had sustained the injuries.

That evening McGrath, Bennett, and Robins boarded an Air America C-130 bound for Udorn. A few hours later, the remaining crew of JG 54 was back at the Thai Air Force base at Udorn, not quite home to NKP. That trip wouldn't happen at least until the next day as the base hospital's emergency staff planned to admit the three for overnight observation. However, before that could happen Air Force intelligence wanted to debrief the crew.

"Can the bird and the drone be retrieved?" asked one of the officers.

"Yeah, if you've got an armada flying cover, a backup bird . . ." began Bennett who was so tired, he couldn't finish the sentence. The crew was obviously weary, but the officers had a strong interest in that drone.

Many years later and after piecing together elements of the classified RPV operations of Southeast Asia, Bennett finally came to the conclusion that the RPV likely contained reconnaissance of parts of China. At the time President Nixon was preparing for a much-heralded diplomatic trip to the communist nation. The data in the U.S. hands would have been valuable. However, had it been recovered by the Chinese or their communist allies, such as the North Vietnamese or Laotian Pathet Lao, it could have sparked international accusations of spying and unraveled any diplomatic talks.

It was close to midnight when the crew finished the debriefing. Several of the 40th ARRS's remaining PJs at Udorn made their way to the base hospital to visit with Jolly Green 54's survivors, and more importantly, to let Chuck McGrath know that Candy had been calling for him all day.

Earlier that afternoon when it was determined that Chuck was not the seriously injured PJ from the crash of Jolly Green 54, fellow PJ Chuck Salome took another phone call from Candy. He told her that Chuck was "working" and was not expected to return to base until late in the evening. McGrath knew he had to check in with his wife. He called Candy in Korat. Clearly she could sense something had happened. He denied there was anything wrong, but it was hard to mask the seriousness in his voice. It gnawed at him that he couldn't be more direct with his wife. Undoubtedly, back in the States at that very moment there were newlywed couples having some similar conversation: "How was your day at work?" met with an ambiguous "Fine." But Chuck wasn't punching a clock and Candy wasn't some idle housewife. They were serving in the midst of a war. While that carried a professional responsibility, they had also taken vows to each other, and there was a personal accounting that needed to be done.

Even with these feelings, Chuck eventually said good night to Candy, hung up the phone and sought out a shower before sleep. His fatigues had been completely covered with Jon Hoberg's blood, but in that harrowing mission, Chuck had proven he belonged with the 40th.

As to the fate of Jolly Green 54 and the RPV, the next day Jim Roper in his U-17 led another attempt, this time by the 21st Special Operations Squadron, to retrieve the drone and the wreck from the hillside. It ended in failure as a CH-53 came under fire as it hovered over the site. Some Sandys came in and blasted the area as the helicopter retreated. Finally, several F-4s were called in to strike the area, destroying the remains of JG 54 and the RPV with their ordnance. If the U.S. Air Force couldn't recover the RPV, no one else would either.

Several weeks later Candy managed a three-day pass and a ride from Korat up to NKP. Chuck had neatly tucked away the details of his first combat mission into his own mental compartment. He didn't like it; Candy was his wife. They were taking a journey together, and secrets weren't good between a husband and wife, even if military protocol suggested otherwise.

As Chuck and Candy were sitting at a snack shop at the NKP base, they started chatting with a flight engineer assigned to the 21st Special Operations Squadron. While the engineer knew the pretty woman next McGrath was Candy, his wife, he perhaps didn't exercise absolute discretion as he shifted the topic of the conversation.

"McGrath, it is amazing that you survived that crash in your Jolly Green," the flight engineer said. "Usually when the rotor slices into the tail like that, it takes out everyone in the aft section of the cabin," he continued matter-of-factly. "I still don't understand why the bird just didn't blow up with all the fuel onboard when it crashed."

Chuck noticed a hint of shock on Candy's face, but the couple gave no indication to the engineer, and the three continued their conversation, until Chuck saw an opportunity to excuse themselves. It was time for some explanations, and they left the shack for Chuck's barracks.

"Chuck what really happened?" Candy asked directly. Chuck then handed her a copy of his after-action report. As the two sat, Candy read the details of Jolly Green crashing, the severe injuries to Hoberg, the gunfire as Chuck went up the hoist line. The war came all too close to home for her, and she teared up.

Chuck knew it was a lot to handle at once. "Honey, I'm sorry I didn't tell you sooner," he said. "I should have known I couldn't keep it a secret."

There was something reassuring in Chuck's voice that eased Candy. Nothing could be said that would eliminate the danger of the war for them, but his voice put perspective where it was needed. As husband and wife,

Looking down a hillside in northern Laos, this photo shows Jolly Green 54, belly up with its crumpled tail section, where Chuck McGrath had been in the PJ2 position. Slightly uphill from the crashed HH-53C (toward bottom of photo) lies the Buffalo Hunter drone and the clearing from which Air America helicopters would rescue the crew. The day after the crash of JG 54 a CH-53 from the 21st Special Operations Squadron came to retrieve the abandoned cargo sling. The ground fire was so intense that the mission was aborted. The Air Force later bombed the site, destroying what was left of Jolly Green 54 and the drone.—*C. McGrath*

they had been inserted into some fantastic story, the kind of tale you might read in a magazine or novel and think, "How could they manage?" But they were not just husband and wife but also a pair of airmen assigned to Southeast Asia as the latest installment in a long and difficult war. They each had a mission and Chuck seemed to have accepted that on any given day, on any given assignment, he could be killed. That's what he signed up for and worrying about it wouldn't change what fate had in store. Candy realized she had signed up for it too. The U.S. Air Force may have assigned her as a medic at Korat, but with her wedding vows came a second assignment as a PJ's wife. With the better pert of a year left for both of them in country, they would just have to make the best of a tough situation.

And now, almost a year later, by this late June morning, that was exactly what the couple had done. Chuck had served his year of combat. Candy still had a little time left, and then they would put in for a new duty assignment. As Maj. Leo Thacker diverted JG 73 to Udorn and some other crew moved from being on alert to their assigned orbit just outside North Vietnam, Chuck wondered whether he would see any action today.

At this stage maybe he had seen as much of the war as he was going to. His combat tour had started perilously with the crash in northern Laos. Who knew, maybe it would finish uneventfully.

NOTES

15. This account of the crash of Jolly Green 54 is based on *Quoth the Raven* by Jim Roper (Roper Books) in addition to interviews with Chuck McGrath, J.D. Adams, Clyde Bennett, and Jim Roper.

CHAPTER FOUR

THE GOOD MISSION

As the 7th Air Force's strike package was crossing into North Vietnam from Laos, back at the 40th ARRS home of Nakhon Phanom Royal Thai Air Force Base (NKP), Capt. Dale Stovall was where he often could be found in the spring of 1972, hovering around the operations desk, tracking the progress of the air war. As a pilot with the 40th, if Stovall wasn't flying a mission, he was trying to find a way to fly a mission.

When Captain Dale Stovall originally received orders to transition to helicopters, the heretofore fixed-wing pilot entertained breaking a leg to get out of the assignment. However, by June of 1972 he had come to love not only flying the HH-53, but also the search and rescue mission of the 40th ARRS. *—D. Stovall*

"We all really, really wanted to fly missions," explains Ben Orrell, a fellow pilot in the 40th. Today, on June 27, Orrell was already airborne in Jolly Green 52, flying the HH-53C to an orbit over northern Laos, just east of North Vietnam. He'd be joined there by Jolly Green 56, flown by Stanley Zielinski. Normally, complementing this pair of helicopters would be another backup pair of alert birds, often airborne, but closer to NKP over southern Laos. At the moment, however, there was no backup alert team. Orrell and Zielinkski's HH-53Cs had started the day as alert helicopters but were pressed into the lead roles when JG 60 and JG 73 both experienced problems after takeoff and had to be diverted to Udorn.

The routine for the 40th was to fly to their orbits in the morning, ahead of the Air Force strike package. Typically the Air Force would hit their targets in the morning, and the fighters and bombers would return to base well before the Navy launched their strike in the afternoon. The 40th, flying the HH-53C with mid-air refueling capability, would hold in their orbit until everyone was accounted for or they would be called on the scene of a rescue. Not until late in 1972 would the 40th have the resources to conduct night rescues.

The 40th's home, NKP, was about four hundred miles south of Hanoi, tucked into the eastern corner of Thailand, where Laos creates a narrow buffer between Thailand and Vietnam. With a top speed of about 170 knots (almost 200 mph) it could take the better part of two hours to get a Super Jolly Green airborne and over a rescue site in North Vietnam, but NKP was also within a hundred miles of parts of North Vietnam's major supply routes, the Ho Chi Minh Trail, which wound through Laos and Cambodia into South Vietnam.

The 40th's bread and butter aircraft, the HH-53C Super Jolly Green Giant, was a specialized model of the H-53 family of helicopters, which were used by the U.S. Air Force, Navy, and Marine Corps, as well as several foreign countries. Between 1967 and 1973 the Air Force ordered seventy-two of this Sikorsky airframe, the majority of which, forty-four, were the HH-53C, used primarily for search and rescue and other special operations. Amazingly, the H-53 models, with the help of various modifications, would go on to serve nearly four decades in the Air Force before being retired in 2008.

As compared to the CH-53 model, the HH-53 variants had a midair refueling probe. This was an enormous asset to search and rescue operations, a feature that would play a critical role in the events that would unfold in the next few hours for the members of the 40th ARRS.

As Stovall hovered around the operations desk this morning, weighing the impact of possibly two helicopters grounded with some mechanical fault and only two birds in the air should the day start to unravel, the HH-53C that carried the call sign JG 57 sat on the NKP flight line.

In most but not all respects JG 57 was identical to the other forty-three HH-53Cs that comprised the Air Force's fleet of search and rescue Super Jolly Green Giants in June 1972. The Sikorsky serial number 68-10357 identified this Jolly Green as having rolled off the production line in 1968. Exactly when it arrived in Southeast Asia is hard to ascertain, but it was part of the 40th's fleet by at least late 1970 when it took part in war's greatest rescue that wasn't.

By 1970, the military believed that as many as five hundred Americans were held as POWs in North Vietnam, most of them Air Force and Navy pilots, WSOs, and other aircrew who had been shot down. At the same time, there were numerous reports of inhumane treatment. North Vietnam did not adhere to the international standard of treatment known as the Geneva Conventions. Diplomatically, the North skirted this fact by playing a game of semantics. Since the U.S. had not formally declared war, the POWs were not international combatants but a form of spy or criminal, "American air pirates," as the North Vietnamese propaganda would say.

During the summer of 1970 planning began in earnest for a raid on the Son Tay POW camp, just west of Hanoi. Leading the mission, code named Operation Ivory Coast, would be U.S. Army Special Forces officer Col. Arthur "Bull" Simons. Eventually, following months of rehearsal and training in the States, fifty-six special operations troops would take part in the raid.

In November 1970 the assault group arrived at their staging base, Takhli RTAFB, the same base Lynn Aikman and the other members of 4th TFS had flown from this June morning. The last piece of the assault was to line up four additional PJs to serve on the HH-53Cs that would be carrying the raiders into the camp and, if all went according to plan, be returning with between fifty and sixty POWs, some of whom were believed to be in need of urgent medical care.

As part of the planning, Simons had assembled HH-53 crews, complete with PJs, but once in country the leadership chose to add four more PJs, who could also man the guns on the Jolly Greens. It also would be an asset to have some member of the crew be current on the ever changing landscape of the war, someone up to date on the lay of the land.

Simons turned to the 40th for volunteers, which included Jon Hoberg, the same PJ who eight months later would be maimed on a Laotian hillside by a disintegrating Jolly Green rotor and would have to rely on his junior PJ, Chuck McGrath, to get him and the rest of the crew to safety.

The four had been told that the odds of survival were probably 50 percent at best, but to such men, statistics were secondary to the mission. According to Ben Orrell, pilot of JG 60 on June 27, odds were irrelevant to the bold, young airmen. "At the time, you think you are invincible."

On November 20, each of the 40th's late additions to Operation Ivory Coast took a position on the HH-53s that would fly into the Son Tay camp, which was located about twenty-three miles west of the "bullseye," aka downtown Hanoi. Hoberg would fly on the command helicopter alongside Colonel Simons himself. Call sign Apple 1, the Jolly Green that had this honor was JG 57, the very same helicopter sitting on the NKP flight line on the morning of June 27, 1972.

As it turns out, the POWs had been moved from Son Tay during the previous July. However, the camp was still occupied by enemy soldiers. In the planning, intelligence officers had also identified a "secondary school" about a quarter of a mile south of camp. They warned the helicopter pilots not to mistake the facility for Son Tay since it was very close and similar in layout to the North Vietnamese prison camp. On the night of the raid, JG 57, Apple 1, which was carrying Colonel Simons and Technical Sergeant Hoberg as a PJ, was the trailing Jolly Green. Its pilot, Colonel Warner Britton, made the very mistake he had been warned against and landed at the front of the school. Simons and the crew quickly realized that the location was neither Son Tay nor a school. The building was full of enemy soldiers that engaged Apple 1's two dozen or so raiders in the most intense fighting of the raid. It was over within a few minutes with about a hundred of the enemy killed and no casualties sustained by the raiders and crew of Apple 1. Britton then managed to rendezvous JG 57 with the other helicopters for their egress, dodging surface to air missiles on the way out. For his role piloting JG 57, Britton was awarded the Air Force Cross.

The Son Tay assault lasted slightly less than thirty minutes. While it was a major disappointment in that no POWs were rescued, tactically, it was a major success. The raid, with its months of rehearsal, had no casualties. It sent a message to the North Vietnamese that U.S. military was not only watching the POW camps, but they might in fact come again. Many American POWs report the conditions of their captivity began to improve after the death of Ho Chi Minh in 1969, but the news of the Son Tay raid, which eventually filtered to the POWs, buoyed their spirits, and they noted a change in their conditions. After Son Tay, the POWs were generally collected at one of two major prison camps. This reduced some of the isolation. It is not that the North Vietnamese fully complied with any international standard for prisoner treatment, but while Son Tay didn't rescue the POWs, the raid likely contributed to an improving of conditions for them.

One other upshot from Son Tay is that it helped establish H-53 airframe. It proved to be a great resource. Whether in an assault or rescue capacity, an HH-53C, with its mid-air refueling, meant that a helicopter could be sent on a roundtrip of hundreds of miles, maybe even beyond Hanoi. As would be proven 18 months later, how far an HH-53 could venture into the North may have simply been a matter of 7th Air Force's will and the guts of the pilot of flying it.

Back at NKP in June 1972, Dale Stovall, a tall, red-haired Air Force academy graduate from Washington state, had quickly established himself as talented Jolly Green pilot who got the job done since arriving in Southeast Asia earlier in the year.

"We called him Ricochet," recalls Frank Mason, a second lieutenant who on June 27 was copilot of JG 73, currently diverted to Udorn. "Whenever there was a mission that would go on, and he was around the ops desk, he would be on full-on mode. He would just go 90 miles an hour, one phone in one ear, one phone in the other, talking to maintenance guys, talking to air crews."

Stovall had established himself as a noteworthy helicopter pilot in Southeast Asia, but originally he never wanted the assignment. In 1970 he was flying C-141s out of McChord Air Force Base in Washington, and hoped that when the call came to go to Southeast Asia it would be in anything but a helicopter.

On June 27, 1972, Frank Mason, early in his year-long tour with the 40th ARRS, flew as the copilot on JG 73, which had PJs Chuck McGrath and Chuck Morrow in back. When JG 73 finally landed on June 27, Mason recollects a single thought crossing his mind: "This is going to be a long year." *—F. Mason*

"I knew I was going to Vietnam when I went to 141s," he explains. "We knew half the guys would go over there in helicopters and about half would go over in fixed wing, and that's what you really wanted," he adds explaining he had hoped to draw an assignment flying OV-10s, turboprop planes that served as forward air controllers. By Operation Linebacker, OV-10s were playing a critical role in the evolution of military ordnance. They would be equipped with lasers to "paint" targets for laser-guided bombs fired by other aircraft.

When Stovall got his orders, the avid skier half-thought of breaking a leg to get out of the transition. "So my skiing partner and I came up with the plan that we would drink a bottle of wine, put another in our rucksack, and drink it on the way up the mountain. When we got to the top, we'd point our skis straight down, and the first guy that turned or fell, lost."

The plan didn't work. Stovall had two good legs when he reported for his transition to HH-53s, but in the end, it worked out for the future Brigadier General. "When I came back, I never wanted to go back to fixed wing," he says. "I fell in love with the aircraft. I fell in love with the mission."

About three weeks into his tour, on March 2, 1972, Stovall had his checkout flight as an aircraft commander. The checkout process was part peer review, part local briefing. It was the opportunity for an experienced pilot to confirm someone was ready for duty and to also share what information they had about the region. As it turns out, the HH-53C Stovall flew for the checkout ride was Jolly Green 57, the same helicopter that Bull Simons had flown on in the Son Tay raid.

The commander doing the checkout, Bob Paul, had just signed off on Stovall, who was already in the pilot's seat and starting to head back to NKP. Then the call came over the radio. An OV-10, call sign Covey 219, had been shot down in southern Laos, near Saravan. The OV-10 had been serving as a forward air controller directing fire when it was struck by some antiaircraft fire.

"We were already airborne, and we raced toward the location," recalls Stovall. "We ended up beating the alert birds from NKP."

Stovall was excited to get his first combat rescue as an aircraft commander.

"This is going to be great," Stovall said to Paul.

"Yeah, but you're the copilot," answered Paul.

"Wait a minute you just made me the aircraft commander?"

Paul wasn't about to pass up the opportunity for a combat pickup. That was the culture of the 40th ARRS. As risk-laden as their missions were, they embraced them fully. JG 57 made the pick up of the OV-10 pilot, Captain Jon Long, but it wasn't easy. The weather had deteriorated and the enemy that Long had been directing fire against now had a new target, the lumbering Jolly Green. "Visibility was terrible," says Stovall. "We were getting shot at and didn't know it."

After picking up Long, Paul tried to head out of the area but flew right into antiaircraft artillery. "That was the closest I ever came to getting hit by triple A," Stovall says. "So we flew up to thirteen thousand feet into the clouds. They were firing at us the whole way up."

Paul managed to fly JG 57 back to NKP avoiding any catastrophic hits. While Stovall didn't get the credit as aircraft commander for the pickup, both Paul and Stovall were awarded Silver Stars for their role in the rescue of Covey 219. But in the days that followed, the pilots learned that if they had taken a route that was a mile left or right of the one they chose, they would have avoided the AAA sites.

"I didn't know the intel for the area," Stovall says. "I went in there without fully knowing where the guns were. For the next two weeks I spent at least two hours every day studying in the intel shop, memorizing where the guns were. I wanted to know every position of every gun in Laos."

Stovall may have been "ricochet," but he wasn't a loose cannon. If there was some bit of information that could help him. He was going to find it and use it. "Never again did I fly somewhere and not know where the guns were," he says.

Stovall would have to wait four weeks before he had his next shot at his first rescue as an aircraft commander.

At the very start of the North's Easter Offensive, Thursday, March 30, 1972, an AC-130 gunship, call sign Spectre 22, was shot down by the enemy near the Ho Chi Minh Trail. The Air Force's AC-130 Spectre, and its AC-47 Spooky or Puff the Magic Dragon predecessor, was an early precursor of "shock and awe." With a 132-foot wing span, a fifteen-man crew, and a multitude of ordnance delivered through its cannons, it was a truly awesome weapon of war. At this juncture in the Vietnam Conflict, with the departure of ground forces, the AC-130 could function as a substitute for ground-based artillery, providing a targeted and devastating attack. This was of particular concern in trying to disrupt the North's flow of weapons and resources to the South. The network of roads that comprised the Ho Chi Minh Trail wound through parts of Laos, a country that both the United States and North Vietnam had agreed to treat with neutrality, at least publicly. As such, attacks on the supply route had to be precise. A stray bomb or missile into the Laotian countryside could spark a public uproar both internationally and among an American population that had grown weary of the Vietnam war.

Enter the AC-130 with the apt call sign of Spectre. During night raids on the Ho Chi Minh Trail, when it was most active, the gunship's cannons could target and destroy vehicles coming down the route into the South. However, for all its firepower and reinforced fuselage, the highly modified Hercules had vulnerabilities.

The night before, on March 29, a SAM brought down an AC-130 near Tchepone, slightly north of where Spectre 22 was now headed. There were no survivors from the March 29 shoot-down. At the time, few recognized the size of the North's offensive that was massing in preparation of sending both troops and weaponry into the South. On March 30, it was apparently a barrage of antiaircraft artillery that struck the left wing of Spectre 22, causing a fuel leak and an eventual fire in one of the plane's four engines. Losing power, pilot Capt. Waylon Fulk instructed the crew to bail out as he turned the gunship toward Udorn.

The AC-130 was a menacing giant of an aircraft. Adapted from the C-130 Hercules cargo plane, these gunships featured a variety of cannons, all mounted on its portside. Flying under the call sign of Spectre, AC-130s, with a 132-foot wingspan and crew of fifteen would attack positions along the Ho Chi Minh Trail. On the eve of the North's Easter Offensive, Spectre 22 was brought down by antiaircraft fire. All fifteen crew managed to bailout. In the early morning a massive rescue effort was launched.—*U.S. Air Force*

Spectre 22 never made it, crashing just southeast of Saravan, but all fifteen of the crew managed to bail out. What followed through the night was a massive effort involving four other Spectre gunships, some of which had early night-vision technology, Air America forces, and other resources in the area to pinpoint where the crew had come down.

In those early morning hours, back at NKP, Stovall had wandered into the operations shack. "As the junior officer in ops office, I had two jobs. One was the *Stars & Stripes* newspaper, make sure everyone could read that when it would come in at 11:30 in the morning. And two was to get up at midnight and go down to the tactical control center and get the frag [order] for the next day because it would have all the missions for the next day, and if there were any taskings, it would be on that. Then I would come back and post that with the ops clerk on duty."

On the night of March 30, Stovall was carrying out this junior-officer responsibility when he caught wind of the AC-130 crew bailing out. "I was sitting in the office at about 12:30 in the morning and I hear on the HF [high frequency] radio that Spectre 22 had just been shot down."

As other squadrons were experiencing at this point in the war, good leadership wasn't a guarantee. It had been almost eight years since the Gulf of Tonkin resolution that permitted Lyndon Johnson to significantly escalate the war, but it had also been three and a half years since Johnson, as he departed the presidency, declared a bombing halt on North Vietnam. The Air Force needed officers to command the many squadrons in Southeast Asia. The problem was there weren't enough experienced ones to go around. This fact encouraged the Air Force to frequently rotate in new leadership in an attempt to build up that experience, but it also created a revolving door for such commanders, a continual reinventing of the wheel, often at the direction of an officer who just didn't have the experience to lead.

While other squadrons may have been saddled with this phenomenon, the men of the 40th ARRS were a bit of a different make up. Perhaps it had to do with the fact that the very need for rescue meant that the rules had already been broken. If everything went according to plan, every mission would end with everyone coming back safely. To embrace the mission of search and rescue perhaps meant embracing a recognition that rules and protocol didn't always apply.

Whatever the case may have been, at least during Stovall's time with the 40th, leadership was something to be seized, not assigned. As he heard the fate of Spectre 22 unfold, he knew there were fifteen Americans on the ground and that SAR forces would be leaving at first light.

He drew up a plan for eight Jolly Greens to take part in the SAR. The two HH-53s currently on alert were assigned as the primary low bird and high bird. Stovall penciled himself in as the low bird on the next set of helicopters and assigned Ben Orrell as his high bird pilot. "Ben was one of those guys you wanted to fly with," Stovall says of the Orrell, who at this point (on June 27) was in an orbit over northern Laos. "Whenever I had the chance, I tried to fly with him."

"Then I had the operations clerk type up these orders, and I signed them as assistant ops officer," says Stovall. "Well, I was no more the assistant operations officer than the man on the moon," he confides. "Nobody questioned it. I told them to wake everybody up at 3:30 in morning for first light, a 4:30 briefing, and I went to bed."

When he awoke and checked the board, there were the eight crews, just as he had written them up. One of the PJs joining Stovall's crew, this time on JG 60, would be Chuck McGrath, the same PJ now on Leo Thacker's diverted-to-Udorn JG 73. McGrath's roommate, Chuck Morrow, would be a PJ on Orrell's high bird.

Throughout the early morning of the Spectre 22 rescue, aircraft in the area had worked to locate all fifteen survivors who seemed to have been dispersed in an odd pattern. Critical to the success of the mission would be Spectre 22's fellow AC-130s, which had the latest technology for identifying targets, or survivors, in the night. An Air America pilot, Allen Cates, who joined the effort, dubbed the rescue "The Easter Egg Hunt."

"They had taken 37mm fire in one of the engines," Stovall explains about the downing of Spectre 22. "So the pilot tells the crew 'prepare to bail out.' Well the copilot came out of the cockpit, fell down the stairs going into the bay of the 130 and knocked himself out temporarily. When he came to, he looked out the window of one of the guns and saw the engine on fire and thought everyone else was gone already. He didn't know how long he had been out, and he had his parachute on, and he just dove out the gun port.

"Also, one of the gunners in the back grabbed a parachute and ran off the back ramp before anyone could stop him. So these two guys were out fifteen miles before everyone else started the actual bailout. Then they bailed out ten people in one group. The aircraft commander and two others were the last to bail out, and they were another ten miles away."

This resulted in three distinct groups for the pick up. The first two Jolly Greens concentrated on the group with the pilot.

"The first two went after the aircraft commander," says Stovall. "They were the most experienced guys in the squadron, and they were nearly fighting over who was going to make the pick up." As the next set of Jolly Greens, with Stovall flying low bird, they were directed toward another area. Stovall assumed that he was picking up just one survivor.

"I am going as fast as that helicopter would go. I was going 180 knots, red line was 170 knots and I was going right over the tops of the trees. I made a big circle, came in, and got into a hover. Then the flight engineer, who was the oldest flight engineer in the squadron, says 'Captain if you take your feet off the rudder pedals, the nose will quit shaking.' My legs were shaking so badly that the nose of the helicopter was shaking because

I was pumping the rudder pedals. I mean I was really hyped," says Stovall. The pick-up was easy. The hoist went down, the survivor hopped on and was pulled on board. The young captain was then ready to head out of Laos, due west, a heading of 270 degrees.

"So we pick up the first guy, and I think to myself that I have made my pick up for the war, my combat save," says Stovall.

The forward air controller comes on the radio, "Turn to 270." Stovall puts the Jolly Green on a heading due west, 270 degrees, assuming its his exit route. With adrenaline still pumping, he is flying the HH-53 as fast as it will go. The FAC comes on again, "12 o'clock." Believing the FAC is calling out a gun position directly in front of the helicopter, Stovall quickly breaks off the route. He then realizes, the FAC was calling out the position of another survivor. Stovall comes back around gets into position. "Hey Jolly Green," came from the FAC. "You got nine more people here on the ground. You don't have to go that fast between them. Remain calm, and we'll get them all."

After that Stovall took things easy, falling into a pattern of hovering over a survivor, picking him up, and then moving on to the next man on the ground.

"They all were just lined up," recalls Chuck McGrath, who would have to go down the hoist line to help one of the survivors who had an injured ankle. "The Air America FAC did a great job moving us from one to the next."

A while later, airborne control came on the radio and asked Stovall how many survivors he had picked up. "I've got eight on board," answered Stovall as he piloted toward the remaining two survivors.

Airborne control told Stovall to head back and let one of the other sets of Jolly Greens pick up the remaining two. At that point Orrell, who was piloting the high bird for Stovall chimed in, wanting a shot at the last two pickups.

"A month later I would have said 'you are all garbled' and picked up the other two myself," says Stovall. "But I got out of there, and Ben came in picked up the other two." And just like Chuck McGrath, PJ Chuck Morrow had to go down the hoist line to help one of the injured crew.

All fifteen crew members were recovered with eight of them on Stovall's Jolly Green. At the time, it was probably the most involved combat rescue of the war. However, it would soon be overshadowed by one of the most difficult rescue operations in Southeast Asia. In the midst of that operation, however, Stovall and Orrell would team up again for another successful rescue.

The challenges facing the U.S. Air Force on June 27, 1972, and in particular search and rescue operations , were cast clearly by an arduous, eleven-day rescue operation three months earlier. Known simply as "Bat 21" for the call sign of the downed EB-66 and its navigator/electronic warfare officer (EWO), Lt. Col. Iceal "Gene" Hambleton, the rescue and the failures that preceded it highlighted the great risk and heroism of air operations in Southeast Asia at the time.

Bat 21 was an Douglas EB-66C assigned to the 42nd Tactical Electronic Warfare Squadron (TEWS), which at time served under the 355th Tactical Fighter Wing and was based out of Takhli RTAFB. The EB-66C's assignment centered on defeating surface-to-air-missile (SAM) sites. To lure out the SAMs, the crew of Bat 21 would allow the enemy to lock onto the craft, and, once the missile was fired, the pilot would execute a "SAM break," a hard dive, in this case to the south away from the battery. The maneuver would cause the EB-66 to pull about 5 Gs, well within tolerable for the craft and crew with their training. The SAMs typically faltered at about 2 Gs and would shoot off into nothing. At this juncture in the war, Hambleton and the crew of Bat 21 had probably executed this maneuver more than sixty times.

This day, as the crew of Bat 21 went into their ten-second count, they only had five seconds before the first SAM hit.

At the first hit, the pilot ordered an ejection. Hambleton, who as navigator was positioned right behind the pilot, pulled his handle just before a second SAM struck the wounded craft. Only Hambleton managed to eject. To this day the other five crew are listed as missing in action, presumed to have died in the destroyed EB-66 having never ejected.

Over the eleven days, five aircraft and sixteen men were lost trying to rescue Hambleton. In addition, three other men were shot down and taken as POWs.[16] A devastating component of the casualties was that six of the fatalities comprised the crew of an HH-53 Jolly Green rescue helicopter.

It seems evident that the North Vietnamese, in addition to seeking out

Hambleton, took advantage of their firepower in the area and the desperation of the U.S. forces seeking to rescue the downed navigator. While they were unable to locate Hambleton precisely, the North Vietnamese were able to mobilize tremendous firepower in the area, including additional SAM batteries. They seemed to be using Hambleton as bait.

The massive cost of rescuing Hambleton may have been enough to discourage search and rescue operations or at least convince the command structure that oversaw them that the cost was too great for some rescues, but before such notions could take root, as a matter of fact, even before Hambleton was safely retrieved by a Navy SEAL, search and rescue was given an opportunity to prove that it could adapt as well.

In the midst of the Bat 21 rescue efforts, on April 9, 1972, at about 1800 hours, Marine aviator Clyde Smith had launched off one of the U.S.S. *Coral Sea*'s catapults in the Gulf of Tonkin. He piloted his A-6 Intruder toward the Ho Chi Minh Trail, the notorious path that wound from North Vietnam, through its border with Laos, down to areas of South Vietnam. It was the pipeline through which the enemy was moving supplies and troops across the DMZ.

By this juncture, the American high command was aware of the Easter Offensive, which had launched a week earlier, but it was still unclear on just how many troops and firepower the enemy had funneled south.

Smith's mission was a relatively straightforward bombing of targets along the trail, timed to disrupt the north's routine of advancing supplies during the cover of the approaching night.

After a few successful passes, Smith heard what he would later describe as sounding like a door being slammed behind him. Progressively, he lost control of the A-6 and eventually ejected. Smith parachuted down to the jungle, next to the fireball that had been his aircraft. Much like Hambleton, Smith was able to find adequate cover despite being surrounded by the enemy. However, at best, this bought Smith some time. At worst, the tenuous cover Smith may have found was just part of a larger scheme by the enemy to bait the U.S. forces, much the way the North Vietnamese lured the Jolly Green and its crew during its attempt to pick up Hambleton.

"Stovall and I were on alert, and we heard a guy had been shot down," recalls Orrell. "We assumed we weren't going to be a player in the thing because the call never came in."

Again, in early 1972, search and rescue was very limited in terms of night capabilities. The next morning, April 10, an OV-10 FAC Nail 17 managed to pinpoint Smith. Later in the afternoon, the on-scene commander for the SAR, Maj. Jim Harding, flew his A-1 Skyraider into the area. Coordinating with the FACs, F-4s, and other A-1s in the area, Harding, as Sandy 01, tried to identify the various enemy gun positions.

In the meantime SAR command had gone looking for a pair of Jolly Green crews. "They told us we're not going to order you in there because there is a good chance you're not going to come back alive," says Orrell. That was all the marketing the two young pilots needed.

"My biggest fear going over to Vietnam was with the bombing pause, I would get over there and there would be nothing to do," says Orrell. "That never happened." There was always something to do given the multi-front air war throughout Southeast Asia. And now that North Vietnam had launched its massive invasion of the South there would be plenty of action, especially if Orrell kept hanging around a guy like Stovall.

The pair stepped up to fly the birds that would pick up Clyde Smith, but they needed to assign low bird and high bird. They stole a play from the PJs protocol. Flipping a coin, the winner would take the first stint as low bird. After two days, they would switch. Stovall won the toss.

Each member of the crew had a clear sense of what they were facing. "We threw out the Playboys, packed everything up, wrote our last letters home," Stovall says. Just in case the crews forgot what they were facing, each morning, the Sandy pilots exercised some gallows humor, reminding them that the breakfast they were eating might be their last. The combination of enemy defenses and poor weather prevented a pick-up attempt on the 10th, 11th and 12th. In the meantime Stovall's turn at low bird had expired and it was now Orrell who would be making the pick-up.

Finally, after four days of planning, waiting for the weather, and trying to suppress the enemy in the area, Jim Harding, as the Sandy lead, called for the Jolly Greens to break from the orbit and make a run in for Smith. At the peak of activity, Harding was coordinating some twenty-five to thirty aircraft that were dropping ordnance or otherwise supporting the rescue.

The Jolly Greens started taking some ground fire from the enemy positions below. PJ Bill Brinson took a round in the leg as he was firing from the rear minigun. Injured, but not in a life-threatening manner, he continued firing while Orrell came over Smith's location. Smith had released his flare, but the downwash from the rotor blades dissipated the smoke

Dale Stovall listens intently to one of the morning briefings for the Bengal 505 mission. Stovall and fellow pilot Ben Orrell had flipped a coin to determine who would get the first shift as the primary "low" bird on this harrowing rescue. Stovall won, taking the low-bird assignment for the first two days. However, the combination of weather and enemy ground fire stalled rescue attempts until the fourth day, when Orrell had taken over as low bird. Despite predictions that one or both Jolly Green crews might not make it back, no aircraft were lost in the hotly contested rescue. As Orrell and other members of the 40th relate, despite the immense risk, all the members of the 40th ARRS wanted to fly missions: pilots, copilots, flight engineers, and PJs in the "good mission" of rescuing their fellow servicemen.
—D. Stovall

quickly, and Orrell wasn't sure he was over Smith's location. After four days on the ground, Smith recognized this might be his only shot at rescue. He decided to make a run for the helicopter, leaping and hooking on to the lowered forest penetrator without even unfolding the paddles to sit on. As he made his dash, Smith noticed a red cloth wrapped around a tree, like a trail marker. It had him wondering whether the North Vietnamese had in fact marked his position and were using him as bait.

Despite the odds, all the craft returned safely. Orrell's Jolly Green had sustained at least eleven hits from ground fire. All in all, mere scratches for the SAR warriors while they managed to snatch one of their own from one of the hottest areas of the Ho Chi Minh Trail. Sometime later, Smith found out through military intelligence sources who had intercepted enemy communications, that indeed, the North's commanders had instructed those in the area to suppress their fire until the rescue aircraft came in to get him.

For his efforts in executing the well-orchestrated rescue, Harding received the Air Force's highest honor, the Air Force Cross. Orrell also received an Air Force Cross for his role in the rescue of Bengal 505. Stovall, despite winning the coin toss, had lost out on the combat rescue. "Dale was a man of his word," Orrell says with a laugh, recalling their agreement.

Of course, Stovall would get his due almost two months later in one of the most heralded rescues of the war.

May 10, 1972, marked first full day of Operation Linebacker, which was an extension of the resumed bombing of targets in the North due to the ongoing offensive. Just like Orrell and his crew were doing on June 27, Stovall had done the same on May 10, pilot to an orbit over the uninhabitable mountainous area of Laos. From this relatively safe perch, the Super Jolly Greens would wait for a SAR call and then be escorted into the rescue site by a flight of the prop-driven A-1 Skyraiders, the Sandys.

Linebacker was the evolution of the initial response, known as Operation Freedom Train, to the March 30 Easter Offensive by the North. While Freedom Train marked the first sustained attacks on the North since Lyndon Johnson suspended bombing three and a half years earlier, Linebacker had the more focused intent of separating the North from their

Captain Steve Ritchie records another MiG on his F-4. The brash pilot would become one of three Air Force aces and the only Air Force pilot ace, during the Vietnam War. While an upperclassman at the Air Force Academy, Ritchie had been a mentor to Dale Stovall. By June 27, 1972, Ritchie had recorded two of his eventual five MiG kills, and the North Carolina native was one of the better-known pilots to both U.S. and North Vietnamese forces.—*M. Cavato*

benefactors. The mining of Haiphong harbor and sustained attacks from the Navy helped shut down seaborne imports to North Vietnam. But roads and rail lines connecting the North to countries like China were still a major supply route. By some estimates, in the spring of 1972 as many as 22 thousand tons of supplies were coming into the North monthly from the People's Republic of China.

On May 10, 1972, the morning's mission was a 120-aircraft strike against the Yen Vien rail yard and the Paul Doumer bridge, both near Hanoi. One of the F-4 flights that morning protecting the strike force as MiGCAP was call sign Oyster, a four-ship flight of F-4s from the 555th TFS, better known as the "Triple Nickel" squadron. Oyster was led by one of the Air Force's most experienced crews, Maj. Robert Lodge as pilot and Capt. Roger Locher, the backseater WSO. Oyster 3 on May 10 was piloted by Captain Steve Ritchie, a talented aviator and an upperclassman when Stovall was at the Air Force Academy, where Ritchie had been a standout on the football team and Stovall an all-American in track as well as a football recruit.

Ritchie would eventually emerge as the Air Force's first ace of the Vietnam air war with five confirmed kills. Like Stovall, he would rise to the rank of brigadier general in the years that followed the Vietnam Conflict. Stovall credits Ritchie with being a great mentor.

"When I got to the academy, everything was negative motivation," says Stovall noting how the upperclassmen leaders favored criticism and humiliation. "Ritchie was the first one I saw that used positive motivation. He taught me a lot about leadership."

On May 10, as the Air Force strike force headed North, Red Crown, the call sign for the Navy ship monitoring the airfields of the North, reported a flight of MiGs had launched and were tracking toward the bombing package. The Oyster flight had been patrolling at a relatively low altitude. When the report of the MiGs came in, Lodge, as flight lead, had the four F-4s turn to engage the oncoming MiGs head-on but from underneath, a strong attack position.

As the Oyster flight closed within range, Lodge fired a Sparrow missile, but it detonated prematurely. Firing a second Sparrow while still slightly below the oncoming MiGs, the missile tracked to his target, demolishing its left wing and giving the team of Lodge and Locher their third kill of the war. Lodge's wingman, Oyster 2, piloted by John Markle, had also fired a pair of Sparrows and nailed another MiG. In short order, the Oyster flight had cut the attacking enemy force in half, or so they thought.

Of the two remaining MiGs, one scattered and Lodge and Locher pursued it with their wingman Oyster 2. Ritchie and DeBellevue in Oyster 3 had fired at the third MiG as it was closing on them but missed, as the MiG flew right overhead, Ritchie had turned around to follow, firing again, and this time striking it. Of the four MiGs, three had been taken out, but what none of the Oyster flight knew is that the second set of enemy jets had been trailing the lead MiGs.

Lodge had closed on the remaining MiG-21, too close as a matter of fact. Flying an F-4D, a model that had no cannon, Lodge had only air-to-air missiles at his disposal. Being too close for their use, Lodge had to ease off to fall back into missile range. Just then, a pair of MiG-19s sprung from below coming in between Oyster 1 and 2. One of the MiG-19s hopped on Lodge and Locher's tail. The other members of the Oyster flight radioed to the Oyster 1 crew, but it was too late. The MiG-19 fired its cannons and struck the right engine of Oyster 1. Lodge and Locher were instantly in trouble, spinning out of control, with the burning craft eventually rolling over as it plummeted toward the earth.

Martin Cavato, a lieutenant with the Triple Nickel at the time, remembers the loss of Lodge. "He was a fantastic fighter pilot," says Cavato. "He was always encouraging us to improve our tactics. I remember one night I was doing an AC-130 gunship escort with Bob Lodge, and he says, 'I am going to ask for a fuel check, and you are going to tell me you're bingo fuel,'" Cavato recalls noting the pilots' term for minimum fuel. "Then he says, 'and then I am going to chew your ass out on the radio for being bingo fuel. Then I am going to radio the 130 and tell them we are going off station because you're low on fuel. Then we are going to turn toward the base and drop down low altitude.' And we did that, and sure enough they launched MiGs to go get the gunship. They were listening to what we were saying."

Lodge and Cavato returned to their escort and the MiGs went away, but the lesson, which as the events unfolding on June 27 would eventually prove, was learned; the bad guys were always listening, and sometimes you could use that to your advantage.

Lodge wasn't just a clever tactician. He had a great deal of knowledge about the U.S. air strategy and technology including the Combat Tree technology, which would use a MiG's transponder to reveal its location to Air Force fighters.[17] By several accounts, he had told others he would never eject and run the risk of capture. "There's a lever in the backseat of the F-4," explains Cavato. "If you pull it out and rotate it, then basically you each are on your own in terms of ejecting. The word was he always made sure Roger had that pulled. He didn't want Roger ejecting him."

The rationale for such insistence wasn't some they-won't-take-me-alive boast, but a more quiet and stark reality. It was well accepted that the North Vietnamese and their colleagues the Viet Cong in the South and the Pathet Lao in Laos had no qualms about using torture to get information. Lodge, undoubtedly, would be a known asset to the enemy, and while the prospect of inhumane treatment was unpleasant enough, the greater burden for those with military secrets was knowing that at some point, they would break and divulge critical information to the enemy.

Lieutenant Martin Cavato was a squadronmate of Maj. Robert Lodge, one of the Air Force's best pilots and tacticians in 1972. On one mission, Lodge showed Cavato how the North Vietnamese would listen to Air Force radio transmissions. On June 27, 1972, Cavato and his backseater Tony Marshall have their F-4 "FastFAC" retasked to search for a pair F-4s shot down during the morning bomb strike. The four crews of the Valent flight would be assigned to MiG combat air patrol (MiGCAP) for the FastFAC, which Cavato and Marshall felt was unusual.—*M. Cavato*

As Oyster 1 disappeared, no chutes were seen. For Stovall orbiting in an HH-53, there was nothing for him to do. By some measures, May 10 was a military success. The Oyster flight alone had taken out three MiG-21s. Eight other enemy jets had been shot down by Navy fighters. The air strikes that day, one from the Air Force, two by the Navy, were successful. It was an auspicious start to Linebacker. And yet, there was a cost to the success, as if such a thing could even be measured. At what point did the scales between benefit and risk tip? To what extent should the Air Force go to prevent the loss of or commit the rescue of an individual?

In just three weeks, Stovall and the rest of the 7th Air Force would be given the opportunity to answer that question.

On June 1, Stovall was back in his orbit, and his fellow academy graduate Ritchie was in his role, leading a flight of F-4s protecting a strike package into the North. Not far away from Stovall was Captain Ron Smith, a Sandy pilot, providing support for the HH-53s. All had their radios listening on open frequencies, a common practice in case any downed pilots were trying to communicate with them.

Suddenly, the radio cackled, and a voice announced the call sign of "Oyster 1 Bravo." Stovall, Smith, Ritchie, and the others in the air were confused. There was no Oyster call sign that day. The voiced repeated, identifying itself as Roger Locher.

"And I remembered that, yes, Lodge and Locher had been Oyster 1 when they were shot down," Stovall recalls. "The transmission was very clear. So Ron Smith said to me, 'Let's head up there.'"

While other personnel went about trying to confirm that it was indeed Locher on the radio, Stovall and Smith cautiously flew north. "We were saying this has to be trap," explains Stovall.

One of the lessons SAR forces had learned is that the North Vietnamese would use downed airmen as bait. For Stovall, the idea that the enemy had captured or come across the remains of one of his comrades and was now attempting to lure slow-moving rescue craft, like the Jolly Greens and A-1s, seemed far more plausible than Roger Locher had somehow managed to evade capture for three weeks.

Stovall and Smith continued to fly north, tracking the signal. Not only were they heading toward enemy territory, following a voice that they weren't sure they could trust, but they were heading toward Hanoi without the benefit of much additional air support.

Progressively, the man on the ground correctly identified the personal information of Roger Locher. Doubts turned to exuberance. Roger Locher was alive and apparently healthy enough to move. But as Smith and Stovall began to get a better fix on Locher's location, they realized that, despite the clarity of the signal, Locher was several miles north of where they had hoped. As a matter of fact, it looked as though he was in the vicinity of one of the North's most active, most protected, air bases, Yen Bai, home to some seventy-three MiGs.

As the Jolly Green and A-1 lumbered, suddenly Smith radioed Stovall, "Get down, get down!" A MiG was on them and Stovall hit the deck with his Jolly Green. Recognizing it was only going to get worse the farther north they went, Smith and Stovall turned around. Locher was going to have spend one more night on the ground as his fellow airmen orchestrated a rescue plan.

As Stovall attempted to get away from the hot area, one of the F-4s that had been flying RESCAP for the impromptu rescue effort was struck by a SAM in front of Stovall. Its pilot, George Hawks, and WSO, David Dingee, much to Stovall's disbelief manage to fly the F-4 almost all the way back to Udorn.

The following day all the resources of the Seventh Air Force were directed toward North Vietnam, including an unprecedented bombing of an air base: Yen Bai.

The mission of the day was retasked from the normal bomb strike to rescuing Locher. Part of the rationale was that when the rescue planners added up all the resources the rescue would need, it was 119 aircraft, about the same that would be involved in a normal bomb mission. Within the 40th ARRS, a big question was who would fly the low-bird Jolly Green. "Leo Thacker actually was supposed to fly low bird that day," Stovall says, referring to the same Leo Thacker who was piloting JG 73 on June 27. "But I had already been up there. I wasn't going to pass this up." Both wanted the assignment. The mission meant flying deeper into North Vietnam than any Jolly Green had done before. Yen Bai was Hanoi's backyard, some three hundred miles from the DMZ.

Stovall won out. Then it came time to pick his copilot. "John Gillespie came up to me, and he had all these maps of the area," recalls Stovall. That made the decision easy for the pilot who spent weeks studying Laos gun positions after his first combat pickup.

Next on Stovall's list was to pick the Jolly Green to fly, JG 57, the same Jolly Green that flew on Son Tay and that Stovall had "copiloted" in the

Covey 219 rescue. During the spring, the Air Force had tested a new Electronic Location Finder (ELF) system on the HH-53s. The ELF could identify a survivor's radio signal and provide the Jolly Green pilot feedback on his location: in front, behind, left or right. JG 57 had the ELF package on it, and Stovall wanted every resource available.

The massive rescue strike began with the 7th Air Force attacking the Yen Bai base. Ron Smith was back in his position too, flying his A-1, leading Stovall and JG 57 to Locher's position. Locher popped his smoke flare he had been holding onto for twenty-three days. The Jolly Green lowered the hoist and brought him aboard.

On the way out, a North Vietnamese train with troops on flat beds was crossing close to the egress path, the A-1s used their ordnance, with one pilot, Maj. Jim Harding, firing a pair of rockets into the engine of the train, blowing it up and sending a plume of steam several hundred feet into the air.

For his role in flying deeper into North Vietnam than any HH-53 pilot had done before, Stovall was awarded the Air Force Cross, marking the second time JG 57 had been on an assignment that was recognized for such heroism.

In many ways, the rescue of Locher became an answer to Bat 21, both explaining and affirming why the Air Force would go to such great lengths to rescue just one of its own. The commander of the 7th Air Force, General John Vogt, who flew up to Udorn to greet Locher as he stepped off Stovall's Jolly Green, offered the following, oft-quoted, explanation of the mission, in many ways defining the purpose of search and rescue:

> I had to decide whether we should risk the loss of maybe a dozen airplanes and crews just to get one man out. Finally I said to myself, "Goddamn it, the one thing that keeps our boys motivated is the certain belief that if they go down, we will do absolutely everything we can to get them out." If that is ever in doubt, morale would tumble. That was my major consideration. So I took it on myself. I didn't ask anybody for permission. I just said, "Go do it!"

The junior officers of the 40th, pilots like Stovall and Orrell, perhaps

Roger Locher after his Sawadee flight (final flight before DEROSing). Left to right: Marty Cavato, Sandy Babos, Roger Locher, Jim Bunson (555th TFS commander), and George Nunez, summer 1972. Roger Locher is congratulated after his Sawadee with the Triple Nickel, the 555th TFS. On May 10, 1972, F-4 Phantom pilot Maj. Bob Lodge and his WSO Roger Locher were shot down over North Vietnam only forty miles from Hanoi. With no one realizing that he had successfully ejected, his fellow airmen were elated to hear his voice three weeks later on June 1 having successfully evaded capture all this time. The following day, in what was the deepest SAR mission of the war, Locher was rescued by Jolly Green 57, piloted by Dale Stovall, the same combination of aircraft and pilot that would play a key role in the June 27 rescue of Captain Lynn Aikman.—*M. Cavato*

exemplified that "go do it" attitude as best as anyone. They didn't ask for permission. Their mission was more important than protocol. "They let two young captains run the operation which is like having the prisoners run the prison," Stovall says, referring to how fellow pilot Jim Grant and he assumed the roles of acting operations officer and his assistant, respectively. "It was a huge deal for us because we had experience, or at least we thought we had experience, and we are running this combat squadron."

But that seemed to be the attitude of the entire 40th, everything was geared toward the mission. "I wouldn't say Dale and I had a rivalry," explains Orrell who traded off with Stovall for some of the high-profile, high-risk missions in 1972. "It was more that we all really wanted to fly. We were all about the missions." The new officers coming into 40th picked up on this attitude that was prevalent from pilots to the flight engineers to the PJs.

"We never had to worry about air crews," says Frank Mason, who on June 27 was Thacker's copilot in the diverted JG 73. "People would go down to ops and say 'Hey do you need someone? I will go.' That would be for pilots, engineers PJs, any of us. It was a good mission," he says simply of their task of rescuing their own.

Rufus Hutchinson, who on June 27 was one of newest members of the 40th as young second lieutenant copilot, agrees there was a special makeup to the men who took on that mission. "Let me put it this way," he says. "If you were down, we were the sons of bitches you wanted to come after you because we were crazy enough to do it. We all were that way.

"You want to know how good I felt after a survivor pickup?" said Hutchinson rhetorically. "I couldn't sleep for forty-eight hours. It was as good as sex," he says. "And it lasted longer."

Before the sun goes down on June 27, Hutchinson will have a moment where he is certain he is about to be killed.

An easy going West Virginian, Rufus Hutchinson had only been with the 40th ARRS twelve days when he was tapped by Dale Stovall to join an impromptu HH-53 crew that was thrown together when a second pair of F-4s were shot down on June 27, 1972.—*R. Hutchinson*

As the morning of June 27 continued with the dozens of Air Force fighters and bombers making their run into the heart of North Vietnam, Route Pack VI, the 40th was functioning without backup. It had sent two birds into their normal orbit over northern Laos, but its two other crews were potentially grounded at Udorn. In a short amount of time, the 40th would once again turn to a "Ricochet" and a lumbering helicopter that had already produced two awards of the Air Force Cross.

NOTES

16. There is some disagreement as to the losses surrounding the Bat-21 rescue due to the fact that aircraft may have been serving multiple roles—was their downing a result of the SAR or their original mission. For our purposes, the aircraft lost are Nail 38, JG 67, Blueghost 39, Mike 81 and Covey 282.
17. *Vietnam Air Losses*, Chris Hobson, Midland Publishing, p. 224.

CHAPTER FIVE

A BAD DAY FOR F-4s

If you were to ask retired Col. Jim Harding what June 27 means to him, he'd give you a sly farm boy smile and tell you it's his birthday. However, if you qualified the question by specifying June 27, 1972, his expression would flatten. "Let's just say it was a bad day for F-4s," he answers.

On this June day, Harding, then an Air Force major, is a flight lead with the 1st Special Operations Squadron based at Nakhon Phanom Royal Thai Air Base, better known through the Air Force as NKP. The 1st SOS

Major Jim Harding stands beside his Douglas A-1 Skyraider, named Priscilla's Phoenix, at NKP in 1972.
—J. Harding

flew Douglas A-1 Skyraiders, a large prop-driven airplane that could carry an array of ordnance. Just like the A-1, Harding was a large, strong, throwback of pilot who pulled no punches.

Raised on rural farms in Pennsylvania and North Carolina, Harding attended Penn State University on scholarship to play offensive line for the football team. Enrolled in the ROTC program, Harding graduated in 1956 and chose to pursue his commission in the Air Force rather than an offer to play football for the Los Angeles Rams.

During his first tour in Southeast Asia, Harding served as a forward air controller, making eighteen combat jumps into forward positions to radio in air strikes. He also flew an unarmed O-1F Bird Dog and received a Silver Star when he broke up a Viet Cong ambush in July 1965. After observing the Viet Cong massing on a road where the South Vietnamese army would be traveling shortly, Harding called for an air strike, but realizing the support wouldn't make it in time, he grabbed his M16, pointed it out the window, and fired it at the enemy while making several low passes. Despite being shot in the left arm, Harding managed to fire off a hundred rounds and single-handedly thwarted the ambush.

If Harding could inflict that kind of damage on the enemy flying an unarmed aircraft, one could only imagine the value he might have in an armed one. Perhaps that is what the Air Force was thinking when it issued orders returning Harding to Southeast Asia for another tour, this time as an A-1 pilot.

The 1st SOS was primarily tasked with two ongoing missions: attacking various positions in Laos that were part of the Ho Chi Minh Trail and joining its fellow NKP resident, the 40th ARRS, in conducting search and rescue. In this latter capacity, the 1st SOS flew under the call sign of Sandy.

The strength of the A-1 in search and rescue was a combination of its airspeed and ordnance. With a cruising speed of about 170 knots, the Skyraiders were only slightly faster than HH-53s, the Super Jolly Green Giants that were the primary rescue craft in the latter portion of the war in Southeast Asia. In an age of supersonic jets, the Sandys and the Jolly Greens were slow, lumbering buddies, and the most welcomed sound possible to service men who unexpectedly found themselves in hostile territory.

The A-1 also had fifteen different stations, seven on each wing and one under the centerline, where it could mount ordnance. In addition it carried four 20mm cannons in its wings. The vision of an A-1 fully loaded gave rise to various nicknames like "Flying Dump Truck" and "Old Miscellaneous," but you wouldn't want to speak ill of the A-1 in front of Harding.

Major Jim Harding's A-1 fully loaded with miniguns, cluster bomb unit (CBU) and rockets in addition to a centerline fuel tank. With fifteen different stations for ordnance and a reinforced fuselage, the A-1 was ideally suited for its search and rescue mission of trolling for ground fire and then returning it.—*J. Harding*

"It was just the absolute best plane for the job," says Harding. Not long after this June day he had a face-to-face meeting with Gen. William Momyer, Tactical Air Command commander, so that he could receive his branch's highest award, the Air Force Cross, for being the on-scene commander for the rescue of Bengal 505. At the time Harding had also caught wind of General Momyer's plan to replace the A-1. He gave his superior such an earful about the A-1 and the foolishness of replacing it, according to Harding, Momyer essentially said, "Here's your Air Force Cross. Now get out."

Not quite a month after Bengal 505, Harding's airplane was hit over hostile territory by an SA-7, a shoulder-fired SAM. He managed to eject, but landed not far from enemy foxholes. Leaning on the rural experience of his youth where he learned how to stealthily track and hunt animals,

Harding, who as a college student dreamed of being a rancher, sneaked up on the foxhole and took out the enemy with his sidearm. Seizing the North Vietnamese AK-47, he proceeded to take out two more of the enemy in nearby foxholes and called in his own rescue and that of his wingman, who had also been shot down.

While Harding, like the A-1, may have been a bit long-in-the-tooth compared to their fellow warriors in Southeast Asia, neither knew how to hold back. "We finally stopped asking him to play football with us because he was beating everyone up," jokes Dale Stovall, an HH-53 pilot who flew on the Bengal 505 rescue.

However, for all the strengths of the A-1, it had one weakness for SAR missions: No midair refueling capability. While the A-1 could carry external tanks, typically it would only have about six hours flight time. Unlike the HH-53C helicopters that could orbit on alert indefinitely so long as they could hook up to a tanker, the Sandys would have to move in and out of their orbits in shifts, one flight going out to relieve those that had to return to base for fuel.

On this, his thirty-eighth birthday, Harding is on alert at NKP. Already there is a flight of Sandys orbiting over the uninhabited areas of Laos, simultaneously supporting the Jolly Greens, which are in their own orbit and being on guard for any report of a downed aircraft.

Typically if a plane went down in Southeast Asia, the remaining members of the flight would try to pinpoint the location while calling in the SAR forces. If the flight couldn't fix a location or a SAR effort couldn't be mounted right away, the Air Force might send in a FastFAC, a single F-4 whose job in a SAR was to race over the downed airman's suspected location trying to raise a survivor on the radio. With the coordinates fixed, the Sandys would be called in to troll for ground fire and put ordnance on anyone who might fire back at them. While the Jolly Greens had three miniguns, they weren't a match for large caliber weapons, antiaircraft artillery, or SAMs. Even just a few minutes of ground fire from AK-47s could do serious damage to a HH-53C hovering over a survivor.

"Our job was to come in and soften the area up," says Harding referring to the array of ordnance the Sandys could dump on a position to kill the enemy and chase others away from a survivor. He offers no qualms about the nature of the work. "If they picked up a gun and pointed it at me or one of our guys, to me they were fair game," says Harding.

Meanwhile on June 27, at 0919 hours local time, from Udorn RTAFB an F-4 crew of pilot Marty Cavato and backseater Tony Marshall, had just launched off the runway. Cavato and Marshall were an unusual team in that they weren't even members of the same squadron. Cavato was a member of the 555th TFS, the famed Triple Nickel that was home to MiG killers such as the teams of Lodge and Locher and Ritchie and DeBellevue. Marshall, on the other hand, was a member of the 13th TFS, a squadron he had sought out as senior at the Air Force academy because of its reputation for being well run and, perhaps most important, not losing planes. "The rules were pretty simple," Marshall of the 13th TFS. "You did the mission. You got everybody in the flight home. And if a MiG got in your way, and it was a nuisance to navigation, then shoot it down. But you didn't sacrifice your wingman to go chasing after MiGs, and you didn't take stupid chances."

While the two knew each other, this would be the only time they would fly together in Southeast Asia. Their connection, in addition to both being stationed at Udorn, was that they both were members of special program run out of the F-4 bases. While they had their turns flying in typical four-ship flights, just like the men of the Valent flight out of Takhli this morning, they were also part of the F-4 Forward Air Controller program, better known as FastFAC, a sort of lone-wolf assignment that drew on the best crews in Southeast Asia. Typically, a FastFAC would fly on their own, with no wingman or additional element, in most cases not even an additional flight providing some sort of CAP (combat air patrol) for them.

FastFACs were a necessary evolution during the fighting in Southeast Asia. Throughout the war, the military relied on relatively slow, prop-driven airplanes as regular FACs. However, during the Rolling Thunder years, as the defense of North Vietnam and areas of Laos improved, particularly around the Ho Chi Minh Trail, the FACs became too vulnerable to these enhanced defenses.

The Air Force began experimenting with jets, initially F-100 Super Sabre, flying as FACs in 1967. Success of that experiment encouraged the Air Force to see if they could adapt this emerging FastFAC program to the ubiquitous F-4. The challenge fell to the 480th TFS, a member of the "Gunfighters" of the 366th TFW.

The job of a FAC was to identify targets and mark them with things like white phosphorous rockets so that ensuing flights of fighters, bombers or gunships could unload their ordnance on them. FACs also were essential to search and rescue. As happened in the case of the Spectre 22 gunship "Easter Egg Hunt" rescue, where Dale Stovall and Chuck McGrath picked up eight survivors, FACs would identify the location of survivors and relay the information back to one of a fleet of airborne HC-130s, call sign King, that would coordinate the rescue with the airborne A-1 Sandys and the HH-53 Jolly Greens.

The hazard of being a FastFAC was that in order to perform these tasks, the jet would fly close to the terrain, greatly testing a pilot's skill. During Rolling Thunder, the 480th found a willing guinea pig for this experiment of using the F-4 as a FAC in the form of a talented young pilot, first in his training class at Laredo, Texas. In 1968, Steve Ritchie, the same pilot who had mentored Dale Stovall at the Air Force Academy and would eventually join the Triple Nickel, became the first Air Force pilot to fly an F-4 FastFAC.

From this point the F-4 FastFAC program grew with various bases hosting their own teams drawn from their resident squadrons. At Udorn, where Cavato and Marshall both had recently joined the program, the FastFACs flew with a call sign of Laredo. This morning, while other members of the 7th Air Force were making their strike on targets in the North, including the truck repair facility just north of Hanoi, Cavato and Marshall would be flying to mark targets.

At this point in the war, particularly for the Air Force, there continued to be an ebb and flow in the success of the F-4 against the North Vietnamese air force. Operation Linebacker started with some measurable success for U.S. aviators. While the May 10 loss of Lodge and Locher cast a pall over the squadrons in Southeast Asia, between the Navy and the Air Force, eleven MiGs were shot down on May 10, three by the Air Force.

Throughout May and up until early June, F-4s from the Navy and the Air Force had enjoyed success against the MiGs, but the North Vietnamese, with a hand from the Soviets, would continually adapt their tactics. In addition, their ground control intercept system gave the North very good data to use and coordinate so that ground-based controllers could direct their MiG pilots into optimal situations.

Meanwhile, on the morning of June 27, despite Aikman and Hanton getting airborne late as the number 4 plane, everything seemed to be running smoothly for the Valent flight as it eventually met up with the chaff bombers they were escorting into Route Pack VI. As they neared the heart of North Vietnam, the skies came alive.

"We got into the area. Of course it was a phenomenal, tense situation," says Aikman. "You could hear the radio going everywhere. You could see the triple A and SAMs fired at a couple of other flights, but they didn't appear to be directed at us. So they weren't a threat." Then Aikman spotted a couple of bright flashes well beneath them. "The rules of engagement were that an escort must stay with the flight you are escorting unless there was some direct threat," Aikman says explaining that Valent flight held its position and didn't even have absolute confirmation that the shiny dots below were enemy MiGs. "They were just bright objects," he says. "Many of the MiGs weren't painted camouflage. So we surmised they were MiGs."

With roughly fifty missions flying the F-105 Thunderchief into North Vietnam on his first tour and another ten or so in the F-4 so far on his second stint in Southeast Asia, the array and intensity of the North's defenses were nothing new to Aikman. In general the F-4s flew high enough that the antiaircraft artillery wouldn't touch them. While they certainly were in range of the high flying SAMs, not only would they have some warning when the SAM radar targeted, but the weather was decent enough that they should be able to see the flying telephone poles coming at them. With enough warning, the F-4s could evade the SAMs.

The effectiveness of the Soviet missiles was only a little better than 1 percent: for almost every hundred SAMs launched the U.S. would lose one aircraft.[18] "Slow movers," such as, prop-driven FACs, A-1s, Jolly Greens, and refueling tankers tended to be most susceptible to the SAMs while "fast movers," the jets, had the power to evade the ground-to-air missiles if they had enough warning. Still, the low effectiveness rate of the SAM was offset by the multitude of missiles launched against American and South Vietnamese forces. Throughout 1972 the North would launch more than fort-two hundred missiles and bring down forty-nine aircraft.

With the antiaircraft guns generating their tell-tale puffs of white smoke below him, the occasional SAM in the distance, and constant chatter on the radio, Valent 03's pilot, Craig Miller, grew concerned about the situation. The experienced element lead was already worried with the weaving formation the 4th TFS favored while escorting the line-abreast chaffers, which, as he recalls, were an unusual three, not just two, flights of four. "We already were doing something we weren't too comfortable with," Miller says of him and his backseater McDow.

On Miller's wing, in Valent 04, Aikman and Hanton were still just getting to know each other, and neither of them had flown with the other six members of the flight. Similarly, McDow doesn't remember flying with the other members of the Valent flight other than with his regular frontseat Miller. Despite all this unfamiliarity, the Valent flight and the chaffers they were escorting had made their way into North Vietnam, but getting to the target was only half the mission, and in some cases, the less dangerous half.

But whatever unity Valent flight and strike package had at this juncture, it was about to fall apart.

Given the typical Route Pack VI flight path, the North had plenty of advanced warning of an incoming strike. For the most part, the United States shunned attacking airfields, but the lead time alone, was enough for the North to get its MiGs off the ground and in the air. Still the ground-controlled air force of the North tended to be cautious, waiting for an optimum situation or perhaps laying a trap with a decoy flight. As Cavato learned when he flew with Lodge, the North would listen for "bingo" calls. With the long distance the F-4s had to cover in and out of North Vietnam, an F-4 running low on fuel or perhaps straggling behind due to some damage or mechanical fault could be easy pickings for the MiGs.

"As the chaff birds made their turn," Miller explains, "it all just kind of disintegrated. It was Katie bar the door, and we lost unit integrity real quick." Contributing to the disarray was a set of unguided SAMs launched right up through the chaff corridor. As such, they were no immediate threat, but it helped it scatter the flights of F-4s.

"Somehow we ended up at low level right along the Red River," says Miller. "I look up, and there's our lead, up above us, probably five thousand feet, and I am thinking this isn't good." Miller then sees a dust cloud kick up behind them and calls to his backseater, McDow.

"What the heck is that?" he asked.

Suddenly, Miller and McDow see a fireball coming out the cloud. SAMs, and this time they are guided. Miller urgently radios to Aikman to execute a SAM break—a quick dive and turn to dodge the SAMs—while McDow continues to look back, counting five SAMs in all, turning toward them.

Suddenly, as Miller goes into the break he senses an explosion behind him and fears that either one of the SAMs caught Aikman and Hanton in Valent 04 or they crashed trying to dodge the missile. Then he catches sight of his wingman. The explosion was just the first SAM detonating. With the SAMs still trailing and the two F-4s trying to lose them, McDow watches the missiles and cautions his pilot to tighten the turn. "There I am pulling probably a six-and-a-half-G turn, and Rick says very calmly 'You better pull it in,'" Miller says.

"We broke right and went down to the deck," Aikman recalls of following his element lead. "Then we came back up left, and there was a ridgeline so we went behind ridgeline, down a valley, where the SAMs lost us."

SAM attacks may have been routine by now for the Air Force, but they routinely remained trouble. For element lead Miller, Aikman's handling of the quick SAM-break maneuver demonstrated his ability to fly the Phantom in combat. Once clear of the SAMs, Miller led the element through a 180-degree turn around Hanoi. He looked up and saw Valent 01 and 02 ahead of him and was able to bring the second element back together with its lead. Miller recalls calling the lead, asking if they had any issue with the SAMs. To Miller's surprise, the lead element didn't even see the salvo of five missiles that had chased away Valent 03 and 04.

Guided SAMs could be lethal for the F-4s especially if a crew was unaware of the oncoming missiles. "They didn't see them," says Miller of Valent 01 and 02 and the SAMs. "If they had locked onto them, they would have got them. "

For Aikman, there was a fighter-pilot's bittersweetness to leaving the target area. "Each time we egressed the target area, there was always a little disappointment in my mind when I would realize that I had still not had the chance to hassle with a MiG," he would reflect a few years later. "And this was my second tour!"

What Miller and Aikman didn't know at the time was that as they were heading west, at almost this very moment, in two separate areas of North Vietnam, two F-4s were on the losing end of a battle with a MiG and a SAM.

The 308th TFS out of Udorn had contributed several F-4 flights to the morning's mission. One of those flights, call sign Troy, was part of a simultaneous attack on the airfields near Hanoi.[19] Another flight from the 308th, call sign Dobby, was part of a second wave of the chaff-bombing flights.

Piloting Troy 04 was Captain John Cerak with Captain David Dingee as the backseater WSO. Only three weeks earlier, on June 1, Dingee, flying backseater for Captain George Hawks, and had the close call with a SAM, being lit up like a fireball in front of Dale Stovall's HH-53C after the Jolly Green dodged a MiG in the first, thwarted, attempt to pick up Roger Locher. Miraculously, Dingee's F-4 had held together almost all the way to Udorn, when Dingee and Hawks ejected and were safely rescued. This morning, Cerak and Dingee and the other members of Troy flight received a SAM warning about forty miles west of Hanoi as they were heading east toward the airfields. At the same time, a pair of MiG-21s, which had been scrambled from a base near Hanoi when the strike was initially detected by the North, turned west to meet the Troy flight head on.[20] One of the MiGs fired a pair of missiles striking Troy 04. Cerak and Dingee managed to eject.[21] At nearly the same time, the second wave of chaff bombers were laying their corridor and were making their 180-degree turn back toward Laos. One of those chaffers, Dobby 01, was piloted by Lt. Col. Farrell Junior Sullivan with Capt. Richard Logan Francis in the backseat.[22] Flying at about 17,000 feet, Dobby 01 was struck by a SAM about twenty miles west of Hanoi, not far from Son Tay. Francis, the WSO, managed to eject, but whether the pilot, Sullivan, managed to get out was unknown.

Just three days earlier, June 24, the Air Force had lost two Phantoms as part of a strike against the Thai Nguyen iron and steel plants, not far from Hanoi. Both of those F-4s had been lost to MiG-21s and the fate of their crews wasn't known as of June 27.

Air-to-air combat had reignited in earnest with the Linebacker response to the Easter Offensive. During all of 1972, the Air Force would launch almost 38 thousand sorties against North Vietnam. In contrast, this was about 10 thousand more than the total number of sorties in '69, '70, and '71 combined. In terms of losses, in 1968, the Air Force lost twenty-two aircraft in aerial combat. During the bombing halt from 1969 to the start of 1972 it lost only one.[23]

At the outset of Linebacker in May, the Air Force enjoyed an upper hand. During the first full day of the operation, May 10, the team of Lodge and Locher was shot down, but only after they and two other crews of their Oyster flight managed to kill three MiGs. At the same time, the Navy managed to shoot down eight MiGs while losing three F-4s. Most notably, one of them was flown by Lt. Randy Cunningham with Lt. Willie Driscoll in the backseat; they managed three MiG kills that day, making the Cunningham-Driscoll team to the first aces of the Vietnam Conflict. However, as they were egressing North Vietnam, their F-4 was struck by a SAM. Cunningham managed to pilot the badly damaged jet back to the vicinity of their aircraft carrier. They then ejected over the water, abandoning the mortally wounded jet, and were promptly picked up by a Navy helicopter.

In late May, the North Vietnamese convened a conference of commanders of its MiG regiments and other senior officers. Within two weeks, they produced a report analyzing U.S. tactics making several recommendations to counter the North's shortcomings.[24]

One of the tactics adopted by the North was to introduce low-flying attack flights, traveling at fewer than 2,500 feet above the terrain. Complementing these "in the weeds" MiGs would be a higher flying, 25,000 feet or so, set of MiGs, traveling at less than 500 miles per hour. The low-flying attack flight would fly faster, and there would be about six to ten miles between the two flights,[25] a gap that a set of MiG-21s could close in less than half a minute in a supersonic dash.

This tactic wasn't revolutionary. From the early days of Rolling Thunder the North seemed to grasp that the small, nimble MiGs, especially the Mach 2 capable MiG-21, were suited to make fast, single passes from the rear.[26] Again, the North's ground controllers were cautious with their airborne resources. They sought optimal attacks.

Generally, the low-flying MiGs could evade the U.S. early warning resources both airborne (Disco) and seaborne (Navy's Red Crown). Even the secret Combat Tree technology that would could identify the MiG transponders did not provide complete coverage and could be circumvented if the North's pilots turned off their transponders, undoubtedly a possibility if their ground-based controllers wanted to make the low-flying attack MiGs as stealthy as possible.

One other factor involved in the dynamics of the air war over Southeast Asia, which were influenced by everything from political rules of engagement to technological advancement, was whether or not these resources were fully at the hands of U.S. aviators. A few months before this June day, Tony Marshall was flying backseater in a Combat Tree enabled F-4D that had been scrambled to intercept some MiGs heading to targets over northern Laos. As they neared the border with North Vietnam, they received a "minimal threat" call and were asked to hold an orbit thirty miles west,

Patrolling the skies of Southeast Asia would be an EC-121 with the call sign of Disco. With large radomes on top and below that housed advanced electronics, the Air Force plane attempted to provide pilots with updated information on the whereabouts of enemy aircraft. However, many Air Force pilots felt the best information often would come from Red Crown, the Navy cruiser, stationed in the Gulf of Tonkin, in part due to better technology aboard the ship.
—National Museum of the U.S. Air Force

near the Plain of Jars. Marshall had been tracking some MiG indications on the radar scope off to the right of the flight. While the shortest and expected turn to make at the border would have been left, back into Laos toward the Plain of Jars, Marshall asked his pilot to turn right to see if he could get a radar fix on the MiG.

"As we rolled out right into the turn, we got a warning on the radio to break now," explains Marshall. The radio call, whose origin wasn't clear to either Marshall or his frontseat, reported the MiGs were on their tail. After some evasive maneuvering, Marshall still wasn't able to get a fix on the radar. They were descending from about twenty thousand feet at this point, increasing speed and trying to get to a better altitude for an engagement. Marshall then looked out the cockpit and saw at their 1 o'clock position the MiG. As the MiG passed, it fired an Atoll air to-air missile, missing the members of the flight. Marshall then saw two more Atolls pass over them from a second MiG that had turned tail.

At that point, the wingman called out "bingo" fuel, and the members of the 13th TFS headed back. "That's what we did," he said of the 13th. "If someone called bingo, we didn't stick around or go chasing MiGs."

When Marshall got back to Udorn, he made a few phones calls and probably cashed in a personal favor or two to find out exactly where the "break now" radio call had come from. What he was most interested in knowing from the person he eventually was put in touch with is why they only got the warning at the last moment. "He said they weren't allowed to say anything because it would let the enemy know what our capabilities were," says Marshall.

To add to the situation, once back at Udorn, members of the flight were looking at the radar film from the incident with the 13th's film interpreter. When they broke right, rather than the expected left turn, the radar indicated MiG-19s on both sides of the scope. "Had we made the normal left turn initially, we would have fallen into the trap by rolling out in front of them, and they would have been in position to shoot us down like sitting ducks," says Marshall.

While Marshall recognized the need for military secrecy, the incident left him wondering how much more information was there that the aviators on the front line weren't getting. "People had great information," says Marshall. "But they sat on it because they didn't want anyone to know that we knew it."

By the time he would land back at Udorn on June 27, Marshall would have even more reason to wonder if somebody knew more than Phantom crews were being told.

About ten in the morning of June 27, while Chuck McGrath waited with his roommate, Chuck Morrow, on Leo Thacker's diverted HH-53C at Udorn, Dale Stovall listened to the radio at the 40th ARRS's operations shack, Ben Orrell held his Jolly Green in an orbit just outside North Vietnam, Jim Harding sat on alert at NKP, the Valent flight was heading for the refueling tankers over Laos, and FastFAC Cavato and Marshall were on their way to mark targets.

Little did they know, this was the calm before the storm. Over the next several hours, the lives of these men would intertwine against a backdrop of what could be considered the worst day for F-4s in terms of air-to-air combat.

With two crews reported being down, the airborne command and control center (ABCCC) needed to assemble the early stages of the rescue force. As Cavato and Marshall recall, not long after they had left Udorn, they received the call to start searching the area west of Hanoi, to see if their FastFAC could bring up any survivors on the radio.

At about the same time, ABCCC radioed Valent flight. "They asked us if we were configured for escort," recalls Lynn Aikman, pilot of Valent 04. "Our flight lead said we were, and they assigned us to fly MiGCAP for a FastFAC."

Back at NKP's operations desk, with the near simultaneous reports of F-4s down, Captain Dale Stovall started assessing the situation. The 40th was working without a backup right now. He needed to figure out the status of the other birds, including Thacker's JG 73, which was currently diverted to Udorn.

A lone F-4 races over the jungle and mountains of Southeast Asia. When flying as a FastFAC seeking out a survivor, the aircraft would fly at low altitude through a set of coordinates, trying to raise the survivor on an emergency radio channel. Typically, an F-4 would perform this mission without any immediate escort so as to not identify the position of the low-flying F-4 or survivor and also because the flight profile of the FastFAC made it very difficult to escort, as Valent flight would discover on June 27, 1972.—*National Archives*

Meanwhile, the Valent members raced to the refueling tankers. "We took a full load of fuel," explains Aikman. "Normally we would only take what we need to return to base." Instead, the four jets and eight crew of Valent flight would be in for an extended mission, providing cover for Laredo 12, the FastFAC team of Cavato and Marshall.

Aikman and other members of the Valent flight recall a second flight also being assigned to MiGCAP. Presumably, the two flights would cycle in and out the search area. Typically, the gas guzzling F-4s would only have about twenty minutes time-on-station before they would reach "bingo," the minimum amount of fuel necessary to safely recover to a friendly base.

Under the direction of their lead, the four Phantoms raced toward a rendezvous with Laredo 12.

NOTES

18. "The Vietnam War Almanac," John T. Correll, *Air Force Magazine*, September 2004, p. 56. The reported effectiveness was 1.15 percent.
19. *Vietnam Air Losses*, Chris Hobson, Midland publishing, p 230.
20. Ibid
21. MiG-21 Units of the Vietnam War, Istvan Toperczer, Osprey Publishing, p. 57. It is worth noting that *Vietnam Air Losses* and *MiG-21 Units of the Vietnam War* differ somewhat in the account of this shoot down. First, Hobson identifies the serial number as 67-0248 and Toperczer indicates it as 67-0243. Hobson's account states that the Troy flight received the SAM warning and was orbiting some forty miles west of Hanoi. Toperczer's account, drawn on the records from the MiG units, indicates that the MiGs engaged Troy flight not long after it crossed the Laos border, which would place the shoot down closer to some seventy to eighty miles west of Hanoi.
22. *Vietnam Air Losses*, Chris Hobson, Midland publishing, p 230.
23. "The Vietnam War Almanac," John T. Correll, *Air Force Magazine*, September 2004, pp 53, 58
24. *MiG-21 Units of Vietnam War*, Itsvan Toperczer, Osprey Publishing, p. 55
25. Ibid, p. 53
26. *F-4 Phantom II vs. MiG-21*, Peter Davies, Osprey Publishing, p. 52

CHAPTER SIX

FOUR IS ON FIRE!

As the Valent flight raced to meet up with Laredo 12, the FastFAC's crew felt a little uneasy about their impromptu escort. "It was very abnormal," says Tony Marshall, the backseater WSO on Laredo 12. According Marshall, he couldn't recall any other time he had flown with a four-ship MiGCAP. The Laredo 12 pilot, Marty Cavato, agrees it was an unusual situation, but it was one that they had all been thrown into by the airborne controller rather than something the F-4 aircrews had chosen.

"I was supposed to be doing something else and these guys were supposed to be doing something else," says Cavato referring Valent's and Laredo 12's original assignments for the day. "And then all of sudden they are CAPing for me."

In his experience flying escort for reconnaissance flights, "recces"(pronounced wreck-ees) as they were called and which were similar to flying a FastFAC mission, there was never a four-plane escort says Cavato. "We might have a two-ship escort a recce, but never anything like this," he explains. "Where a four-ship is trying to CAP for a single ship, it's very unwieldy. It was not a usual situation. We were all kind of thrown into this thing and trying to make do the best we could."

Craig Miller, Valent's second element lead, wasn't a fan of the four-ship MiGCAP either. "It was absolutely ridiculous, stupid and dangerous," he says.

Even before Valent and Laredo 12 made their first cycle through the search area, well west of Hanoi, a call of MiGs came in. "We got a call that there were two F-4s being chased out of North Vietnam by a pair of MiG-

21s. They were heading southwest," recalls Laredo 12 backseater Marshall. "What I did was get on the radar, and I picked up four targets. We asked if we could shoot at the two in the back, and they said no."

Marshall decided to keep working the radar to better identify the two MiGs. At that point the two F-4s went by to the north of the Valent flight and Laredo 12. Feeling confident that the only jets trailing would be the enemy MiGs, Cavato radioed the airborne command once more. "Again he asked if we could shoot, and they said no," recalls Marshall "At that point, we figured the only thing we could do was identify them for Valent, and let Valent have a shot at them. Our mission wasn't shooting down MiGs. We were supposed to find these downed guys."

Marshall admits he was so uneasy with the four-ship MiGCAP over them that he was hoping the Valent flight would chase the MiGs and leave him and Cavato to handle their FastFAC mission on their own. However, the Valent flight lead and airborne command decided to the let the MiGs pass. The lead then briefed the rest of Valent on the approach they would take to the escort. The original mission of Valent that day was escorting a group of twelve, line-abreast chaff bombers. Quite possibly, in the arsenal of U.S. Air Force flight techniques, there is nothing closer to being the opposite of escorting a large group of chaff bombers flying abreast than flying MiGCAP for a FastFAC. Chaff bombers try to fly at a steady speed and altitude, which is essential to setting up the ground-radar-obscuring chaff corridor. A FastFAC races over the terrain immediately below it. Especially when searching for downed aircrew, a FastFAC makes quick passes to avoid giving away a survivor's location to the enemy. Being low to the terrain and over potentially hostile territory, a FastFAC wants to be able to move unpredictably. As a single aircraft, it has no formation.

For the four Valent crews, who had virtually no experience flying with each other, this daunting assignment of escorting Laredo 12 may have been too much from the get-go. It didn't take Valent flight long to lose some cohesiveness. "Our lead element was down low level with them" says Miller referring to Laredo 12. "And they told me that we were to stay up high to act as a radio relay. So I feel like I am hanging out there trolling for flak or SAMs or anything else. And then I am trying to keep track of those three green F-4s against the jungle," Miller says noting the camouflaged jets.

Meanwhile Orrell and Zielinski have piloted Jolly Greens 56 and 52 up to their holding point where the A-1 Sandys are keeping them company.

With two F-4s, four crewmen, down between the Laos border and Hanoi, it may only be a matter of time until a survivor comes up on radio.

At NKP, Dale Stovall is listening to the initial search and rescue effort at the operations desk. As is the habit of members of the 40th, several men have begun to gather around. News of downed jets travel quickly. While the 40th has two birds up in their orbit over northern Laos, Stovall is trying to get word on the status of the 40th's other Jolly Greens that morning.

JG 60 still wasn't checking out. Its problem was a "chip" light—the HH-53's equivalent of the "check engine" warning on the dashes of cars produced decades later; the warning could mean anything from nothing to pending catastrophic failure. The concept of the chip light was simple. Sikorsky used a series of magnetic chips as a sort of early-warning system for mechanical failures. The idea was that the magnets would attract metal debris in the engines and gears of the helicopter. This would be the kind of debris that would come from worn bearings or other components that could precede some major failure. When the chip collected enough debris, a light on the instrument panel would go on. The only problem was that these chip lights tended to be very sensitive, producing a lot of false positives.

If a chip light came on in the middle of an operation, as pilots and copilots in the 40th tell it, their tendency was to roll the dice, putting faith in the HH-53's dual engines. Considering many of the H-53s served four decades worth of combat, such a gamble on Sikorsky engineering may have been a safe bet. However, a chip light early in the morning, such as with JG 60, was a different story. As the crews of the 40th were demonstrating in 1972, they had no qualms about taking enemy fire during their mission, but they also knew how quickly the tables could turn on them, with the rescuers needing to be rescued themselves. This not only exposed the crew involved to certain danger, but the larger concern for many members of the 40th seems to have been how such a catastrophe could prevent them from accomplishing their mission, saving downed airmen. If a pair of Jolly Greens were trying to pick up a survivor, and one of the helicopters crashed to the jungle, the protocol was for the backup high bird to rescue the low-bird crew first.

For a moment, there had been a report that JG 60 had to make a forced landing, but the helicopter had managed to stay airborne and make it to Udorn. In any case, it looked like it would be grounded for the day while the mechanics went to work to fix whatever caused the chip light.

Meanwhile, the warnings with the hydraulics on Leo Thacker's JG 73 seemed to be checking out. Thacker, copilot Mason, and the crew with PJs McGrath and Morrow, a flight engineer, and a combat photographer were still at Udorn. With the two F-4s having gone down in North Vietnam, if the search and rescue operation was able to raise survivors, the two Jolly Greens orbiting over northern Laos might be able to handle the pickup. Still Stovall started looking at the faces hovering around the ops desk. A bespectacled young flight engineer Rick Simmon was in the room, and not far away was 40th's newest copilot, a young second lieutenant named Clifton Hutchinson, although he preferred the more informal "Rufus." Finding PJs for a crew would be easy as they always seemed ready to go and managed their own scheduling. As Stovall started filling slots for another bird to head north, just in case, there was no doubt in his mind who would pilot the HH-53C. Just as a player-coach, or in this case, pilot-assistant acting operations officer, knows when to call his own number, Stovall wasn't going to sit on the bench at NKP.

Just before noon on June 27, 1972, Valent flight had refueled for the third time of the day. With the lead element of Valent flight at low altitude over the Laredo FastFAC and Valent's second element, the crews of Miller and McDow, and Aikman and Hanton at higher altitude trying to shadow the three aircraft below it, the F-4s would burn fuel quickly as they needed to use their engines to keep getting back into formation.—*M. Cavato*

About this time, now a little before noon on June 27, 1972, Laredo 12 along with their unwieldy four-jet Valent MiGCAP had made their first cycle through the search coordinates with no luck in pinpointing in either Troy 04 (Cerak and Dingee) or Dobby 01 (Sullivan and Francis). Low on fuel, the five F-4s egressed the search area and headed out to the refueling tankers orbiting over Laos. It has been more than five hours since Valent flight left Takhli. They have already flown into the heart of the most heavily defended air space in history, dodged a salvo of guided missiles, refueled, and come back over North Vietnam to fly what seems to be an impractical, if not near impossible escort for a FastFAC. And now they were topping off their tanks to do it one more time.

As Laredo 12 backseater Tony Marshall ponders years later, while also acknowledging an uncanny ability to "rationalize anything," there may have been some big-picture reason for the unusual MiGCAP. "I'll be generous and say that someone knew something that we didn't," he says. Partly influenced by the close call with some MiGs lying in wait from earlier in his tour, Marshall surmises that someone with more information than they had may have intentionally created their current scenario. Of course as the members of the Valent flight point out years later, if there was some orchestrator of their extended assignment, and it wasn't just a haphazard tasking that had been cobbled together for Valent flight to begin with, that person or group of people undoubtedly had never flown an F-4 Phantom in combat. Pulling off the tankers and coming back into North Vietnam, now for Valent flight's third time of the day, Cavato and Marshall in FastFAC Laredo 12 flew to a second set of coordinates. They are attempting to alternate between the reported locations of Dobby 01 and Troy 04, searching for one on the initial cycle and the other on the next.

It's high noon over the North Vietnam jungle, not too far from where the border of Laos and North Vietnam form an outline almost like the profile of an ape, giving rise to the moniker "gorilla's head" for the location. Meanwhile one of the Air Force's rescue coordination centers (sub-RCC), call sign "Jack," in Thailand is monitoring the rescue forces over Southeast Asia and notes that one of the airborne rescue command craft, King-21, advises pulling back search and rescue forces due to reports of MiGs in the area. Ten minutes later, King-21 relays back to Jack sub-RCC that it doubts that any aircraft can get to the area due to MiG activity. Five minutes later, another King bird, King-27 performs a headcount of all search and rescue forces and eventually reports to Jack, at about 1220 hours that all aircraft are accounted for.

During this same time, from noon until about 1220, Valent flight is back on its wild ride of trying to keep up with Laredo 12 in the weeds below. Each member of the trailing element of the flight recalls somewhat different details of what transpired in these twenty minutes.

"One [the lead] was trying to keep the Laredo FastFAC in sight," says Valent 03B, McDow. "Well, that is not very conducive to keeping 3 and 4 in formation. We were getting thrown out. Four was getting thrown out." In this jet-propelled mission of follow-the-leader, as the second element tries to keep position with the first element, which is trying to keep up with Laredo 12 racing over the search area below: flight integrity disintegrated. McDow's frontseat Miller agrees that the two elements weren't working together, and in a few moments they won't even be communicating with each other.

Valent 04B, Hanton, vividly recalls all the turning was causing them to burn fuel. "There is no fuel gauge in the back of an F-4, so I kept asking Lynn how we were doing." Hanton knew how important the calculation of "bingo" could be. Not long before June 27, he had been on a flight where they flamed out on landing, sucking the tanks dry to make it home. He didn't want to take that chance again. "Lynn told me we were bingo fuel, and I must have made three or four bingo calls myself."

"After we had been in the area for about twenty minutes, I told my flight lead that I was getting low on fuel," recalls Aikman who believes the flight then started making a turn to the west.

At about this time, all four members of the Valent's second element recall receiving reports of "blue bandits," from the airborne early warning aircraft, call sign Disco; these are MiG-21s that are about fifteen miles ahead of them crossing from west to east. These may be the MiGs that had chased the two Phantoms into Laos when Valent flight first rendezvoused with Laredo 12. As Valent flight is flying north, apparently preparing to make a westerly turn toward Laos, these MiGs, which are now some fifteen miles out, will be crossing in front of them, coming from Laos toward their bases in North Vietnam. For Aikman and Hanton in Valent 04 the MiGs seem to be of little concern.

"Nobody paid much attention to the call," says Aikman, who with the rest of the flight has been airborne for more than five hours at this point. "I was getting a little fatigued. I guess I was tired enough to not realize that if the MiGs had decided to come after us that fifteen miles was only about two minutes away."

Hanton recalls checking the radar for the MiGs, calculating them to be, indeed, about fifteen nautical miles out and not a threat. His worry remains Valent 04's fuel status, but still he asks Aikman to roll up on the wing as they turn so they can check their rear, six o'clock position.

Miller doesn't recall Aikman and Hanton's bingo calls, but he doesn't discount them either. On their first cycle through the search area, Miller had burned through most of his fuel trying to keep the elements together. If he, as the 3 plane was burning that much fuel, it stood to reason his wingman, Aikman, would have burned through more. Miller remembers the MiG calls, but he also remembers at this critical moment in the flight, the unwieldy four-ship MiGCAP was not in full communication with each other. Throughout their escort of the FastFAC, the flight lead was switching among radio frequencies, apparently talking to Laredo on one, the rest of Valent flight on another, and maybe also monitoring the guard frequency that would have been used by the emergency radios of the four men who had been shot down earlier, the men who they were trying to rescue.

Miller believes the lead had gone off Valent's frequency to talk with Laredo 12, but Miller says he never heard back from anyone in the lead element as to whether they were going to pursue the MiGs crossing to the north of them, egress the area for refueling, or stay on the MiGCAP for the Laredo FastFAC.

"At this point I was kind of drifting to my right," says Miller explaining he was hedging his bet—trying to stay in formation while also trying to keep the MiGs crossing in the distance in front of him should the lead decide to engage them. The lead never came back up on the radio to let Miller know. The switching of frequencies might also explain that while Aikman and Hanton remember issuing bingo calls, the flight lead may not have heard all of them.

As Miller drifts right, Aikman, anticipating the turn to leave the area dives from being on the right of Miller to cutting across the flight's turn left (west)

After retiring from the US Air Force, Robert Craig Miller worked for a number of years as a government test flight contractor. Miller had flown F-105s during Operation Rolling Thunder in addition to returning to Southeast Asia for Operation Linebacker. Miller reflects that during the three-and-half-year bombing halt between these operations, not only did some of the Air Force tactics atrophy, but with the turnover in leadership, whatever had been learned during the first part of the war would have to be relearned through many of the same mistakes in the latter portion of the war. "A lot of what went on cost a lot of aircraft and lives," he says.—*C. Miller*

toward Laos. Miller said Aikman was doing a good job as his wingman.

"Lynn was in good formation with me," Miller says. "He was flying a good fluid four, right where he was supposed to be."

As Aikman crosses underneath, he plans to roll up on the wing to give Hanton a view out the back to check that no MiGs have sneaked in behind. McDow, who had lost sight of Valent 04, asks Miller to perform a similar maneuver.

"Miller was an exceptional pilot," says McDow. "Seeing out the back of an F-4 isn't easy, but Craig could get the plane to stand up on wing and you could see all the way back and deep."

Both McDow and Hanton describe the way a backseater checks their six o'clock the same way. As the pilot banks the jet up onto the wingtip, the backseater props himself up, pushing a hand against the instrument panel or even the throttles in rear of the cockpit. He can then can crane his head all the way around and get a good view of what's behind them. As practical as this cockpit yoga may be, the consequence is that in order to have this kind of mobility, the backseater WSO likely doesn't have his shoulder harnesses secured, which can lead to problems for the WSO if the jet is hit by enemy fire or the ejection sequence is started.

———

As McDow perches himself up, he is worried that he has lost sight of Aikman and Hanton.

"In a typical fluid four, our responsibility was clearing the area behind 1 and 2," McDow says of the 3 plane's role in protecting the six o'clock of the lead element. "But I knew that at this point that typical responsibility had gone down the drain. I wanted to make sure I could clear 4 [Aikman and Hanton]."

While members of the trailing Valent element may have been unclear or uncertain as to the direction of their lead at this point—were they engaging the MiGs or leaving the area—Marty Cavato, piloting Laredo 12, says he recalls the entire flight was moving to engage the MiGs.

"I was alongside the Valent flight," he says explaining he was still very low to the jungle below and off to Valent's left. "Basically, I was just trying to stay out of their way." At this stage, Cavato believes the lead element had come up level with the trailing element of Valent 03 and 04 but was to the right so that the two jets closest to Cavato were Valent 04 and then Valent 03.

Aikman and Hanton remember the flight was turning west toward Laos and the tankers to refuel; the MiGs in front were a nonissue. Miller was anxiously awaiting word from the Valent lead as to whether they were going to engage the MiGs. Cavato believes the entire Valent flight was proceeding north to engage the crossing MiGs. However, the one clear recollection of all the aviators was that there had been only one call at 1220, just a minute or two earlier, of MiGs in the area, the ones about fifteen miles in front of them.

The next moment is seared into Cavato's memory. "Jesus Christ, Tony!" he exclaimed over the intercom of Laredo 12. "Four is on fire!"

As Aikman crosses, he becomes the left-most jet in the formation, the one closest to Cavato, who is below and trailing the Valent flight, which gives the FastFAC pilot an unobstructed view of the fireball that had been Valent 04's left engine.

Marshall, who has been looking at the radar, lifts his head just in time to see a missile strike Valent 03 in its engines. Cavato then follows the path of the missiles back trying to find their source and sees a pair of MiG-21s high over his shoulder passing at a high rate of speed.

"This was one of their tactics," says Cavato "An airplane, high altitude. Meanwhile they would have two other planes coming from low altitude."

Cavato and Marshall give chase to one of the MiGs, going into a climbing turn right and becoming nearly inverted as they get a radar lock on the enemy MiG. Armed with Aim-7 Sparrow air-to-air missiles, Cavato has the MiG lined up and pulls the trigger.

"Nothing happens," he says. In a tale quite common among pilots in the Vietnam Conflict; the missile malfunctions.

"When we got home, the maintenance and weapons guys looked at it," Marshall says. "No wonder the damn thing didn't come off. The cable was corroded. They looked at the records, and sure enough, the thing had gone a couple of years without ever being bench checked."

Cavato comes back around and sees Valent 03 almost hanging in the sky. "Imagine you had some child's miniaturized version of an F-4 and it was just hanging by a string and you tapped it, spinning it around," he says.

Valent 03 has gone into a perfectly flat spin as it falls almost straight down. Scanning the area, Cavato and Marshall count four chutes and mark the coordinates, passing the information onto search and rescue command. Low on fuel and with at least one dud for a missile, they head for Udorn.

Moments earlier, in the cockpit of Valent 04, Aikman began his diving turn to cut across the formation and roll up on his wing. He never got a chance to finish the turn and Hanton never got the full view behind them.

With his head craned all the way around to the left, out of the corner of his eye, Hanton sees Valent 04's engine explode. A heat-seeking Atoll did exactly what it was designed to do and buried itself in the F-4's left engine. To Hanton, it feels as though some giant had just slapped the back of jet.

"It was like we hit a wall in midair," recalls Aikman.

The entire jet lurches right. Aikman's instrument panel lights up in a way he has never seen before. Aikman shouts over the intercom, "Let's get out!" Hanton never hears him. The missile must have ripped out the intercom's electronics. Still Hanton has already gone into the ejection sequence, checking the altimeter and getting himself into the ready position.

Meanwhile, in the frontseat of Valent 04, Aikman's mind and body are fighting each other. His left hand starts reaching for the handle next to his seat. "It was like a slow motion movie. My mind was saying 'No, that's not right,' but my hand kept moving." For nearly all his Air Force career, in the T-38 trainer, in the F-105, and the F-106, the ejection handle had always been on the left of the seat. Aikman's brain keeps trying to intercept the reflex, to tell his left hand to stop. If it pulls the wrong handle, his fate will be sealed. To the left of the pilot's seat in the F-4 is the release that separates the pilot from the ejection seat.

As they are flaming toward the ground below Aikman's brain finally wins out and his hands move to the ejection handle between his legs.

In the backseat of the F-4, there is a command selector valve whereby a backseater can eject only himself. Otherwise, the normal ejection sequence in the F-4, regardless of whether it is initiated by the WSO or the pilot, first ignites the explosive bolts that send the canopy clear and then launches the WSO a split second before the pilot.

The Phantom's ejection seats were made by the Martin-Baker company. At its simplest, the ejection seat is a chair strapped to a rocket. When a plane has been damaged beyond recovery, pulling the ejection handle can be like going from a frying pan into a fire . . . at speeds that could kill an untrained, unprepared individual. Neck and back injuries in addition to broken arms and legs were a common consequence of ejecting. While these types of injuries ranged from painful to life threatening, they were better than the alternative of staying with the aircraft all the way to the ground. Still, ejecting was no fun. Among crews who worked on the F-4s and pilots who had the misfortune to ride the seats out of the cockpit, these thrones to safety had earned the nickname "Martin-Baker Widow Maker."

Hanton has no idea that the intercom had been lost, and thus, he has no warning when Aikman initiated the ejection sequence. However, as he is already preparing to eject, he has gotten himself into a good position.

The wounded F-4 is still probably traveling at least 400 knots, 460 mph, when Hanton goes up the rail and out of the aircraft.

"You can imagine the wind blast," says Hanton. "Overall I was in pretty good position, but I had my head tilted a little bit to the left because I watching the altimeter."

That slight tilt of his head may have been enough to allow the wind to awkwardly catch Hanton's custom-fitted helmet and rip it straight from his head, exposing his right eye to the full force of the vortex he has been thrown into.

Aikman on the other hand, concerned about grabbing the correct handle and punching Hanton and himself from the craft before it is too late, shoots up the ejection rails in an awkward posture. His head is slightly forward, and he is whipped back into seat as his body experiences what he estimates to be seventeen Gs of force.

Like Hanton, Aikman looses his helmet instantly. The force of the ejection causes him to black out. Unconscious, his body flails in the 400-knot windstream. While Aikman's parachute will deploy automatically, being unconscious he won't be able to steer his chute to a safe landing.

In the seconds that seemed like minutes to the crew of Valent 04, Rick McDow in the backseat of Valent 03, has been propping himself up to try to get a view of Valent 04. Miller has rolled up on his right wing as Aikman and Hanton were crossing underneath. Feeling Miller getting ready roll back left, McDow catches view of the nose of their wingman. In the next moment McDow sees Valent 04's engine explode, and the jet snap roll to the right from the devastating strike. At the time, McDow has his shoulder harness off so that he can prop himself up to get a peek out the back of the jet. He has his left hand on the throttles, which also feature the switch for the intercom. As he watches his wingman roll violently right, suddenly the giant that had slapped the back of Valent 04 now strikes Valent 03.

Over the ensuing months Rick McDow would talk to other aviators shot down in battle. Many would describe their shoot downs as almost like flying through jet wash. An Atoll missile with a proximity fuse would detonate below the aircraft, sending shrapnel into the fuselage, causing the progressive damage that would cause the engines to flame out.

"That was not the case for us," says McDow. The Atoll flew right into the engine, apparently detonating on contact. The F-4 was hit violently as though some giant sledgehammer had descended from the sky. Leaving the jet in a completely flat spin, the second Atoll had basically stopped Valent 03 in mid air, causing it to fall straight toward the hilly terrain below. As had happened to Aikman and Hanton, Miller and McDow also lost their cockpit intercom.

McDow, who has been turned around looking for Valent 04 when the

Atoll hits, injures his left shoulder. "Whether my shoulder hit the cockpit rail or my left hand had somehow gotten tangled up with the throttles and I hyperextended my shoulder somehow, I don't know," says McDow. All McDow does remember is that in the moments he was still in the cockpit, he couldn't move his left arm or shoulder.

"The airplane was vibrating so significantly that I couldn't read any of the instruments," says McDow. "And we were rolling and tumbling so violently, I couldn't tell if we were up or down." McDow remembers that at the time of the shoot down it was a perfectly clear day, and, yet, Valent 03 was in such a spin that he couldn't get a visual reference.

The altimeter is a three-hand model and McDow can see it rotate through the falling feet past the number eight, but he can't tell if it marks 18,000 or 8,000 feet.

"When you are flying in combat, you get your mind prepared for these options," McDow says of the scenario of being shot down and having to eject. "I think I can honestly say that there was nothing that surprised me." But while his mind goes through the sequence for ejecting, his body has difficulty. He distinctly remembers moving his left hand to change the command select valve to ensure both he and Miller will eject when he pulls the handle between his legs, where he also presumes both hands now were. Instead, when he looks at the valve, it hasn't been touched, and when he looks for his left hand on the handle, it isn't there either. Whatever injury he sustained when the Atoll exploded, it is keeping his left arm from cooperating with his brain. With one good arm and knowing he is running out of time, he pulls the handle.

With the intercom dead, McDow can't know that his pilot, Miller, has started going through the same sequence, pulling the ejection handle. Miller senses the canopy blow, and McDow eject, meaning his seat should go momentarily. Then he notices his left hand is still on the mic button on the throttles.

"And the throttles are under the cockpit rail," Miller says, explaining when he ejected, his hand slammed against the rail. "I didn't break any bones in my hand, but it got cut up pretty good."

With Valent 03 in a flat spin, the one benefit for Miller and McDow is that their airspeed has nearly fallen to zero when they eject. Unlike Aikman and Hanton, who are thrown into a 400 knot windstream, they have little windblast to confront.

The area where the four ejected is about eighty miles west of Hanoi right on top of the "gorilla's head," over mountainous, rocky, terrain. The area has a few small villages. While it doesn't quite represent the defenses of Hanoi, for the four American air pirates now descending from the air, hostile villagers armed with AK-47s can be every bit as deadly as a SAM. In these remote areas outside the domain of the regular North Vietnamese Army the villages in the region organize themselves into militia whose weaponry can include guns up to the caliber of antiaircraft artillery.

As Miller is descending his chute is spinning, disorienting him somewhat, but right between his feet, he can see his F-4 still in its flat spin. Eventually, he watches it crash into the ground below.

Still strapped into the ejection seat, Miller feels a sharp pain in his legs. "My first thought was that the G suit for some reason had inflated," he says. "But I wasn't hooked up to anything anymore. That didn't make any sense. I tried to rationalize it, and I couldn't."

He takes out his survival knife and starts cutting his G suit, but it is not inflated. The pain intensifies and then he notices an orange bubble popping out from under his leg. The one-person life raft in his survival kit has started to automatically inflate, and it is trapped between the seat and his body. He quickly stabs it with the knife, but the inflating dinghy has the effect of putting his upper legs in a vise, giving him a serious hematoma on each thigh.

He then spots another chute above him and off to the side. "I see that and I say good, Rick got out." But then he sees another chute. Valent 03 was hit before McDow could tell Miller that Valent 04 had been hit. Of the crew members of the trailing element, McDow is the only who knows that both jets were hit.

Even the lead element, which apparently notices the fireballs behind it, seems to be unclear on what just transpired. The flight lead reports Valent 03 and 04 have collided in midair.

As Miller gets himself oriented, he sees a parachute on either side of him but still doesn't grasp that Valent 04 was shot down, too. Miller then steers his chute toward a hillside and the elephant grass. Once on the ground, he sees what looks to be the denser coverage of a jungle at the top of the hill and he starts running, but the injury to his legs wears him out. "I got probably about seventy- five feet and quit. I just ran out of steam," he says. Miller then lies down on the hill and gets out his emergency radio.

Once free of Valent 03, McDow descends in the ejection seat until the parachute deploys. He then starts seeking out a good spot to land, but may be getting ahead of himself. "I steered over this one spot, but then I kept drifting and I was too high," says McDow. "So then I pick another spot, and again I am too high."

Finally, he manages to land on the side of a hill where he removes his helmet and throws it down the hill while he starts heading for what he thinks is a ridgeline. "In survival training, one thing they tell you is that you need to get over a ridgeline." He hopes that by sending his helmet to the bottom of the hill that if any pursuers see it they will think he is near the base of the hill and not moving to the top of it.

However, when McDow reaches what he thinks is the top of the ridge, he realizes that it is just a wide-open plateau. While going up the hill he notices his left arm is still not working. One other consequence of the ejec-

A-1 Skyraider Sandys, so-called because their call sign was Sandy when flying SAR missions, would troll for ground fire as part of their search and rescue mission and then return it with the wide array of ordnance typically carried by this propeller-driven workhorse. For all the strengths of the A-1s, they had one shortcoming for search and rescue operations: no midair refueling capability although centerline drop tanks served to substantially increase their mission time. Still, for a downed airman the sound of a Sandy was welcome because it meant there were A-1s in the area that could keep an approaching enemy at bay. It also meant that the rescuing Jolly Greens couldn't be far behind.—*J. Harding*

tion is that his ears had become blocked up in the rapid descent. Still, he is able to pull out his radio, and like Miller, make contact with the Sandy overhead who tells him to stay put. McDow then crouches low in the grass, trying to hide from any nearby militia.

While McDow will have additional radio contact with the Sandys, what he doesn't notice, in part due to his compromised hearing, is a couple of militiamen creeping up on him

"They had long-barreled rifles, and one had a bayonet on the end of it. It had to be eighteen inches long," says McDow. At that point, he did something that he admits probably came from watching one too many John Wayne movies. "So I stood up and still had the survival radio in my hand," says McDow. "I keyed the mic and said, 'Sandy, 03 Bravo, strafe, strafe.'" His captors hit him with the rifle, and McDow falls to the ground, realizing the foolishness of his asking the Sandy to make an attack. "I said to myself 'Oh geez, I hope they don't try to strafe. These guys are only three feet away from me.'"

As the Sandy makes another pass, McDow has his hands raised over his head as he is led at bayonet point. He tries to make a wave to the passing Sandy, to signal he has been captured. From this point, McDow will start a several day and night journey that will end at the Hoa Loa prison, or as has been coined by American aviators, the Hanoi Hilton.

Valent 04B Hanton manages to eject in fairly good shape despite losing his helmet. However, the windblast damage to his right eye affects his depth perception. "When I was coming down in the chute, I ended up thinking I was a lot higher than I was," says Hanton, "and that impacted where I came down."

Trying to avoid a village in front of him, Hanton steers toward a rice paddy, but then he notices a group of men with rifles there. He continues to steer for a karst formation before coming down in a stand of bamboo that hangs up his parachute. In this less than ideal locale, he seeks out a nearby overgrown bush. "It wasn't the best place," Hanton says of the compromise he had to make. "It was obvious. Anyone that was looking for somebody, this is where they would be."

Hanton crouches down and turns on the survival radio by fully extracting the antenna. Then he hears the Sandys on the radio "That surprised me," says Hanton who didn't expect the Sandys to be in the area so quickly. "But I was kind of happy to hear the Sandys because I thought if they were that close, maybe they can get these guys off my back." Believing the bad guys are right on top of him, Hanton doesn't try to talk to the Skyraiders above, afraid he will give himself away. He stays low in the tenuous hiding spot.

While the four airmen aren't completely aware of where each of them has come down, it appears that they came down east to west. First is McDow, then Miller. Maybe a mile west of their locations is Hanton, and then somewhere past him is Aikman.

In addition to the survival radios that the four men carry, emergency beepers are attached to the parachute systems. When the chute deploys, the beeper will automatically turn on, transmitting a chirping sound that can be picked up on the radio. Once on the ground, a survivor can manually turn it off.

Shortly before the MiG-21s jumped Valent 04 and 03 from behind, the Jolly Greens and Sandys that had been orbiting over Laos were pulled back due to the reports of enemy aircraft in the area. However, when the Valent shoot down is first logged, at about 1225 hours, the initial report, apparently from Valent lead, is of a midair collision.

The only people in all of Southeast Asia who knew the full picture—Valent 03 and 04, had been shot down by two MiGs—were the FastFAC crew of Cavato and Marshall, who at this time were on their way back to Udorn. McDow (Valent 03B) knew both jets had been shot down but not that it had been two separate MiGs. By now he has already been captured by the local militia. Hanton (Valent 04B) and Aikman (Valent 04A) have no idea that their lead has also been hit, and Miller (Valent 03A) is only beginning to piece together what had happened, as he hunkers down on the hillside waiting to hear from the Sandys again.

Sandy 03 pilot Byron Hukee is one of the first on the scene. His belief, based on the initial report, is that the two Phantoms had a mid-air collision. Had the SAR forces known that a pair of MiG-21s jumped Valent 03 and Valent 04, very likely their approach to the area would have been different. As it is, the Sandys are picking up what they believe to be four good beeper signals from the chutes of the downed crews. Also in the area is a Laredo FastFAC, presumably a jet that Laredo 12 has been cycling with on the initial search for Troy 04 and Dobby 01.

Back at NKP, the ricochet has begun. The moment the ops desk hears that two more F-4s have gone down, Stovall and the others in the room know they need another crew.

"I happened to be standing at ops counter when the second call came in for another downed aircraft," recalls Flight Engineer Rick Simmon, who had been with the 40th about 10 months. "Stovall was forming a crew for the next go round. I was standing there, and I volunteered to go on it."

Stovall grabs the new guy Hutchinson to be copilot. "Here was the new guy, and this would be an opportunity for him to get some experience," says Stovall.

Hutchinson had already been on one combat SAR despite only being with the 40th about two weeks. When he was supposed to be on a training mission, the crew was diverted to pick up Triple Nickel pilot John Markle, the same man who had taken out a MiG on May 10 as part of Oyster flight. During the pick up, a group of SAMs were launched at the Jolly Green. The sight of the rockets going up on either side of the helicopter had been harrowing, but the easygoing West Virginian recognized it as part of the growing pains that come with the assignment. "Listen, there are two kinds of pilots," Hutchinson counseled years later. "Those who have been sick and those who will be sick."

Volunteering for Stovall's crew are PJs Mike Nunes and Al Reich. For good measure, Stovall also grabs Kelly Schulman, a combat photographer. As Schulman's counterpart, Robbie Wellborne, on Orrell's JG 56 would demonstrate in about an hour, the emphasis in that role was as much combat as it was photography.

The plan is to get airborne as soon as possible and rendezvous with Thacker's JG 73, which is coming from Udorn, at a refueling point over Laos. As Stovall takes this crew out to the NKP flight line, they step aboard a familiar helicopter, Jolly Green 57, the same aircraft that carried McGrath's mentor, Hoberg, in the Son Tay raid and that had brought Roger Locher back from deeper into North Vietnam than any other rescue helicopter had previously flown.

The "Jack" log for June 27, indicates that Laredo 11 and the Sandys have had contact with three of the survivors. Ben Orrell's Jolly Green 56 and Stan Zielinski's Jolly Green 52 are being called back into the area. The initial reports indicate that everything looks good for a pickup.

In retrospect, however, there seems to have been confusion, perhaps

On June 27, 1972, Lt. Rufus Hutchinson was the newest member of the 40th ARRS. When the report of a second pair of F-4s down came into the 40th, Hutchinson joined the cobbled-together crew of Jolly Green 57 as it headed to North Vietnam-Laos border. Later in his career, Hutchinson would become commanding officer for the U.S. Air Force's Helicopter Pilot School at Fort Rucker, Alabama.
—R. Hutchinson

between the Sandys and the Laredo FastFAC, as to which survivors they had voice contact with. Hanton never transmits to the Sandys. In reports that McDow would read years later, it seems that when McDow spoke with the Sandys overhead, while they heard his transmission, they may have been looking at Hanton. Upon initial contact with the Sandys, they told McDow to stay put, but then in follow-up transmissions he was surprised to hear them encourage him to move. McDow, with his ears blocked up from the ejection, opted to stay put, crouching low until the militia snuck up on him.

The picture painted by the Sandys is that one of the survivors, whom they presume is McDow, has stayed very close to his visible parachute and refuses to move. It's likely that the Sandys are observing Hanton, who by his own acknowledgement was in a poor location near his chute, which had been hung up in bamboo. Knowing there are militia nearby and with a bad eye from his ejection, Hanton had little opportunity to stash his parachute and instead tries to evade as best he can, finding nearby overgrowth as the only cover in the area. He never speaks to the Sandys.

To the Sandys' dismay, the survivor with whom they are speaking, probably McDow, responds that he prefers to stay put as originally instructed. However, it's likely they are looking at Hanton's position with the nearby parachute. During this confusion McDow is captured by the militia. Although he keyed his mic, asking for the ill-advised strafing run, and believes the Sandy overhead saw him wave as the militia held him at bayonet point, the Sandys still think McDow is evading capture.

While at this juncture the Sandys believe they have voice contact with at least three of the survivors, in truth they only have contact with Miller and McDow. A further complication arises when the fate of Lynn Aikman becomes known.

Aikman's first recollection after being blown from the cockpit is hanging from his chute, tied up in a tree. Very groggy he looks below. All he can see is a scene of bamboo. It's as though he's suspended in air, and he can't make sense of his predicament.

"I thought I must have been dreaming," Aikman recalls. "So I went back to sleep, thinking when I wake up, I'll just climb out of bed and everything will be just great."

Things are far from great for Aikman. He is actually hung up in a dead tree with several broken bones and other injuries that not only will prevent him from being able to evade capture, but undoubtedly lead to shock and death without competent medical treatment.

With little idea as to whether it has been seconds or minutes since he dozed off while hanging in the tree, Aikman comes too again, and the same scene affirms that it is not a bad dream but a bad reality Aikman is experiencing. Most confusing to Aikman as he hangs in his harness is that as he looked at the ground, his mind seems to be registering different heights. He will take a look, and it seems to be only a two-foot drop; he will look again and it seems to be fifteen feet. He can't make sense of it.

With only one good arm, releasing his parachute harness is a struggle for Aikman, and he still isn't sure how far up in the tree he is. As part of the ejection gear, there is a lowering device for this very circumstance, but Aikman doubts he can work it with only one arm. He takes his chances, releases the harness, and hopes that his eyes were right when they saw a two-foot drop.

He comes free of the harness and quickly hits the ground, but any elation over not falling fifteen or more feet is replaced by pain, particularly in his left leg and knee. Sitting down, leaning against the base of the tree, he looks around, and discovers why he had such a difficult time assessing the height: he is on a steep hillside. The large tree had grown straight up, and as he hung there, if he looked left toward the uphill slope or straight down toward a level patch immediately below, it was only a two-foot drop. It was when he looked downhill off to his right that the fall was much farther.

He reaches into the survival vest that several hours earlier he had first strapped on at Takhli and pulls out the emergency radio. With the antenna fully extended, he is relieved to hear someone already transmitting on the frequency. He waits for the chatter to clear and then tries to reach the Sandys overhead.

Miller's recollection is that Aikman had first come up on the radio maybe half an hour after Miller had put his feet on the ground. Of the four ejections, Miller is probably in the best shape, at least at this time. The inflating life raft caused such severe bruising in his upper legs that he will need a hospital visit, but for the time being he is mobile.

McDow had been captured sooner than anyone realized. Despite his believing that the Skyraider pilot saw him when his captors had him at bayonet point, at this point the Sandys thought all four survivors could be picked up. With his damaged left shoulder, McDow was not capable of fighting his captors.

Hanton believes it had been about half an hour before he had turned on his emergency radio, but with the bad guys nearby, he wasn't able to transmit, and the windblast injury to his left eye was hampering his vision.

Miller's recollection from listening to the traffic on his emergency radio is that when Aikman came up on radio, the Sandys had to regroup. There was another survivor on the ground, and before they could bring in the Jolly Greens, they had to know where everyone was in case things got hot, and they had to lay down some ordnance.

One of the aspects of search and rescue is that the rescue forces needed to confirm the identity of those on the ground. The first step is checking call signs.

As Aikman comes up on the radio, he hears the Sandy ask for his call sign. Still quite dazed from his ordeal, Aikman thinks and thinks, but it just doesn't come. He opts to hope for the best.

This photo shows the landscape of northern Laos, not unlike the remote terrain where the crews of Valent 03 and 04 landed after ejecting from their disintegrating F-4s. Despite the steep hillsides, the location where the four airmen came down was also heavily cultivated for farming and was home to a well-armed local militia.—*R. Hutchinson*

"I can't remember my call sign," he says.

Experienced Sandy pilots know this isn't unusual. Being flung from a fast moving jet that has just been blown up by a missile has a tendency to jostle the mind. Aikman then hears the Sandy transmit, as if to anyone listening, "Valent 04 Alpha, come up on voice."

It was a pretty good clue to drop, and it clears away some of the fog induced by his ordeal. "Roger, Valent 04 Alpha," Aikman responds immediately. The next stage involves a series of identifying questions, including items such his wife's name, which, coincidentally, happens to be Sandy.

Meanwhile Hanton is still crouched in his poor hiding spot, yet to make a transmission for fear of being heard by the nearby militiamen.

It takes the Sandys some time to sort out where the survivors are so that they can confidently bring in the Jolly Greens, knowing where each survivor is located. McDow is probably the easternmost of the four survivors, but he has already been captured. Miller is hiding in some tall elephant grass, perhaps one hillside away from where McDow came down. About a mile to his west is a small village, and Hanton is hiding nearby in

Barely visible in the middle of this photo taken from Jolly Green 56 during the rescue mission is Valent 03A Robert Craig Miller, hidden in a field of tall elephant grass. JG 56 pilot Ben Orrell managed to get the helicopter to within about fifteen feet of Miller, who then made a run for the hoist as small arms fire erupted around him. Both JG 56 and its high bird, JG 52, sustained damage from the ground fire. What had initially looked like an easy pickup of all four survivors had turned difficult. Unknown to rescue forces at this time, Miller's backseater, Valent 03B Rick McDow, had already been captured by the local militia. Valent 04B Tom Hanton would also be captured shortly after McDow. Valent 04A Lynn Aikman, was semi-conscious, lying in a steep ravine with serious injuries following his ejection. The two shot-up Jolly Greens had to return to NKP, leaving it to the ad hoc second set of birds, JG 57 joining up with JG 73, more than two hours away at this point, to make the next attempt at rescue.—*B. Orrell*

overgrowth. The Sandys only have intermittent contact with Aikman, but it appears that he is farther west than Hanton, beyond the village and maybe in the hilly ravines below it.

It's now getting on to about 1400 hours, and Orrell and Zielinski have reached a holding point just outside the area. The Sandys plan is to bring them in to pick up Miller. They have yet to realize that McDow has been captured. Hanton's position appears to be marked by his parachute. Past Hanton there is a village and then a steep ravine covered with jungle growth and a solitary distinguishing characteristic: a very tall, almost 200-feet, partially dead tree. While the Sandys don't yet have an exact location for Aikman, the pilot has been able to tell them of his injuries; he can't move on his own; he'll need a PJ. It becomes clear that Aikman's location is somewhere past the other three survivors, perhaps down in the ravine past the village.

Now, with the situation becoming clearer, the Sandys call in the Jolly Greens.

Orrell pilots JG 56 into the area as the Sandys radio Miller to pop one of his smoke flares. Orrell hovers over the area, and the flight engineer lowers the forest penetrator on the hoist line. The minigun on the hoist side, the right side, of the Jolly Green is now inoperable as the door is open.

Miller initially waits to see if the hoist will come to him but sees the PJs on board signaling for him to run to the line. In survival training "they tell you don't run," says Miller. "But they were telling me to come, and it was about fifteen feet."

As Miller breaks for the penetrator, gun fire erupts from the surrounding jungle. The local militia has been lying in wait.

As Miller makes his dash to the hoist line, he looks up and sees Robbie Wellborne, the combat photographer, with a camera in his hand. A moment later, a step away from the hoist, he looks up again, and Wellborne has traded his camera for CAR-15 rifle (a version of the M16) and takes out two of the enemy behind Miller who were shooting at the helicopter, undoubtedly angling for a shot against the defenseless side of the Jolly Green and the open doorway into which Miller will be pulled seconds later.

Orrell turns the helicopter and climbs quickly with JG 52 swooping in to provide support. Both helicopters take ground fire but manage to pull up. JG 52 reports a fuel leak but nothing else serious. The Sandys come in make strafing runs while also trying to bring the Jolly Greens around to what they believe was McDow's position, but they can't raise him on the radio.

Amid the sounds of the Sandys making their runs, Hanton decides to try a radio call. As he prepares to transmit, he feels the butt of a gun hit the back of his head. "Then the next one hit my hand where I was holding the radio." The radio's lanyard, wrapped around Hanton's wrist, causes it to bounce back into his hand. "And that kind of freaked them out," he says of his captors. "Then they just started pounding me. They were pointing at my sidearm, my pistol, and it really wasn't until I handed that pistol over to them that they got less skittish."

What had initially been considered an easy pickup of all four downed aviators has now gone terribly "sideways," to use the slang of the military.

The two Jolly Greens are shot up. Of the three survivors still on the ground, only one still has contact with the Sandys, and that is Aikman, who is intermittent at best and reports that he is badly injured.

With the Sandys low on fuel and the Jolly Greens shot up, the A-1s will escort Orrell and Zielinksi back to NKP. Sandy lead Byron Hukee passes on-scene command to Randy Scott and his wingman, who have flown up from NKP to be the next duo of Skyraiders supporting the rescue. Scott calculates that they have only about three hours until they reach bingo fuel and will have to hand over the scene to the next set of Sandys.

About an hour before Miller jumped onto the forest penetrator hanging from Orrell's Jolly Green, Laredo 12's team of Cavato and Marshall landed safely back at Udorn. Cavato immediately went through a debrief where he told the intelligence officers precisely what he witnessed: a pair of MiG-21s coming up from the weeds take out the rear element of Valent flight with air-to-air Atoll missiles.

The next morning, attending a mission brief with a different intelligence officer, Cavato is incredulous when he hears a report of two F-4s colliding on a MiGCAP the previous day. "And so I told them, 'Yeah, it was a mid-air collision all right . . . with an Atoll missile!'"

On their separate journeys to Hanoi, McDow and Hanton were led by their captors through different villages along the way. Their shoot-down happened so close to the Laotian border that McDow says he had no idea whether he would end up in the hands of the North Vietnamese army or perhaps the more fringe factions, such as the notorious Pathet Lao. "I had no idea whether we were walking east or west."

The two Valent backseaters took different paths over the next few days, occasionally being displayed in villages along the way for the angry amusement of the populace. After about five days, they reached Hanoi where they became residents of the Hanoi Hilton for the next nine months. After an initial internment in solitary confinement, the now POWs were released into the larger population.

One day Hanton is with others in his cell when they are given a new cellmate who Hanton vaguely recognizes from the mission briefing of June 27: it's McDow! "Honestly I didn't even recognize Tom when I saw him," says McDow, underscoring the lack of familiarity the members of Valent flight had with each other. It is only at this point that Hanton becomes aware that both Valent 04 and its lead, Valent 03, had been shot down.

Not long after this meeting, the WSO (aka Guy In Back) population at the Hanoi Hilton grows by one more when Hanton and McDow meet a new POW who seems to know a heck of a lot about them. On July 3, 1972, thanks to a collapsing centerline tank, Laredo 12 backseat Tony Marshall found himself ejecting over North Vietnam and being readily scooped up by his captors. Marshall eventually finds himself at the Hanoi Hilton where he meets Hanton and McDow. It is telling that while Marshall has never met the men, he knows their names. As seems to be the case for many airmen in Southeast Asia, when a colleague went down, especially if you were in the air that day, you make note of it. Marshall takes care not to reveal too much too quickly. As Hanton explains, as much as prisoners want to know what is going on in the war, ignorance also helps sell their captors on the fact that the POWs really don't know that much.

Eventually, Marshall is able to round out the story. While McDow knows that both F-4s of the trailing element had been hit, Marshall provides the additional detail of it being two separate MiGs that jumped the flight from the weeds below. He is also able to tell the two WSOs about the fate of their frontseats.

CHAPTER SEVEN

TAKING FIRE

Decades later, Leo Thacker still remembers June 27, 1972: "That was the day I thought I would drown in my own sweat."

At this point on the 27th, Thacker has left Udorn in JG 73 and is racing toward a rendezvous with Stovall's JG 57.

Over the hilly, remote area that was the crash site of Valent 03 and 04, Randy Scott takes over as the Sandy on-scene commander while Ben Orrell's Jolly Green with Valent 03A, Craig Miller, on board makes its way back to NKP, escorted by Sandy lead Byron Hukee and his wingman.

On his 101st mission since coming to Southeast Asia in September of 1971, Scott makes progressive passes over Aikman's location. The gunshots in the area have quieted. The role of a Sandy in regard to a search and rescue site falls on that fine line between bravery and bravado. Part of Scott's job over the next two hours is to find out where the ground fire might be coming from, and there is really only one reliable way to do it.

"Their job was basically to fly as low and as slow as they could, just troll for fire," says Rufus Hutchinson, copilot on Stovall's JG 57. "When someone shot at them, then the other guy would come in and pound them."

But Scott and his wingman, despite the ground fire that had battered the first two Jolly Greens, haven't been able to stir up much in the time since. While they keep making their trolling passes, Scott also wants to get a better fix on exactly where Aikman is so that the next set of Jolly Greens can get in and out as quickly as possible.

Aikman has been hard to reach on the radio. Not only groggy from his injuries, but the ejection that ripped off his helmet also broke his jaw.

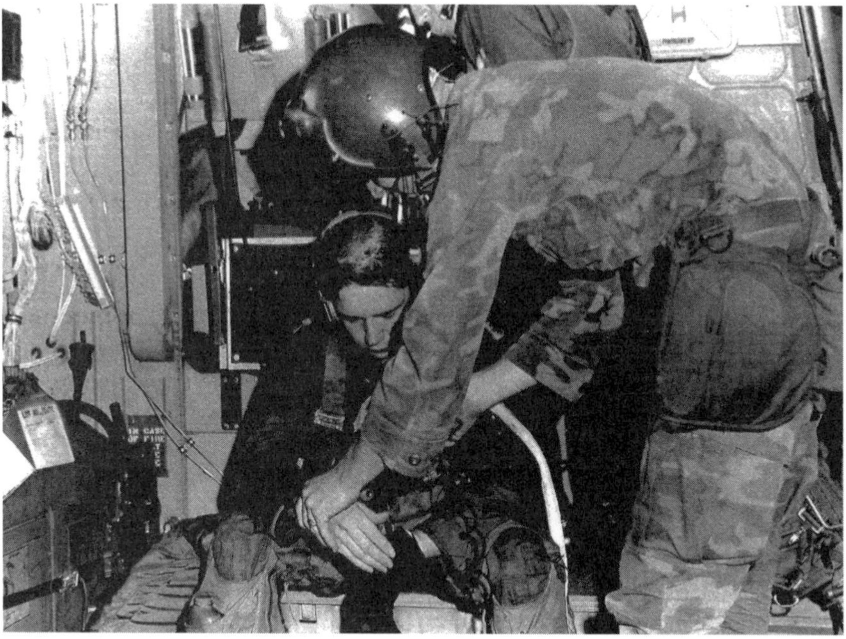

Major Robert Craig Miller is tended to by the PJs while on board JG 56 as it returns to NKP. When Miller ejected, his hand was still on the microphone button on the throttles. As such when the ejection seated rocketed him free from the aircraft, his hand was slammed against the cockpit rail. As his chute opened while he was still in the ejection seat, Miller watched his F-4, in a completely flat spin, spiral directly below him into the earth. He then began to feel growing pressure on his thighs. After a moment he realized that the one-man survival dinghy under the seat had begun to inflate, putting his legs into a vise. He managed to stab the inflating raft with his survival knife, but the severe bruising of his thighs would limit his ability to run once on the ground and require hospitalization following his rescue.—*B. Orrell*

It is difficult for Aikman to speak and equally hard for the Sandys to understand him over the radio. But the larger issue has been that Aikman overshot everyone else. In looking at the grid of where the four airmen of Valent 03 and 04 came down, it appears as though the order is McDow and Miller, and then separated by a little distance, Hanton who came down very close to a village at the top of a ravine. Aikman was past Hanton, down on the steep hillside of the ravine. The order reflects the ejection sequence— backseater first, pilot second. There is no doubt that Valent 04 was hit slightly before Valent 03, but as Miller distinctly recalls and Laredo 12's pilot Cavato affirms, Valent 03 went into a completely flat spin. Even though Valent 04 would have been slightly trailing its lead as both were hit by the MiG-21s, Valent 03's forward airspeed dropped to almost zero while Valent 04, smoking and on fire continued onward at what Aikman and Hanton estimate to be about 400 knots before they ejected.

(Decades later, in looking at an image that has been attributed to the North Vietnamese as Valent 03, looking like a meteor shooting downward across the sky, Miller concludes that likely it has been confused with Valent 04.)[27]

The end consequence of whatever physics led to Aikman overshooting the other members of his element is that every time the Sandys went over a ridgeline, they were losing radio contact with him, on the hillside in the ravine. But the silver lining to this precarious situation, especially as the afternoon wears on, is that the militia from the villages can't find Aikman either.

On one of his passes Scott is able to get Aikman back up the radio. First Scott asks Aikman to try his mirror, but Aikman says that would impossible given the canopy he is under. There are only a few breaks in the trees and brush through which he can see the sky.

Lieutenant Randy Scott gets out of his A-1 holding a seat cushion the pilot would use. On June 27, Scott was on his 101st mission and would need to find a way to not only pinpoint Lynn Aikman's position in a steep ravine but also stretch his fuel until another set of Skyraiders from NKP could reach the scene.—*R. Scott*

"I'm next to this big tree," Aikman transmits before realizing he is in the midst of a jungle. "There were trees everywhere," he says decades later.

But as it turns out, the tree Aikman is next to is not an ordinary tree. It rises probably 200 feet from the hillside and looks dead from the air and helps Scott get a potential fix on Aikman. The Sandy pilot decides he will pass over the location while asking Aikman to peek through a "sky hole" overhead. When Aikman sees Scott's A-1, he will call it out on the radio, giving the Sandy pilot a chance to fix the location.

After a few passes, Aikman sees the A-1 cross above him and calls to Scott. The good news is that Scott has the exact coordinates and an excellent marker in the tall, dead tree. The bad news is that the location is so tricky that a Jolly Green could barely fit in the ravine. Not unlike the location Clyde Bennett had to hover in almost a year earlier when Chuck McGrath and Jon Hoberg went on the mission to recover the downed drone in Laos, when the Jolly Green comes into this spot its rotor will be close to shaving the canopy on either side of the hovering helicopter.

Aikman's location, virtually on the Laos border, resembles a three-pronged valley in the shape of an upside-down T, formed by the conjunction of three steep hillsides. The stem of the upside-down T runs south to north and the base runs east to west. Aikman is somewhere just east of the stem, on the steep side of the ravine. North of his location, past the tip of the upside-down T and outside the ravine, is a grouping of shacks, a small village. To the east of Aikman, up past the steep hillside, is another small village, presumably the one Hanton tried to steer away from as he came down in his chute. Not quite a mile east of this village are the hillsides where Miller and McDow had come down.

As remote as the area is, much of this hilly and mountainous land has been cleared and cultivated for farming, causing difficulty for both Hanton and McDow as they attempted to evade their eventual captors. While there are no large buildings or fortifications, the signs of agriculture indicate some sort of population dispersed throughout the region. As Scott makes his trolling passes, he isn't able to provoke the ground fire that had chased away the two Jolly Greens. Neither has he seen signs of any kind large caliber or antiaircraft weapon. It is not unusual for the North Vietnamese to supply militia, even in remote areas, with such guns, but at least for now, things seem quiet.

Now, with a fairly good fix on Aikman's position, or at least the large tree immediately beside the downed pilot, Scott radios Aikman to sit tight and have some pain pills from the survival kit. In the meantime, he and his wingman will have to stretch their fuel as best they can. They make themselves as light as possible, dumping any ordnance they have, keeping just their guns.

In trying to take Scott's advice, Aikman incurs a minor injury to add to the list of the more serious ones that he was confronting. "I managed to get the three cans of water out of the survival kit," recalls Aikman. "I took my hunting knife out and began to pound a couple of holes in the top of one can. My coordination had deteriorated, and I hit my finger instead of the can."

Minor though it was, it is a clue to how his injuries were catching up to his body. "I guess shock had set in by that time since it didn't hurt that much," says Aikman noting he was more irritated that he had now gotten the top of the water can bloody. He then takes some pain pills from the first aid kid and washes them down with the bloody can of water. He then realizes how thirsty he is. Having awoken at 0400, he had now been up for nearly twelve hours. He finishes a second can of water, saving the last can for later. Aikman then falls asleep.

In the meantime Stovall and Thacker are pushing their Jolly Greens up to the holding point that the Sandys have set up. Also flying up from NKP is Sandy 01, Jim Harding, and a wingman to relieve Scott. By the time the Jolly Greens get into position, Scott estimates he'll be at bingo fuel. He isn't going to be able to stick around long.

With Thacker's JG 73 back in the air, it looks like McGrath and Morrow are going to see some action today after all. The early morning flip of the coin had already designated McGrath as PJ1 who will go down the hoist to pick up Aikman.

While by different accounts, including Morrow's own, he could get along with anybody, the seasoned PJ had struck up an almost brotherly bond with McGrath.

"Chuck and I, I think we hit it off real good," Morrows says of his first impressions of the PJ, who was six years younger. "We've got the same initials so I guess we figured we'd never get lost," he jokes. Morrow was near the end of thirty-eight straight months of combat duty as a PJ. Combined with the twelve-month stint he had during his first tour, Morrow's time in Southeast Asia spans a remarkable fifty months. In his time in the war

Morrow has probably had as much of an opportunity as anyone to fly with nearly every pararescueman in Southeast Asia. While his roommate, McGrath, is just a little past a year in country, Morrow says he had a good sense about him.

"Basically you would probably fly with a guy one time, and you could just sit around, talk with people, and you would have a good feeling, or maybe not, in terms of how you felt you could work with the person," he says. "Everyone has the same type of training, but you get a feeling about some of them."

As JG 73 makes its way up through Laos to rally with JG 57, piloted by Stovall, McGrath and Morrow man their positions at their miniguns. As PJ1, McGrath will be at the left-side window of the HH-53C. Morrow has the minigun facing out the rear from the lowered ramp of the Jolly Green. The flight engineer mans the third minigun on the right side of

PJ Chuck McGrath mans the electrically operated minigun on the lowered rear ramp of an HH-53C while serving as PJ2. On June 27, 1972, McGrath had won the coin flip to be PJ1 on JG 73, meaning he would man the portside minigun and be the PJ to descend on the hoist and assist a survivor on the ground. The other minigun position on an HH-53C on the starboard side was manned by the flight engineer. However, this position became inoperable during a rescue or any activity using the hydraulic hoist as the minigun was swung out of the way in order to open the door.—*C. McGrath*

the helicopter, but in the midst of an operation, this third post becomes inoperable as the door with the minigun must be slid out of the way to work the hoist.

In a hole in the frame of the helicopter, McGrath has stuck an essential piece of equipment, at least as recommended by Morrow: a flat-blade screw driver nearly twelve inches long. The Jolly Green's electric miniguns are a high-speed, electrically-operated Gatling gun. The miniguns had a switch that allowed the gunner to set the rate of fire at either at two thousand or four thousand rounds per minute. By no means precision instruments, the weapons are intended to suppress hostile ground fire for the Jolly Greens, which have no other integrated weapons. Ammunition comes in a three-thousand-round canister, with each round linked together with metal clips, feeding the miniguns an unbroken stream of ammunition. For many reasons, including this limited supply of ammunition, the PJs and others, such as the flight engineer and combat photographer, who man the electrically operated miniguns, fire short bursts rather than continuous fire.

If a gun a jams or otherwise is taken out, it can open an entire side of the helicopter to unsuppressed hostile fire. As the gunners on the rescue helicopters, one thing PJs learned early on with the miniguns is that even with short bursts of fire, the barrels can become intensely hot. Hence, one of the in-country tips that wasn't in the year and a half of PJ training Chuck McGrath went through: Always carry a screwdriver long enough to wedge between the barrels as a lever so you can rotate them to free a jam without burning your hand.

Still, the firing mechanism of the minigun has no manual option. If electricity somehow gets cut to the weapon, it does not function at all.

HH-53C pilots, as aircraft commanders, had final say over use of the miniguns. The Jolly Greens had a switch in the cockpit that could turn off the guns. Typically, pilots would shut down the weapons during refueling to avoid any accidental discharge. Otherwise, the switch was generally left on.

On April 20, 1972, a reconnaissance F-4 had left Udorn to photograph a truck facility near Dong Hoi, a portion of North Vietnam just above the Demilitarized Zone. It was not even a month after the start of the Easter Offensive, and the area was crawling with North Vietnamese troops. SAMs were fired at the F-4, and while the crew managed to avoid one, a second caught it, forcing the crew to eject. The backseater on the F-4, 1st Lt. Ernest "Woody" Clark, broke several ribs as he descended through the jungle trees below. He was able to avoid capture for three days. McGrath and Morrow were the PJs on the Jolly Green sent to pick him up.

As they flew over a road near the Ben Karai pass, McGrath saw what looked like traffic jam below them. Divisions of the enemy pouring from the North into the South. As they came into a hover over Clark's position, McGrath fired the rear minigun into the jungle, prompting a bit of a reprimand from the pilot: McGrath had no target; he'd been firing blind.

The crew that rescued Cosmic 16B (1st. Lt. Ernest "Woody" S. Clark) on April 23, 1972, from left to right: Dennis C. Chriswell (flight engineer), Charles D. McGrath (PJ), Dennis M. Boroczk (pilot), Charles D. Morrow (PJ), Douglas C. McCraw (copilot). Morrow served a remarkable fifty months in combat as a pararescueman and says he and McGrath got along well from the start. "We've got the same initials so I guess we figured we'd never get lost," Morrow jokes. The roommate PJs formed a brotherly bond. On June 27, 1972, as Jolly Green 73 sustained a critical blow to its hydraulics, it would be Morrow, realizing the severity of the situation, who would shear the line of the nonfunctioning hoist, allowing the wounded HH-53C to escape the ground fire. It also meant leaving McGrath and his survivor, pilot Lynn Aikman, behind in an increasingly hostile ravine, but that was the tradeoff between a chance and no chance for the mission to succeed. If JG 73 didn't remain airworthy, the backup high bird, Jolly Green 57, wouldn't be able to come back for McGrath and Aikman. Likely, it would also have fallen on Morrow to break the news to McGrath's wife, Candy, an Air Force medic at another base in Thailand. "I don't think I would have wanted to be in Chuck Morrow's place having to tell Candy if I didn't make it back," says McGrath.—*C. Morrow*

The flight engineer lowered the hoist, which Clark duly hooked onto and was pulled up.

Knowing the survivor had been on the ground for three days, McGrath and Morrow had brought some cans of tuna fish with them for the young lieutenant. The pair of PJs watched as their hungry survivor devoured them.

Some 40 years later, Morrow has a hard time recalling the specifics of many missions, including much of what went on June 27. With 1,000 hours (Officially 999.5 hours. "I'm sure I did that extra .5, but someone probably forgot to write it down," he jokes.) of combat missions as a PJ, details can blend together. Like many pararescuemen, McGrath and Morrow will finish their time in Southeast Asia with a string of ribbons and awards that would make any desk officer blush, but both remember what might seem to others a very small recognition they received relating to the Clark rescue, something that appears to mean more to them than the Silver Star each received for that mission.

"Probably not long after that [the Clark rescue], his parents sent us a

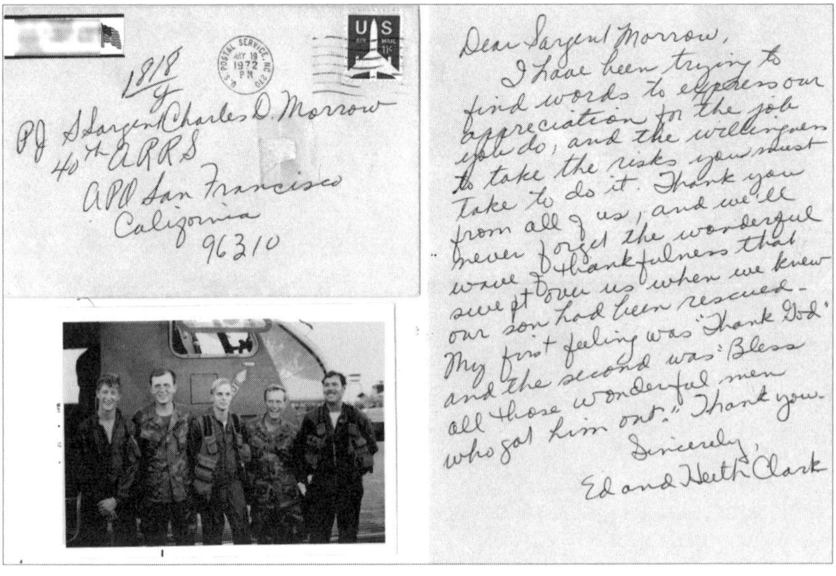
1818
PJ SSargent Charles D. Morrow
40th ARRS
APO San Francisco
California
96310

Dear Sargent Morrow,
I have been trying to find words to express our appreciation for the job you do, and the willingness to take the risks you must take to do it. Thank you from all of us, and we'll never forget the wonderful wave of thankfulness that swept over us when we knew our son had been rescued — My first feeling was "Thank God" and the second was "Bless all those wonderful men who got him out." Thank you.
Sincerely,
Ed and Heath Clark

For the rescue of Woody Clark, both Chuck McGrath and Chuck Morrow received a Silver Star, but each also received something much more personal, a handwritten note from Clark's parents thanking the PJs for bringing back their son.—*C. Morrow* little short letter sayings thanks for picking up their son and bringing him back," says Morrow. "That was something that was very nice to get. It's one of those things you don't expect, and when it happens, it's surprising, but it's very nice."

Each held on to their letter among their commendations and citations from the Air Force. While such formal recognitions are peppered with words like "gallantry" and "bravery," the letter from the Clarks on powder-blue stationary offered something quite tangible, a reminder that behind every mission they flew was someone's son, husband, or father.

The men of the 40th never wanted to leave anyone behind. It would be all the worse if they ever had to leave a PJ on the ground.

"Any mission going on and your aircraft starts getting shot, that can be hard," says Morrow. "Then you have to start having to worry about leaving somebody on the ground, and if that somebody is one of your teammates, someone who does the same job as you do, that comes into play. You don't know if another helicopter is going to be able to come and get him without more people getting hurt. You don't want to be in a situation where you were one of the last guys who saw him because you had to leave him on the ground."

For Morrow, one of the things that distinguished the PJs was how they learned from each other, whether it was something medical, where to stow the gear on the Jolly Green or even why they should always carry a long, heavy-duty screwdriver.

"Chuck was a young person, like a lot of people over there," reflects Morrow "But after a couple months, he wasn't a young person any more. You didn't stay a young person over there very long because you didn't have the time. You took the knowledge someone passed to you, and if you had a question, you asked."

Just before 1700 Thacker's JG 73 meets up with Stovall's JG 57 at a refueling tanker over northern Laos. Aikman is on a steep hillside not far from the Laotian border. Sandy lead Jim Harding escorts the Jolly Greens to their holding point. Between the previously sustained ground fire and the difficult terrain, the pilots are convinced that rather than bringing the two helicopters together, the Sandys will escort just the low bird, JG 73.

Aikman is located in a steep ravine barely wide enough for one Jolly

Green. With the Sandys making strafing orbits and a FastFAC and other F-4s as RESCAP in the area, packing both Jolly Greens into the congested airspace may put too many aircraft in the same area.

At about this time, Aikman awakes, still on the hillside. He starts hearing a tinkling of small bells. Later, he will discover this was the methodical process of the militia trying to alert others in the area of approaching American aircraft. In addition to the awkward hillside location, there is thick underbrush all around. Aikman can only see ten or so feet in any direction except for a few holes in the canopy over head. Gathering his senses, he turns on the emergency radio and immediately starts talking again with Scott.

"He told me the Jolly Greens were on their way and to get some smoke flares ready," says Aikman. The challenge for a survivor in Aikman's situation is to fight impatience. Lighting a flare too early will give away his position to the militia, and that will create a two-fold problem. Not only will he identify his location, but it will reveal the destination of the Jolly Green, and it may afford the bad guys an opportunity to get themselves into better position to open fire on the helicopter. As Aikman will learn by day's end, being a few seconds ahead of the bad guys can be the difference between safety and catastrophe.

Scott and his wingman communicate with Harding and his wingman. They devise a plan to drop smoke on the two nearby villages, trying to quell the militia that may still be near the rescue site. They break off, execute the plan and then fly out to the holding area to bring in Thacker with PJs McGrath and Morrow in the back.

Scott gets back on the radio and tells Aikman to pop his smoke. "I ignited the flare and held it as high as I could from my sitting position," recalls Aikman, who at the time was unsure the smoke could penetrate the dense jungle canopy.

Using white phosphorous rockets, "willy petes" in Air Force slang, the A-1s had marked a path for Thacker to follow. The Jolly Greens had been holding in Laos, just northwest of the rescue site near the border. The path laid out by the A-1s runs in over the cultivated land, over a ridgeline or two then into the ravine of an upside-down T, where along the stem of the T stands this unusual-looking and tall, some two hundred feet, tree.

The situation is tense, but there seems to be no signs of the gunfire that had chased away Orrell about three hours earlier. Thacker takes up a

The electrically operated minigun on the HH-53C featured six rotating barrels and a rate of fire of either 2,000 or 4,000 rounds per minute. Designed and manufactured by General Electric, this minigun would be used throughout the military under various designations, including GAU-2/A in the Air Force and M134 in the Army. There was no manual option for the weapons, meaning that if there was damage to the electrical system to the gun or the aircraft, they were completely inoperable.—*R. Hutchinson*

hover, the nose of the helicopter pointed west. In his right-side pilot's seat, Thacker holds the large tree to his immediate right. The portside [left side] minigun, which will be manned by combat photographer George Holland once McGrath jumps on the forest penetrator, can defend against any fire coming from the south. The rear minigun, manned by PJ2 Morrow, will cover the east. The north will be unprotected during the rescue as the starboard [right side] gun has to be swung out of the way to work the hoist and door. Also completely exposed will be the west-facing nose of the HH-53C, as there is no forward-firing capability in the Jolly Green.

The tight confines of the ravine not only limit the maneuverability of the Jolly Green, but the A-1 Sandys don't have much room for error either in being able to put down suppressing fire.

McGrath gets on the penetrator and rides the hoist down to the jungle floor. At nearly two hundred feet, it will take the better part of a minute for the hoist to pay out enough line for McGrath to reach the ground.

From the holding point about a mile and a couple of ridgelines away, JG 57 copilot Rufus Hutchinson watches as Thacker's Jolly Green follows the white phosphorous path and takes up a hover next to the large tree. "They come in and get Chuck on the ground," recalls Hutchinson. "And then all of a sudden, all hell breaks loose, 360 degrees of fire." For Hutchinson, there was no doubt about what was going on. "It was a trap," he says.

Scott is equally shocked. "I had spent a long time trolling that area, and I was really taken by surprise when we got the Jolly into the hover, and we started taking the fire that we did," says Scott.

At this moment, Frank Mason, copilot on JG 73, looks out at the hillside through the windscreen. "I am sitting there looking down, and I see a muzzle flash, and then I hear a thunk on the helicopter," he says.

As Mason witnesses fire from the indefensible west, nose of the Jolly

An HH-53C flight engineer stands at the ready beside the starboard minigun. The mountainous terrain of areas such as northern Laos or the need to evade antiaircraft fire would often force the Jolly Greens to fly into the thinner, colder air above 10,000 feet, leaving crew such as this flight engineer to use a woolen blanket for warmth.—*R. Hutchinson*

Green, Holland, manning the port-side minigun, fires bursts to the south. Back on the rear ramp, Morrow is using his minigun to try to suppress the small arms fire coming from the rear, the east, of the helicopter. One saving grace of this location is that it is below the plateau that is home to the villages in the area. If there is some large caliber, mounted weapon manned by the militia, they won't be able to aim down at the HH-53C in the ravine. Still Morrow sees tracer fire come from the canopy. Thunk, thunk—more rounds land on the fuselage.

He fires back. In middle of the mission, Morrow says training just takes over, but he admits no pretense when under fire. "Any mission anyone went on, and they say they weren't scared of the situation when they started getting shot at, they are either lying or just plain dumb," says Morrow.

Down below, McGrath hadn't quite hit the ground yet. Initially lowered into a stand of bamboo, he ends up tangled, upside down. Still, he manages to signal the flight engineer to pull him up slightly so that he can right himself.

Thacker maintains the hover shaving off the top branches from the large tree to his immediate right. Thunk, thunk, thunk—another set of rounds peppers the side the aircraft while Mason tries to coordinate some covering fire from the Sandys overhead. Seeing muzzle flashes right in front of him, he calls out, "Ground fire 2 o'clock!" Suddenly he realizes he has transposed his location "Break, Break, That's 10 o'clock, 10 o'clock!" The Sandys correct just in time, laying down fire from their 20mm cannons.

As the firefight begins overhead, McGrath extricates himself from the stand of bamboo and starts looking for Aikman. With the Jolly Green hovering overhead and the sound of fire all around, communication becomes difficult. He can hear occasional rounds being fired in the jungle while overhead he hears the distinct high-pitch sound of the Jolly Green's miniguns as they counter the ground fire. He hears the rifles on the hillside retaliate as he continues to push his way through the underbrush, seeking out his survivor.

For Lynn Aikman, much of the surrounding action is being drowned out by the sound of the Jolly Green's engines and rotor directly overhead. It is probably only minutes, but seems much longer, since Scott had told Aikman to pop his smoke. The F-4 pilot had almost tried to light a second flare when he saw the Jolly Green come over head. "That was a tremendous sight," says Aikman.

A PJ pops a smoke flare during a training exercise. With the triple-layered canopy in Southeast Asia the smoke flares did not always work as intended as the smoke could travel a distance before finding a hole in the canopy.—*R. Hutchinson*

It has to be at least several minutes since the Jolly Green appeared, however. While Aikman has lost his sense of time—his watch was flung off his wrist at 20,000 feet during the ejection—he knew it had been several hours since he blacked out in the windstream. In fact it is going on five and a half hours, and there is only so much adrenaline that Aikman's body can pump to keep him alert.

Aikman can tell there is lot of action on the hillside. If the bad guys are in the area, they have to be getting close. But there is no sign of a PJ.

Just then he hears some rustling nearby. A dreadful thought comes over him. "There I was with the Jolly Green in sight, and I thought 'Oh geez, the bad guys are going to get me.'" As Aikman, limited to just one good limb, his left arm, looks at the jungle something catches his eye: a brown helmet pushing through the underbrush. His panic quickly gives way to relief, when he sees the USAF uniform of pararescueman Charles Damian McGrath.

Chuck had been crawling through the jungle for a few minutes. Aikman's parachute had wrapped around the base of the tall tree next to him. Perhaps that helped explain how in the five hours or so Valent 04A had been there, the militia hadn't found him. But the obscured parachute and heavy undergrowth also made it hard for McGrath to locate Aikman. But now with the Jolly Green overhead, everyone on that hillside, from the members of the 40th to the members of the militia, knew where Aikman was.

McGrath asks Aikman about his injuries. With one leg broken and the other knee dislocated, limping isn't even a possibility. Based on the dense jungle, Chuck knows that lowering a litter won't work either. As banged up as Aikman is, the PJ has to get him to a clearing somewhere. Several yards down the ravine, near its bottom, there is a dried up streambed. McGrath asks Aikman about trying to make it to this flat clearing, "I said he would have to drag me by my left arm," says Aikman, noting it was his only good limb.

While this is going on, Aikman hears what sounds like rocks being thrown through the jungle. Only later did he assess the true source of the sound, bullets being fired through the brush, trying to wound or kill the American air pirates.

Nearly two hundred feet overhead, JG 73 continues to take fire. Suddenly a "pop" comes from the windscreen in front of Frank Mason and Leo Thacker. A round, right from their 12 o'clock, the most defenseless position of a Jolly Green, had shot through the windscreen and into the instrument panel in front of Mason. As the copilot contemplates trying to stick his sidearm out the window of the Jolly Green to return fire, he sees another set of muzzle flashes followed by another set of hits on JG 73—thunk, thunk, thunk.

Meanwhile the crew has lost communication with McGrath on the ground. But Thacker holds his hover in the midst of the summer heat and hot ground fire. It is impossible to know the status of the PJ and survivor until they can get him back on the radio. Despite fire right in front of him, Thacker doesn't flinch.

Seasoned PJ Chuck Morrow is still manning the rear minigun. Like all the men on this rescue, his thoughts are focused on the mission. "Things happen so fast," he says speaking of the many missions in Southeast Asia. "I'm sure everyone panicked some, but so much is going on, you just don't have time for that to set in."

There isn't room to worry about his roommate on the ravine below. If he does his job, it will let McGrath do his. And as the bullets fly by in the jungle, McGrath doesn't pause to think of his newlywed wife a few hundred miles away at Korat. Even the injured Aikman doesn't allow his mind to wander back home to his wife and newborn daughter.

There will be time . . . a day, a year, even ten years down the road, when each man on or over this remote ravine, in a jungle half a world away from home, may take full appreciation of what hung in the balance.

Airman First Class Candy McGrath tends to a patient at the base hospital at Korat RTAB. Chuck and Candy resolved to call each other every night during their tour in Southeast Asia. Occasionally, one of the officers at the base, having been alerted to the next day's orders in the region, would tell Candy not to worry if Chuck called late; it might be a busy day. Given the nature of communication among U.S. forces and bases, bad news could travel very quickly. In all likelihood, if a Jolly Green went down or a PJ was left behind in enemy territory, Candy would hear about it before the remaining rescue forces made it back to their base. *—C. McGrath*

As Morrow now recognizes, while they were all embroiled in that very moment, their fate, by no means would have been a private affair. "If a Jolly Green went down or someone got left behind, word traveled pretty fast," he says. With the radio calls to the 40th being retransmitted to various other locations, including the rescue center and the 7th Air Force headquarters in Saigon, if something went wrong in that ravine in the remote terrain bordering Laos, back at Korat RTAFB, Candy McGrath would hear about it before any members of the SAR force made it back to NKP.

McGrath starts dragging Aikman down the hill, but it is so steep that the injured pilot almost starts sliding on his own toward the clearing. Again, Aikman hears a salvo of what sounds like flying rocks as the militia continues to fire into the jungle near where the Jolly Green is hovering. As the two men continue to make their way down the steep slope, Chuck suddenly hears something out of place overheard. The distinct report of an M60 machine gun from the Jolly Green means only one thing. It has lost one of its miniguns.

Up above, combat photographer George Holland, who had taken over the port-side minigun for McGrath, has been firing bursts in an effort to quell the attack from the hillside to the south. A small barrage of fire has been directed at the left side of JG 73, and one of the rounds nicks Holland in the nape of his neck. By the slimmest of margins, he avoided a fatal injury; in its place a searing but superficial cut. However, the Jolly Green is not so fortunate. Another round from the same burst of fire from the south has severed part of the electrical system, disabling the port-side minigun. Holland immediately retrieves the M60 that is stowed inside the cabin, loads it, and starts returning fire.

As demonstrated in this photo of Lt. Rufus Hutchinson, every member of a Jolly Green crew needed to be checked out on the M60 machine gun, which the HH-53Cs carried as an emergency backup to the electrically operated miniguns. On June 27, 1972, one of the twenty-three rounds fired into the fuselage of JG 73 during its nearly eighteen minutes of hover took out the electrical connections to the portside minigun. Combat photographer George Holland retrieved, loaded, and began firing the backup M60 in an effort to suppress the ground fire from the local militia.
—R. Hutchinson

With the dislocation in his knee, Aikman's left leg was like a wet noodle. "It kept flopping around and getting entangled in the vines," he says. And when it did, he would experience excruciating spikes in pain. McGrath would respond by helping free up the leg, and then they would keep moving down toward the clearing.

After coming down the ravine—at times feeling like going over a cliff recalls Aikman—McGrath places Aikman under some bushes, providing him some cover from the militia that is now crawling over the hillside. McGrath begins to radio JG 73. Despite the ground fire, McGrath must come out into the open to signal the flight engineer who will be responsible for guiding the penetrator down to the PJ and his survivor.

In the HH-53C that is hovering almost two hundred feet overhead, Chuck's transmission comes through. He has Aikman. He wants the hoist with the forest penetrator. The two will ride up from the clearing.

Chuck has been on the ground for fifteen minutes, and all the while the Jolly Green has been taking fire from the enemy on the ground below. Another set of muzzle flashes goes off near Frank Mason in the copilot's seat, and the complementing thunk, thunk is punctuated by a different sound. Mason's instrument panel, which had already taken a hit, is now in shambles. Not only has the Jolly Green taken fifteen minutes of small arms fire, undoubtedly doing damage to the fuel tanks and other systems, but with a shot-up instrument panel Thacker and Mason will be left guesstimating the true condition of their craft.

As they try to respond to Chuck's call for the hoist, one thing does become clear: the utility hydraulics have been shot out. As the flight engineer extended the hoist line down, it only reached about half way to the ground. Now, however, with the hydraulics damaged, he cannot retrieve the line or extend it any farther. While this means that they cannot retrieve McGrath and Aikman via the hoist, a larger concern is the problem the line poses for the aircraft and its crew. In a scenario that could turn like the crash of JG 54, where Jon Hoberg was maimed when the Jolly Green was essentially anchored by the dragging drone below, Thacker can't take JG 73 out of the fire until they sever the hoist line. Should the line snag on the jungle below, it could pull the Jolly Green and crew down. What's worse, one of the few working pieces of instrumentation in front of the Thacker and Mason indicates that one of the engines may be damaged. They needed to get out the fire now.

"Shear the hoist!" Mason shouts into the intercom, instructing the flight engineer to actuate a piston on the hoist mechanism that will sever the line, freeing JG 73 . . . and stranding McGrath and Aikman below.

McGrath, still out in the open, tries to signal the flight engineer for the hoist. Over his radio, the PJ hears the call to shear the hoist. Not fully understanding the situation above, he believes that the command may have come because the line is tangled in the bamboo. "Don't shear it," he shouts into his mic. "Just pull the helicopter up."

Thunk, thunk—more fire hits the fuselage. Mason and Thacker continue to call for the hoist to be sheared. With JG 73 as shot up as it is and with near-constant chatter over the radio, something has gone wrong with communication in the cabin. Frank Mason recalls the flight engineer may have had a hot mic (stuck in talk mode) preventing him from hearing the order.

The problem with the hydraulics is growing worse. There is clearly a break in the system. Any and every time there is an attempt to use the hoist, the aircraft loses more hydraulic pressure, threatening its airworthiness.

Morrow, all the way at the rear of the HH-53C, manning the minigun on the back ramp, can hear the order from the cockpit. Recognizing the situation, he leaves his rear perch and rushes to the hoist, hitting the piston to sever the cable, again, with full focus on the mission and little worry of the personal consequence. Not only is his best friend at the foot of that cable, but if Chuck is left behind in this harsh ravine, it will be up to Morrow to tell Candy her husband's fate.

Leo Thacker, the pilot who after an earlier tour thought he had reached burnout before he found a renewed faith, has now held his Jolly Green in the middle of a fire fight for more than a quarter hour without flinching. He then pulls away from the large tree as Dale Stovall's Jolly Green 57 comes in from its holding position to join up with Jolly Green 73 and escort it from the ravine and the militia's assault.

Down below, in a scene not unlike what Bill Pitsenbarger must have experienced six years earlier, McGrath watches as the helicopters overhead depart in the midst of gunfire. Aikman's condition is worsening, and it is now late afternoon. In moments several dozen angry, well-armed militia, coming from all directions, will be right on McGrath and Aikman. Things seem grim, but for PJs, men accustomed to jumping into the fire that everyone else is running from, over analysis is a luxury they don't have.

Theirs is a facts-only profession. As Chuck watches the Jolly Greens pulling away, the facts aren't good on the afternoon of June 27, 1972.

"I looked up and I thought to myself, 'Well, that's it. We may get out of this. We may not.'"

NOTES

27. *MiG-21 Units of the Vietnam War*, Itsvan Toperczer, Osprey Publishing, p. 61.

CHAPTER EIGHT

SO THAT OTHERS MAY LIVE

Dale Stovall's Jolly Green had been in a holding orbit about a mile from the rescue site, right on the border of Laos and North Vietnam. From this position, Stovall and copilot Rufus Hutchinson had been monitoring the progress of the rescue. From Thacker's radio transmission, Stovall knew that JG 73 was taking heavy ground fire. When the call came in that the hydraulics were lost and they had to shear the cable, it became clear the pilot and the PJ weren't going to be coming back on Thacker's bird.

Worse yet, there was the question as to whether Thacker's JG 73 could hold together for the two- to three-hour flight back to NKP. As Thacker pulled away from the tree, he radioed Stovall to come in and escort the wounded aircraft. They would need all the firepower they could get. If JG 73 were to crash or make a forced landing, protocol dictated that the high bird, Stovall's JG 57, would pick up the survivors from Thacker's aircraft before making any attempt to get McGrath and Aikman. As Stovall's Jolly Green entered the valley he could see Thacker pulling away from a large tree that stood out from all others. Stovall, ever-seeking an edge over the enemy, took note of this reference point and observed where Thacker had been taking fire. If it was at all possible, Stovall was coming back for the two men on the ground.

Thacker's Jolly Green began to gather airspeed to climb. Stovall followed a short distance behind, prepared for the likelihood of JG 73 manifesting some catastrophic damage. The crews of both helicopters fire bursts from their miniguns as they leave the valley and head for the ridgeline.

As Thacker keeps an eye on what is left of his Jolly Green's control panel, he begins to form an assessment of the damage. They are hemorrhaging fuel. The utility hydraulics are damaged, but amazingly they seem to have both engines. They will need a lot of fuel to get home as the helicopter seems to be leaking it faster than the engines are burning it, but that is a manageable problem thanks to the HC-130 tankers and the HH-53C's refueling probe. Thacker plans to put JG 73 into an orbit over the holding area. The next minute or so is critical. If he has control of the craft and can hold an orbit, Stovall can bring JG 57 back into the ravine to pick up McGrath and Aikman.

Back in the valley, the departure of the JG 57, brings a quietness that would be uncomfortably disrupted by the sound of small arms fire. Overhead, Jim Harding and his wingman remain in their orbiting A-1s and continue to strafe the hillside, but the A-1s have limited fuel. They will have to leave soon, too. Afternoon is leading toward evening.

In the ensuing hours since Valent flight lost half its F-4s, the valley had come alive, as the local populace had formed into militia cells. Men, women, and children gathered what weapons they could: everything from AK-47s, Nagant M-44 rifles, and Simonova SKS carbines to farming implements like hoes and axes. The militia was directed to scour the countryside looking for the American air pirates.

McGrath and Aikman's options were limited. Aikman's injuries ruled out their trying to evade possible capture. McGrath was armed only with a .38-caliber pistol, which didn't offer much of a defense against a militia with automatic weapons.

With Thacker's JG 73 shot up the way it was there was a good chance the other Jolly Green would have to escort it all the way back to NKP. Sunset was probably less than an hour away. There wouldn't be another mission today. A night rescue would be impossible, especially with this terrain and the ground fire that had been coming from the militia. While for the moment, the Sandys and the egressing Jolly Greens had attracted the attention of the militia, it would only be a matter of time before the bad guys redirected their focus to the PJ and injured pilot.

Chuck was in exceptional physical condition and trained to handle any circumstance. He could evade the village militia, but this thought wasn't within the framework of being a PJ.

What McGrath knew is if they fall into the hands of the North Vietnamese, Aikman's only chance of surviving his injuries is if the two stay together. Together, McGrath could at least provide some care for Aikman's injuries until proper medical treatment was available in captivity. For McGrath, there was no leaving Aikman. There was a bond of airman to airman even though the two had never met. But there was also the oath, the creed, McGrath accepted when he became PJ. His mission was not about his well-being or survival. It was about doing all he had to so that others may live.

For the time being their lives and fates were intertwined.

McGrath and Aikman are at the bottom of a ravine. As observed by Sandy lead, Jim Harding overhead, the militia have massed on a hillside along the ravine. From atop this hill, only about forty to fifty yards away from McGrath and Aikman, the militia can fire down on the survivors. The enemy are too close to McGrath and Aikman for the A-1s to risk using ordnance such as cluster bomb units. The A-1s will have to rely on their 20mm cannons.

Harding and his wingman position themselves in an elliptical orbit, 180 degrees apart from each other. From this pattern, each A-1 can strafe the hillside. After making a run, the attacking aircraft will climb away, resuming the orbit while the other makes its dive on the militia's position.

The passes from the A-1s drive many militia from the hillside into the jungle where they are able to find ample cover. Those that linger on the hillside learn a fatal truth: behind the stick of an A-1 Skyraider Jim Harding is a deadly marksman. Still, what much of this amounts to for McGrath and Aikman is a slowing of the ticking of the clock. Sooner or later the Sandys have to leave. Not only do the two airmen on the ground know that, but the militia also know that the clock favors them and not the American air pirates.

Just over the North Vietnam border, in Laos, Thacker's wounded JG 73 is showing its grit. Bleeding fuel and with damaged hydraulics and a broken minigun, it is still flying. Thacker manages to hold an orbit and quickly radios Stovall.

"Go back," Thacker transmitted to Stovall. "Go back and get them."

Stovall immediately pivots and radios to Harding that he is returning to the valley to pick up McGrath and Aikman.

"We're going in!" he says tersely.

However, more people than just those over the remote ravine are listening to the action. Back at NKP, where Stovall's friend Orrell has just landed with Valent 03's pilot, Miller, members of the 40th have all gathered around the operations desk, listening intently to action several hundred miles north. As Stovall makes the call, for a moment everyone thinks disaster has struck. The two Jolly Greens have been so shot up that Stovall is crashing into the jungle below.

The crew of Jolly Green 56, which picked Robert Craig Miller up on June 27, 1972: From left to right are TSgt. Robbie L. Welborne (combat photographer), SSgt. Denny Sanders (flight engineer), SSgt. Kenneth L. Musnicki (PJ2), Capt. Bennie Orrell (pilot), Lt. Stephen Connelly (copilot), SSgt Hubert (aircraft mechanic), and TSgt. Michael L. Walker (PJ1). Welborne, the combat photographer, shot two North Vietnamese militia with his M16 during this rescue. *—C. Miller*

"I heard that, and I thought it was time to go to the bar," recalls Orrell.

But Stovall and the crew of JG 57 weren't done by a long shot. Stovall tells Harding that they are proceeding back in to make the pick-up and their approach will be the same as before, coming in from the northwest over the crest, into the valley and heading south to the large tree that marks Valent 04A's position. However, Stovall plans to position his Jolly Green 90 degrees to that which Thacker used. This will face the nose of the helicopter to the south with the aircraft's port-side minigun covering the east hillside and the rear minigun, manned by PJ Mike Nunes, firing north.

As Stovall's helicopter approaches the valley the crew of JG 57 has a clear picture of what they are heading into. They know that the first set of rescue helicopters that picked up Miller had drawn heavy fire and a crew member had been wounded. Thacker's Jolly Green had been riddled with gunfire as it hovered above Captain Aikman and was now barely airworthy. This was a hot location, but unlike heavy-fire rescues like that of Roger Locher or Bengal 505, there is no time to plan or call in additional resources. These rescuers are down to the last tick of the clock, the proverbial final play of the game. If they are going to bring home Chuck and the wounded pilot, they will have to do it now, relying on that special recipe of training, instinct and sheer guts.

As Stovall brings his JG 57 over the northern crest and begins his descent into the valley, copilot Hutchinson believes he sees fire from a large caliber weapon, such as a 12.7mm DshK or some other heavy machine gun, from the ridgeline at the Jolly Green's ten o'clock position. PJ Al Reich, manning the port-side minigun, opens fire, taking out whatever is there.

As the large tree comes into view, Stovall brings JG 57 down into a hover until its rotor-blade tips are touching the canopy cover on either side of the valley. With a rotor span of seventy-two feet, the steep ravine doesn't leave much room for Stovall to maneuver, but dropping low into terrain also gives the North Vietnamese less of a target to shoot at.

With JG 57 coming over the ridgeline and into a hover, McGrath doesn't skip a beat and starts arranging the rescue. He comes into the open and starts communicating with Stovall and Hutchinson. "The whole time he was as calm as can be," Stovall recalls of McGrath. "It was as though it was a training exercise."

In preparing for the pickup, McGrath initially had taken out smoke flare to mark his location, but then thought better of it as it would have put a bullseye on McGrath and Aikman's position. "I figured I needed to put that puppy right out," he says, recalling how he stomped on it and rubbed it into the ground.

As Stovall maneuvers the helicopter lower, the rotor blades are cutting away the foliage from the tops of trees, and branches and leaves come raining down on Aikman and McGrath. The PJ has to clear away several large branches to ensure an unobstructed path for the forest penetrator.

Earlier, as the Jolly Green entered the valley, SSgt. Rick Simmon, the flight engineer, swung his minigun away from the starboard-side window and then opened the door just below the window. He attached the forest penetrator to the end of the cable hoist and began to lower the device as he worked the hoist lever next to the door. Simmon had realized that given the landscape, they would be hovering at nearly two hundred feet. To lower the hoist from that height could take a minute or more. Simmon wanted to get as early a jump as he could on getting the hoist down to minimize the time Stovall would have to hold JG 57 in its sitting-duck hover.

A crew from the 40th ARRS trains for a rescue pickup. Note the forest penetrator being lowered. Flight engineer Rick Simmon began lowering JG 57's penetrator as the helicopter began to approach the ravine in which PJ Chuck McGrath and Lynn Aikman were waiting. The steep, narrow ravine forced the HH-53C to hover some 185 feet above the ground, and Simmon wanted to get the penetrator to the PJ and his survivor as quickly as possible.*—R. Hutchinson*

During the pickup, Simmon in effect would be navigating the aircraft, giving direction to Stovall, who would have to make maneuvering adjustments to get the Jolly Green, with the forest penetrator attached, into position. As such, Stovall would have his hands full guiding the helicopter, and he handed the task of managing the radios to young copilot Hutchinson.

Not even a full two weeks into his tour, Hutchinson is juggling communication with McGrath, the gunners in the rear cabin, Harding and his wingman overhead, and air rescue command back in South Vietnam. All the while, the Jolly Green's nose, right where Hutchinson and Stovall are sitting, remains vulnerable as the helicopter has no forward-firing capability.

Simmon, from his perch in the doorway, can see JG 73's sheared cable and forest penetrator next to the tree on the valley floor. Now in the hover, he is able to pay out the remaining line. As the flight engineer is lowering the hoist with the forest penetrator, he can see McGrath move toward the bushes and undergrowth, where the PJ has stashed the injured Aikman.

Down on the ground Chuck will need to move the injured pilot by dragging Aikman by his one good arm. Just like going down the ravine, each time Aikman's leg moves, the pain is unbearable. Another concern is with the dislocation, too much lateral movement could sever an artery in Aikman's leg, causing massive and possibly fatal internal bleeding. However, in the ongoing fire of the jungle, Aikman's comfort and the worry about the dislocation become secondary to the most prevalent threat, being shot by the militia emerging from all around. McGrath has to get them out of there.

From the cover of the surrounding jungle, the North Vietnamese militia are watching as the forest penetrator descends from the hovering Jolly Green. The militia begins to shed the cover of the jungle and make their way toward McGrath and Aikman's position at the bottom of the ravine. PJ Mike Nunes manning the minigun on the rear ramp of the Jolly Green can see McGrath pull Aikman toward the forest penetrator. Off in the distance, looking at the hillside to the northwest, Nunes can also see two militia making their way down the slope from the back of the ravine. Nunes can tell the foliage and topography are providing some temporary cover for his fellow PJ and his survivor, but he can also see that once the bad guys reach the cleared area at the bottom of the slope, they will have an unobstructed view of McGrath and Aikman, who are unaware of the approaching enemy.

Nunes reaches down and grabs some spent shell casings from the minigun and starts dropping them toward his fellow PJ on the ground. He is hoping to get Chuck's attention and warn him of the route the militia now seem to be exercising. But from nearly two hundred feet above, the casings are landing wide of their mark.

As the two militia near the clearing, Nunes switches the selective rate of fire on the minigun to four thousand rounds per minute. He is going to leave no room for error or doubt in keeping these bad guys away from his roommate and the survivor.

From his pilot's seat Stovall instantly recognizes the squeal of the rear minigun on its higher rate of fire. He breaks from his ongoing communication with the flight engineer to ask Nunes what is happening at the Jolly Green's six o'clock.

"Sir, I had two bad guys approaching from the rear," Nunes told Stovall, who instantly agreed with Nunes's decision to open up the minigun at full throttle.

"Shit, yes. Take them out!" says the pilot.

Once the forest penetrator reaches the floor of the ravine McGrath drags it over to where Aikman is lying. McGrath works quickly to extend the three collapsible paddles on the device. He moves Aikman into position, carefully placing him upon the extended seat and secures the retention

A survivor's-eye view of a PJ and the ride up an HH-53C's hoist line. With Lynn Aikman on the forest penetrator, the six-foot-tall PJ Chuck McGrath enveloped the wounded pilot in a bear hug, providing protection from the ground fire. Nearly 185 feet later, as the two neared the doorway of Jolly Green, McGrath could see bullet holes appear around the door. Unknown to him, another round had come up through the helicopter deck, striking fellow PJ Al Reich in the leg. Then, just as Aikman and McGrath were pulled into the HH-53C, another round hit Aikman in the ankle.—*National Archives*

strap around his body. McGrath then gets on the opposite side placing his legs over the other two collapsible seats and straps himself in.

McGrath and Aikman are now facing each other on the forest penetrator as the PJ gives the thumbs-up signal to the flight engineer. With that Simmon takes up the slack on the rescue hoist and McGrath and Aikman are lifted from the floor of the ravine. As they begin their steady ascent McGrath wraps his arms and legs around Aikman, taking him in a bear hug. McGrath at two hundred pounds and nearly six-feet tall envelopes the smaller Aikman in his embrace.

Using his body as a shield, McGrath covers Aikman as the enemy swarms down the hillsides, sending ground fire toward the two airmen and the lumbering helicopter that is pulling them in. The PJ and the injured pilot are on a nearly two-hundred-foot ride from the floor of the ravine to the waiting flight engineer in the door of the Jolly Green. As they dangle in midair, McGrath and Aikman are completely exposed to enemy fire. McGrath looks up at Simmon as he stands in the door working the hoist and giving directions to Stovall.

Suddenly McGrath sees a series of holes open up around the door as bullets strike the fuselage not more than a few feet from where Simmon had been standing. The starboard-side of the Jolly Green, which is facing west, is completely exposed to fire since the minigun is inoperable as long as the door is open for use of the hoist. The bullet holes also indicate that by this point the militia in the area have managed to burrow into positions on all sides of HH-53C.

The flight engineer can hear the rounds as they pierce the helicopter's skin, but he can't afford to be distracted. This is a critical juncture, he has to keep the line clear of any branches or other entanglements that could snare the survivors and the Jolly Green. He was going to face another challenge too: at 160 lbs., Simmon has to somehow swing both McGrath and Aikman inside the helicopter once they reach the door. He is going to need help from either the other PJ, Reich, or the combat photographer, Schulman, to be able to do this.

As the hoist steadily pulls the two men up to the Jolly Green, Simmon surmises the best tactic for bringing the two into the cabin. He turns to Al Reich, who is manning the port side minigun, to ask for assistance.

From his copilot seat, Rufus Hutchinson watches the hillside to his left and in front seemingly come to life. Militia begin to sprout from the cover of the jungle, emerging onto the hillside and starting to flow down toward the helicopter, right in front of the defenseless cockpit holding Hutchinson and the pilot Stovall. Hutchinson keys his mic, hoping to call in fire before the militia open up on the windscreen. As he radios Harding, time slows down for Hutchinson as his eyes and mind focus on one of the militia at the Jolly Green's ten 'clock position, no more than twenty yards directly in front of him, and sees the militiaman stand up on the hillside and raise an AK-47 to his shoulder.

"Sandy, Sandy ground fire ten o'clock," Hutchinson says into the mic, certain they are the last words he will ever say. The militiaman has him dead in his sights. He sees a burst of fire from the automatic rifle. He hears the rounds hit immediately behind him, and then a scream from the cabin.

As Hutchinson was staring down the barrel of the AK-47, the flight engineer, Simmon, turned toward PJ Al Reich on the portside minigun. Outside the Jolly Green, McGrath continues to hold Aikman in a bear hug, now some 185 feet over the jungle. Just as Hutchinson witnesses the burst of fire from the AK-47, a bullet from a different rifle rips through the deck of the Jolly Green, coming up between Simmon's feet, striking Reich in the right leg, just below the knee. Reich lets out an agonizing scream that Hutchinson hears in his copilot's seat. Simmon instinctively moves to help the PJ.

Reich does an immediate assessment. The bullet seemed to have passed through. He is in pain but his fellow PJ is hanging on the hoist with a wounded F-4 pilot in the middle of this fire fight. Despite the pain, he tells Simmon that he is not badly injured and to get McGrath and Aikman in the cabin.

Simmon moves back toward the starboard doorway with a clear sense of the danger erupting around them. He sees combat photographer, Schulman, firing away with his camera. "Never mind the pictures! Man the minigun!" shouts Simmon. Schulman becoming aware of the crisis, drops his Nikon on the cabin deck and grabs the handles of the minigun that Reich had been firing.

From his position orbiting above the Jolly Green, Jim Harding heard Hutchinson's call for help. He proceeds to roll his A-1 into a dive, heading for the hillside in front of JG 57. The tight quarters will test all the marksmanship Harding has developed in his three and a half years of aerial combat in Southeast Asia. The fighting is so close that for the first and only

The Douglas A-1 Skyraiders of the 1st SOS were well suited to escorting the lumbering Jolly Green Giant HH-53Cs. As the last on-scene commander of the rescue, Major Jim Harding used the guns of the A-1 to counter the ground fire being directed at Jolly Green 57.—*D. Stovall*

time in the war the A-1 pilot actually sees the eyes of the enemy before he opens up on them with his 20mm cannons. The entire hillside in front Hutchinson pops in reaction to the strafing. To the Jolly Green copilot, certain he had just dodged the bullets from the AK-47 a moment ago, the rounds from Harding's cannons shredding the canopy and underbrush look as though the fire is coming from the hillside not into it. For a moment, it seemed as though all the militia had stood up at once, firing automatic weapons. The young second lieutenant, on only his twelfth day in country, is convinced for the second time in just moments that he is about to be killed by ground fire.

As the smoke and fire clear, Hutchinson realizes it has been Harding's cannons, not ground fire. Off in the distance on the hillside directly in front of the helicopter, Hutchinson can see still more militia emerging from the jungle. Despite the rollercoaster moments he has just experienced, Hutchinson surmises that a smoke screen might shield JG 57 while they get the survivors on board and try to make their eventual exit from the tight valley.

"Sandy, this is Jolly Green. Do you have any smoke?" asked Hutchinson. "Negative," replied Harding.

An F-4 pilot who had been part of the high-flying RESCAP for the operation hears the radio transmission between Hutchinson and Harding. "Jolly Green, I have smoke. Where do you want me to lay it?" the pilot transmits.

Harding, as the on-scene commander, tells the F-4 to lay the smoke from east to west. Harding then banks his A-1 and turns north to get out of the way of the approaching F-4. As he completes his turn and levels off, the major, celebrating his thirty-eighth birthday, is suddenly staring the F-4 in the face. The Phantom is closing at better than 400 mph and Harding's A-1, traveling at 185 mph with an altitude of under two hundred feet, has no room to evade in the tight location. There is nothing Harding can do as the F-4 passes directly beneath his aircraft, laying a trail of smoke—north to south, perpendicular to his instructions—and then climbs out of the valley. From the Jolly Green, Hutchinson watches as the smoke drifts down to the end of the valley completely enveloping the hillside obscuring the helicopter's southern position from the militia. It was a near catastrophe, but it worked.

The close encounter is enough for Harding, and he orders all the other aircraft out of the area.

McGrath and Aikman are still just outside the door of the helicopter. Despite all his injuries, Aikman registers a sudden, sharp pain in his uninjured left foot. It is as if someone had taken a sledgehammer and slammed it down on his foot. Aikman thinks he may have hit the side of the helicopter's fuselage while they were dangling outside. Simmon, who unknown to McGrath and Aikman had momentarily been tending to the injured Reich, appears at the doorway. It will be up to him and every one of his 160 lbs. to pull the two men into the cabin.

On the ground, the North Vietnamese militia, who had been seeking cover from Jim Harding's strafing attacks, break from their cover and rush to get clear shots at the hovering helicopter. A number of the militia are in the ravine just beneath the helicopter and are firing directly up toward the aircraft. With the enemy directly below, the miniguns cannot angle down to get a shot at them. Neither can Harding and his wingman make a run at the enemy without risking a hit to the Jolly Green.

Simmon has to get the two survivors in so that Stovall can move off the hover. Otherwise, they are an easy target for the enemy directly below. Swinging the hoist line first back, so that the forward momentum will carry the survivors into the cabin, Simmon manages to pull the pair inside the helicopter, with McGrath, still shielding Aikman, landing on top of the wounded pilot as they hit the cabin deck.

With the two inside, Stovall begins to move the Jolly Green out of the valley, gathering speed and gaining altitude. Simmon closes the door and swings his minigun into position. On the hillside directly in front of him, he can see two North Vietnamese militia preparing to fire on the departing helicopter. Simmon lets loose with a long blast of fire from the starboard minigun. "I don't know if I hit either one or both of them, but I probably scared them to death," says Simmon.

As the Jolly Green egresses the valley, Nunes, from his rear minigun position, fires down at the ravine. Stovall takes a southwesterly heading to rendezvous with Leo Thacker's wounded HH-53C, which is in a holding orbit about a mile and half away. In the meantime, Harding and his wingman provide covering fire for JG-57 as it withdraws from the valley. As the helicopters depart, Harding and his wingman take up escort positions on either side of the Jolly Greens.

Knowing that the site of the rescue is teeming with North Vietnamese militia and believing that they have brought heavy caliber weapons into the area, Harding makes a broadcast request for all aircraft with expendable ordnance to bring it to bear on that location. F-4s laden with cluster bomb units and napalm hit the rescue site turning it into a inferno, killing scores of North Vietnamese militia and destroying any heavy weapons.

In the aft compartment of the helicopter, Aikman looks up at McGrath and motions for Chuck to release him from the penetrator. Once they are free from the penetrator McGrath can see that in addition to the injured F-4 pilot, his fellow PJ Al Reich has taken a round through his right leg. As the Jolly Green begins to climb to altitude Nunes is able to leave his minigun position on the rear ramp and assist McGrath in treating the wounded. Together McGrath and Nunes place Aikman and Reich on stretchers. McGrath reaches for the medical kit box that is attached to the interior of the helicopter. It is riddled with bullet holes. Opening the kit, looking for a tourniquet and bandages, McGrath finds an odd piece of metal, a spent AK-47 round lodged among the medical supplies.

Reich has sustained a painful injury, being shot just below his right knee, but McGrath observes there isn't much bleeding. The round seems to have gone through and through without hitting an artery or bone. Still McGrath puts a loosened tourniquet on Reich's upper leg. It is a precaution. If he begins to bleed it can quickly be tightened.

McGrath then returns his attention to Aikman, who is asking for water. As McGrath gives him a can of water, the PJ starts a head-to-toe examination of the pilot. The whites of Aikman's eyes are red from the windblast during ejection; his mouth is bloody and impossible for Aikman to close, a clear sign of a broken jaw as a consequence of his helmet being torn away in the windstream; there is a large friction burn on the left side of Aikman's neck, likely caused by the parachute harness during ejection; and his right elbow is broken, perhaps having come in contact with the side of the cockpit as the ejection seat fired. Aikman's chest, stomach, and upper legs appear to be free of injury. The pilot's left knee is severely swollen and obviously dislocated, likely due to a hyperextension during the ejection. However, there doesn't seem to be any sign of a severed artery, one of McGrath's fears as he dragged Aikman through the jungle. The PJ immobilizes the pilot's knee and reaches into the medical kit for an inflatable splint, but finds them to be of no use; they can't inflate due to bullet holes. As McGrath examines Aikman's lower right leg, he comes to a pair of holes in front and back, just above the pilot's boot. "When did this happen?" asks McGrath. "Just as we were coming in the door," replies the weary Aikman.

As the bullet ripped through the Jolly Green deck between Simmon's feet and hit Reich below the knee, a bullet from the same assailant may have hit Aikman in the ankle. Getting underneath the Jolly Green, the militia had certainly moved into a dangerous position. If the Jolly Green had to hover any longer, who knows how much more damage the enemy could have inflicted upon JG 57.

McGrath dresses Aikman's bullet wound and applies a pressure bandage to stop the bleeding. He then checks the pilot's vitals; while they are not normal, at least they are stable.

"I can give you some Demerol for pain, sir," McGrath suggests to Aikman.

"No, I just want some more water," the F-4 pilot replies. "Can, I close my eyes and sleep?"

"Sorry sir," says McGrath. "Can't let you do that. I don't want you to drift off to sleep. There's too great a chance that you might fall into shock."

Thus began a routine that would last for the next few hours. Aikman, exhausted from the day's ordeal, would give into his body's demand for sleep, and McGrath would nudge the captain back awake, then commanding his patient to follow his two fingers as he moved them from side to side.

Meanwhile, Schulman, the combat photographer who had taken over the port minigun when Reich was shot, began looking for his camera, which he had dropped on the helicopter's deck. This had been an intense but unique rescue. The 40th had been literally face-to-face with the enemy. This was a mission worth documenting, yet where was his camera? As he hunted around on the deck, reality set in. As the Jolly Green egressed the valley, moving quickly away from the ground fire, the camera must have slid out the open door, crashing to the jungle below.

Once Simmon got McGrath and Aikman on board, he started assessing the condition of the helicopter. There were several visible bullet holes, including the one right under where he was standing when Reich got hit. The intercom appeared to have been shot away, but all the major systems seemed to be working despite having taken close to fifteen minutes of fire.

While Stovall rendezvoused with Thacker's wounded Jolly Green, a request had been made to send not one but two HC-130 tankers to meet them. The contrail of fuel streaming behind Thacker's Jolly Green gave only slight indication of how much damage his helicopter had sustained. JG 73 was leaking fuel faster than it was burning it. Thacker's Jolly Green would need multiple in-flight refuelings to make it back to NKP. This also meant that the HC-130s would have to journey a lot farther north than they would normally venture. Their mission to refuel Thacker and Stovall's Jolly Greens would bring them right up to the North Vietnamese border. This was a perilous flight for these HC-130 crews since their aircraft were slow, unarmed, and loaded with aviation fuel making them a flying bomb, vulnerable to antiaircraft fire and, worse, MiG jet fighters. This was not an irrational fear on these crew's parts. Two years earlier the 40th ARRS had lost an entire crew of a HH-53 Jolly Green Giant on a SAR operation in southern Laos to a MIG-21. Further, as the HC-130s came to meet JG 73 and JG 57, they would have limited protection; all the fighter aircraft that had provided MiGCAP for the rescue were now low on fuel and head-

This photo shows some of the extent of Jolly Green 73's damage. (The contrail trailing the HH-53C is not exhaust but leaking fuel.) JG 73 can be seen hooked up to the HC-130 ahead of JG 57, which was limping back to NKP, leaking fuel faster than it is burning it. The HC-130 tankers came farther north than usual so that they could resupply the wounded birds. However, the North Vietnamese apparently were listening to the Air Force transmissions, and as the pair of Jolly Greens began taking on fuel, they received a report of an enemy MiG closing on their position.—*C. McGrath*

ing to their tankers. During this time, while the fighters and helicopters coordinated their refueling with the tankers, this air armada would be extremely vulnerable to a North Vietnamese aerial attack. The tankers arrived, and both helicopters began taking on fuel.

Off the North Vietnam coast, in the westernmost portion of the Gulf of Tonkin, the USS *Sterett* (CG-31), serving as Red Crown, was using its PIRAZ system to track all aircraft movement over North Vietnam. From their position in the Gulf of Tonkin, the radar operators onboard the *Sterett* observed the launch of MIG-19s from an airfield in the Hanoi area and watched as one headed north climbing for altitude. After a few minutes, the MiG turned west-southwest, streaking toward the Laotian border and was forty to forty-five miles from the refueling that was currently underway.

Cruising at four hundred mph, the MiG-19 settled on a westerly trajectory causing Red Crown to issue an alert to all U.S. aircraft in the area, routinely providing status updates as the enemy jet progressed toward the border and the vulnerable slow-moving aircraft.

"When it got to seventeen miles, we started to get a little nervous," says Stovall. At that stage both Stovall and Thacker began to disengage from the HC-130 tankers. The two pilots could use the maneuverability of the Jolly Greens to their advantage, dropping to the deck to avoid an engagement with the MiG. The HH-53 couldn't match a MiG's speed, but the lumbering giants could maneuver once free of the refueling line. The HC-130s, however, were sitting ducks. Not only were they big and slow, but they had to reel in their fuel lines before they could do much of anything. With the MiG probably less than four minutes out, the situation grew tense.

Farther west of the two Jolly Greens and their tankers, a gaggle of F-4s had begun to queue up on their own midair fuel station, a KC-135 tanker. One of the F-4s was piloted by Captain Steve Ritchie, a member of the Triple Nickel squadron who had two MiG kills in May, and was one of the best known pilots in Southeast Asia, to both the Americans and North Vietnamese.

Ritchie hears the Red Crown call of the MiG tracking on the HC-130 tankers, where his friend from their Air Force Academy days, Dale Stovall, is topping off his Jolly Green. If the numbers coming from Red Crown are right, even with afterburners, which Ritchie could ill afford to use with his low-fuel status, there is no way he can intercept the MiG before it gets in range of the HC-130s. But stealing a tactic from Bob Lodge, the Triple Nickel pilot who once showed Marty Cavato how to bluff a MiG into a trap, Ritchie makes a calculated gamble and breaks off the queue, putting himself on a heading for the HC-130s.

Stovall and Thacker are already off the tankers and start dropping low. Red Crown updates: the MiG is still coming. The two Jolly Greens are helpless to stop the attack. Here they are at the last leg of an arduous battle to pull not just Lynn Aikman out of a ravine, but also grab some consolation from the otherwise very bad day. Four F-4s had been jumped today. Six men were still unaccounted for. The enemy couldn't get the tankers too!

At a moment when there seemed to be no options left, Stovall hears a familiar voice on the radio. "Ritchie's got this North Carolina twang," he says, recounting how he instantly recognized the voice. "And he gets on the radio and starts making a call that he has the MiG on radar. He is making a run on it."

Stovall does the quick math. Ritchie had to be at least thirty miles away. There is no way he can be close enough to engage the MiG.

Ritchie had absolutely no chance of making the intercept. He was bluffing in a high-stakes game of aerial combat and his ante was the drop of fuel left in his tank. There is no doubting that Ritchie was a superb pilot, but along with his skill came a confidence, some of his aviator brethren might call it cockiness, that tempered opinions of Air Force's only pilot ace in Vietnam. But the fact of the matter was it was Ritchie's complete make-up—that combination of talent and attitude—that became the last piece to the complex puzzle of the day's rescue. No other pilot might have thought of such a bluff, and even if they had, no other pilot had cultivated the reputation Ritchie had to sell it.

Undoubtedly when that "North Carolina twang" was heard over the radio by the ever-calculating North Vietnamese ground control, they flinched.

The next update from Red Crown reported the MiG breaking off and

Steve Ritchie recorded his fifth MiG kill on August 28, 1972. Two months earlier, on June 27, Ritchie's combination of talent and attitude may have been the final piece in salvaging something positive out of what may have been the worst day of air-to-air combat for the Air Force during the war. *—National Museum of the U.S. Air Force*

heading back to Hanoi. It had closed to just within a few miles of the HC-130s and the Jolly Greens.

Stovall then heard that familiar voice again. "Jolly Green, I am low on fuel. I might not make to back to the tanker," Ritchie radioed as he nears the helicopters, giving the crew a heads up that he might flame out and have to eject.

"No problem," Stovall transmitted back to his Air Force Academy mentor. "You just tell us where you are, and we'll come pick you up. You can pay up at the bar in NKP."

A KC-135 tanker, racing up from an orbit in Laos, meets up with Ritchie as he was down to just a few hundred pounds of fuel, about as dry as an F-4 pilot would ever want to get his tanks. Among all the factors to a good bluff, luck remained the most important.

Night would be falling soon in the skies over Southeast Asia as the Jolly Greens took a heading south toward Thailand. With the intercom system in JG 57 shot out, Stovall had flight engineer Rick Simmon draw Chuck McGrath away from attending the wounded Aikman and Reich to speak with him. McGrath came forward and poked his head into the cockpit.

"Chuck," Stovall began, "we are going to have to climb to 10,000 feet to make it safely over some of these mountains, and the weather might be a little rough up there. Is your survivor going to make it?"

McGrath thought for a moment. "Reich's wound is okay," he told Stovall. "He'll have no problem, and Captain Aikman should be able to handle it okay."

"McGrath, this is your call," Stovall continued. "Do we need to head for the closer hospital in Udorn or can we keep on going to NKP?"

McGrath understood Stovall's question. Basically, the captain had handed the decision to the PJ. It was up to McGrath to determine where they would land that night. Udorn had a hospital that was larger than the 15-bed dispensary at NKP. By landing at Udorn, they would get Aikman into a medical facility sooner. But it would also mean taking both of these badly shot up Jolly Greens out of service. Once they landed at Udorn, the aircraft would be grounded, unable to continue on to NKP, which is where the 40th had the equipment and crews to keep their helicopters flying. At some point the resources could be flown into Udorn from NKP, but that would take time. Other pilots' lives would be in the balance tomorrow, and these Jolly Greens could make the difference.

Perhaps that was the testament to the men of the 40th. As extraordinary as one day could be, they all knew it would be their job to wake up and do the same thing again the next day.

Confident that Aikman was stable enough for the flight to NKP and from there, likely an air lift to Udorn and then maybe eventually U-Tapao, McGrath offers quick instruction for the aircraft commander.

"Captain," said McGrath, "head for NKP."

As night enveloped the Jolly Green, the crews could make out the illuminated contours of the mountains from distant lightning strikes. The mountain updrafts produced turbulence that buffeted the helicopters on their way over the ridgelines and down the valleys. McGrath kept vigil on Aikman, constantly monitoring his vitals, giving him water, and keeping him awake. McGrath knew Aikman wanted to sleep. The day had been an unbelievable ordeal, and Aikman's body yearned for the relief of sleep. But the PJ was giving orders to this captain. He wasn't about to let Aikman go into shock. "Sir, follow my finger. Stay awake now," the PJ said.

"I'm sick of looking at your damn finger," replied Aikman.

McGrath smiled. "We're close to landing sir. It will be just a bit longer."

With the lights of the airfield of NKP in the distance, Stovall radioed Thacker in JG 73. The pair of pilots figured that with the fire JG 73 had taken, its wheels likely were shot out. Taxiing could prompt a spark, and with leaking fuel tanks, the Jolly Green could be turned into a fireball. "We better call for the fire team to hose down a section of the apron with foam so you can set your bird down there," Stovall told Thacker.

As the two Jolly Greens approached NKP's runway, they could see that the taxi apron was illuminated and full of people. It appeared as though the entire base was turning out to greet them.

Landing, the two Jolly Greens made their way toward the apron. From inside JG 73 Frank Mason could see the fire trucks and a section that had been covered with foam. Thacker put the helicopter down into the foam and began shutting down the engines. Fire crews entered the aircraft, ordering the crew out, fearful of potential fire from all the leaked fuel. Frank Mason was busying himself, collecting his navigational maps and putting them in their carrying case. Just then a fireman put his head in the cockpit looking at both Thacker and Mason, telling them very loudly," Get the hell out of here!"

Mason looked at him saying, "I need to get the rest of my maps."

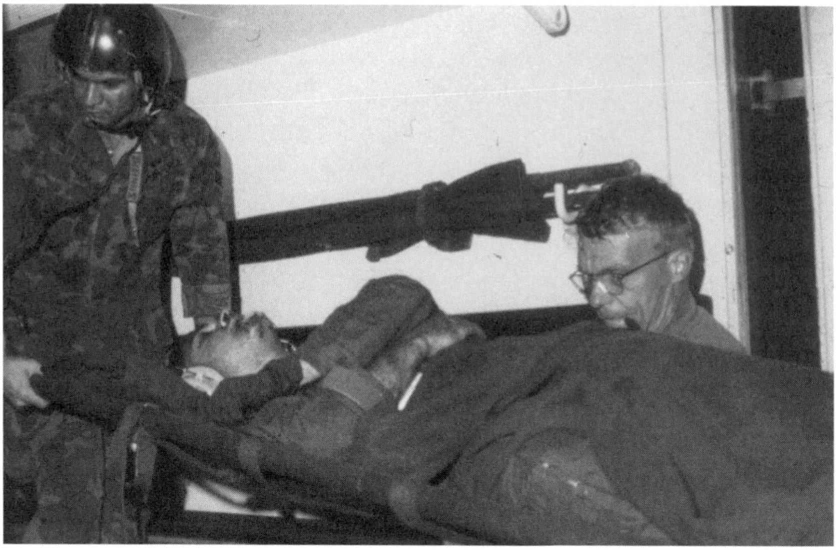

Lynn Aikman is carried to a waiting ambulance by PJ Mike Nunes while Lt. Col. "Doc" Lockridge, the senior medical officer at NKP, looks on. Aikman was taken to a waiting CH-53 and then flown to the base hospital at Udorn.—*C. McGrath*

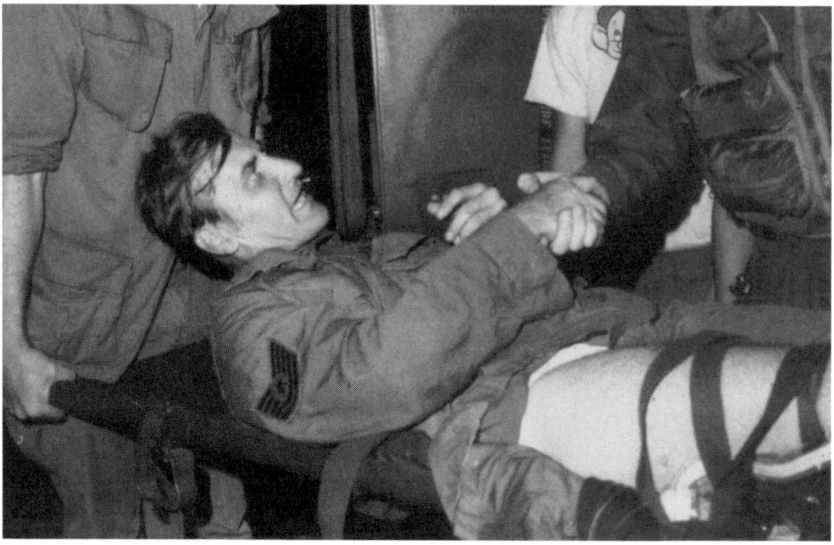

Captain Dale Stovall shakes TSgt. Al Reich's hand as he is carried from Jolly Green 57. In the midst of the firefight with militia in the ravine, a round came up through the deck of the HH-53C, right between the legs of flight engineer Rick Simmon, hitting Reich in the right leg, just below the knee.—*C. McGrath*

"Out!" was the one word reply.

Doc Lockridge was waiting with an ambulance to take Aikman and Reich to his dispensary and begin treatment. Before Aikman knew it, he went from the Jolly Green's cabin to the ambulance, never really laying eyes on the crew that had picked up him and Chuck. The glare of the floodlights and the flash from cameras were the last thing he wanted or needed. He was in pain and wanted rest. From the ambulance, it was then off to another section of the airfield where he was transferred into one of the 21st SOS (The Knives) CH-53s for the trip to the base hospital in Udorn.

From out of the glare of the lights, Jim Harding and his fellow Sandy pilots appeared and were warmly greeted by the Jolly Green crew. Master Sergeant Harold Harvey, the 40th's senior NCO, made his way toward McGrath to shake his hand.

"When do you have me scheduled to fly again," McGrath asked Harvey.

Six of the eight who made it back from North Vietnam aboard Jolly Green 57 stand for a group picture. From left to right, Sgt. Chuck McGrath (PJ), Sgt. Mike Nunes (PJ), TSgt. Kelly Shuman (combat photographer), Lt. Rufus Hutchinson (copilot), SSgt. Rick Simmon (flight engineer) and Captain Dale Stovall (pilot). Over the next thirty-five years, with the Air Force and as a civilian contractor, Simmon would continue to work the H-53s as the helicopters continued their remarkable four-decades of service. Occasionally he would draw an assignment in 68-10357, Jolly Green 57. Seeing the weld patch on the floor where a bullet had come up through the deck, he would reflect on June 27, 1972, the scariest mission he ever flew.—*C. McGrath*

A-1 pilots Lt. Randy Scott (far left) and Maj. Jim Harding (second from left) meet up with Jolly Green 57 copilot Lt. Rufus Hutchinson (second from right) and pilot Capt. Dale Stovall (far right) after all safely returned to NKP with F-4 pilot Lynn Aikman and PJ Chuck McGrath. *—C. McGrath*

PJ Sgt. Chuck McGrath (left) talks with A-1 pilot Lt. Randy Scott while JG 57 copilot Lt. Rufus Hutchinson wraps Scott in a celebratory hug. Pilot Capt. Dale Stovall looks on in amusement. *—C. McGrath*

"The next flight you're on son is the one out of here home," responded Harvey "You're done flying missions for now. Call your wife and tell her that you're okay."

Flight engineer Rick Simmon was thankful that he could step out of JG 57. A few hours earlier, in the midst of all the fire the Jolly Green was taking, the bullet that struck Reich came right up through the floor between his feet. As a member of the Air Force and later as a private contractor, Simmon would spend the next thirty-five years working with the H-53 airframe. While JG-57 would encounter a litany of maintenance and modification as it went everywhere the Air Force did during that period, Simmon was never too far away. From time to time, he'd pull an assignment in the old bird. Spotting the weld patch over where there was now a bullet hole, Simmon would reflect on June 27, 1972, and recall what he would refer to as the "scariest mission" he ever flew.

At the bar that night, it was universally agreed that the tab belonged to Stovall for sending a fright through the 40th. His call of "We're going in" as he went back to pick up McGrath and Aikman became a costly malaprop for the captain.

Indeed, June 27, 1972, had been a disastrous day for F-4s, but for the members of the 40th Air Rescue and Recovery Squadron, theirs was not to worry of the how or why this day came about; theirs was to do their mission, the good mission. When everything else in the day went wrong, theirs was to somehow make it right. A pilot, a husband and a father had come back today. It couldn't be any more right than that.

Sergeant Chuck McGrath describes to A-1 pilot Lt. Randy Scott the close encounter (near miss) that fellow Skyraider pilot Maj. Jim Harding had with an incoming F-4 over the rescue site.—*C. McGrath*

Beginning that night, the aircraft mechanics of the 40th began working on the Jolly Greens that weathered a combined thirty-two minutes of ground fire in the rescue of Lynn Aikman. Stovall's JG 57 had taken sixteen direct hits. Miraculously, none of them compromised the structure or mechanics of the craft. As McGrath had surmised on that long flight home, she'd be patched up, and be back out on the flight line in no time, ready to continue her mission. In fewer than two years, this HH-53C had produced three Air Force Cross recipients. For thirty-six more years, though its call sign, like its airframe, would experience modifica-

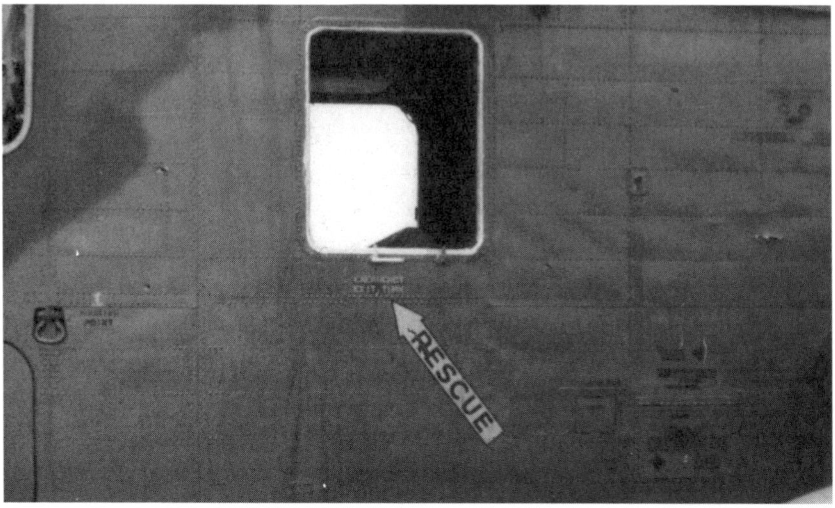

This photo, looking at the port side of Jolly Green 57, shows at least four bullet holes around the minigun window, at least one of them the result of a round from the AK-47 that copilot Rufus Hutchinson saw pointed at him. Despite taking such fire, JG 57 would be patched up and back on the NKP flight line in no time. In 1987, JG 57 would be upgraded to an MH-53 Pave Low and continue to serve in Air Force special operations for another twenty-one years before being retired in 2008. In a little more than eighteen months in Southeast Asia, JG 57 had produced three Air Force Cross recipients.—*F. Mason*

tion, this HH-53C—number 68-10357—would continue to take fire, protecting its crew on missions throughout world.

Thacker's Jolly Green 73 was far more injured, suffering twenty-three direct hits in the firefight. The shot-up instrument panel, from the round that pierced the windscreen directly in front of Frank Mason, was just one of the wounds that grounded the Jolly Green. As was already known, the hydraulic system had been severely damaged and the fuel system more resembled a sieve thanks to the militia's attempt to bring the Jolly Green down. NKP had to call in a special team from the United States to put Jolly Green 73 back together again. It would be a month before it would return to duty. December 27, 1972, six months to the day of the rescue of Valent 04A, JG 73 would be called in for the search and rescue of Jackal 22, a F-111A shot down over North Vietnam five days earlier. During the course of that SAR, the Jolly Green again began taking fire, eventually sustaining an Achilles heal wound to its refueling probe. Unable to replenish itself from the HC-130s, it was forced down near Ban Ban, slightly northwest of the Fish's Mouth in Laos, just behind the Gorilla's Head. The mountainous terrain and enemy activity forced the crew of JG 73 to abandon the helicopter, but they were picked up by another bird. All safely returned to NKP. To prevent the Jolly Green from being cannibalized by the enemy, the helicopter was destroyed by A-7s from the 1st SOS. JG 73 had given all it had so that others might live.

For Chuck McGrath, Sergeant Harvey wasn't joking. Chuck flew his last Southeast Asian search and rescue on June 27, 1972. Harvey and the other members of the 40th knew that the twenty-three-year-old PJ would be in line for some recognition. Protocol dictated grounding him, but it didn't sit well with McGrath, a warrior-guardian born from a brotherhood of men like Chuck Morrow, Jon Hoberg, Tommy Miles, and Bill Pitsenbarger. They weren't there for medals or other such glory. They were men of a special makeup that had then been molded in body and mind so that the unimaginable for most was mere reflex for them.

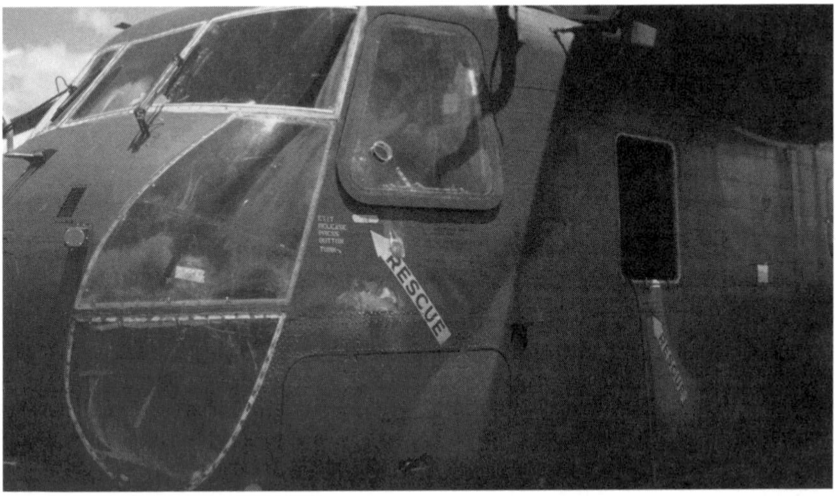

Jolly Green 73 sustained twenty-three hits while hovering over the ravine into which Lynn Aikman had fallen, unconscious in his parachute. It would take a month and a special team flown in from the U.S. to patch up this Sikorsky HH-53C. Visible in this photo are some of the patched bullet holes near the copilot's seat. Also visible is the small window that Frank Mason had entertained sticking his sidearm out of in order to get a shot off at some of the militia firing at the cockpit. Six months to the day after the rescue of Valent 04A, JG 73 would be on another SAR when it would sustain damage to its refueling probe. Unable to refuel itself from a tanker, JG 73 put down in northern Laos where the entire crew transferred to another Jolly Green, and then A-7 Corsairs used their ordnance to destroy the helicopter.—*F. Mason*

Perhaps that is why these guardian angels had to be grounded when the time came; given any opportunity otherwise, they would fly. Chuck had already proven that by passing his DEROS—Date Eligible for Return from Overseas—so that he could leave with Candy, but in the meantime continuing, as much as he possibly could, to be there for his fellow servicemen.

As for Candy, she still had a little time to finish at Korat while her husband fought his idleness. While her assignment was not as dangerous as her husband's, hers had its own difficulties. Working in the medical facility of a major base she would often know, even before Chuck, when the ebbing of the war would be met with a responsive flow. It was just another hard reality. In the military, the early warning for some of the most dangerous actions would not be to the men sent to the battle but to the men and women that might eventually receive their battered bodies.

While Candy and Chuck honored their promise to call each other every day, on occasion she might get word from the officer at the hospital not to worry if Chuck was late with his call tomorrow; reports were that it would be a busy day. Even on June 27, the call may have been late, and it may have been brief, but Chuck still made it.

At this point in late June, the couple knew their next assignment would be at Hickam Air Force Base in Hawaii. Decades later, Candy still refers to their first year of marriage as a "fairytale"—evidence that in even war, love triumphs— even though they had spent their time as newlyweds pretty much apart, and both were now looking forward to truly beginning their married life.

But she didn't want to leave Korat without seizing one opportunity to breathe humor into war's routine. One of the regular responsibilities she drew each morning was the line of young airmen whose in-country indiscretions had led to contracting some form of venereal disease. For her part, Candy says she never passed judgment on the men. She grasped that war removed all pretense of normal, and it wasn't hers to assess or assign morality. But maybe it was hers to teach a lesson or at least provide comic relief.

On this particular morning, one of her last at Korat, she walked into the clinic, hands behind her back, and looked at the line of airmen, some of whom were repeat customers of the clinic's antibiotic shots.

"Good morning," she announced. "I know you are all here because you have contracted a venereal disease, VD. There is a new treatment available that is 100 percent effective against VD. It doesn't require you to use a condom and in fact will ensure that you will never contract VD again." She had the full attention of the afflicted, but perhaps somewhat gullible, airmen. "Is anyone here interested in this treatment?"

Virtually all of the men were nodding their heads in agreement.

"Good," she said. "Those that want the treatment, please stand up and form a line over by the door," Candy instructed.

Almost all of the men rushed over and formed a line at the door. Candy's fellow medics were puzzled, trying to figure out what she was talking about with this new treatment. There was no such thing. Or was there?

"OK, men follow me," said Candy hands still behind her back. And as the eager men prepared to follow her to some presumed treatment room, she turned. All the men stopped, jaws dropping and eyes wide.

She had been hiding in her hands behind her back a giant meat cleaver she had borrowed from the base kitchen.

Amid the hysterical laughter of her fellow medics, the airmen sheepishly returned to their seats with a few wincing at the thought of Candy's radical, yet undoubtedly effective, proposition for permanently treating their affliction.

At the end of the two weeks of Chuck's stir craziness, a C-141 "Freedom Bird" landed at NKP, making its daily pickup of airmen whose DEROS had arrived. McGrath took one last look at NKP and boarded the plane. The Freedom Bird would stop at the various bases in Thailand to pickup other airmen returning to the States. At Korat, Candy joined her husband onboard. The fairytale of a truly American couple wasn't ending. It was just beginning. From Thailand, it was on to Clark AFB in the Philippines, a check through U.S. Customs, and then another flight to Hickam AFB in Hawaii.

Not too long into their assignment at Hickam, Candy became pregnant with the couple's first child, and, as was required at the time, she resigned from duty. With family on the way, Chuck started to refocus his career away from pararescue, returning to the thoughts he had when his birth date was drawn in the 1969 draft lottery. Maybe this time though, a job had opened up in computers.

But before all this happened, there was still a piece of unfinished business from June 27. In January of 1973, the Paris Accords were signed, ending the fighting in Vietnam. Not long after, similar accords were signed

A pregnant Candy proudly looks at her husband, Sgt. Chuck McGrath, following his decoration with the Air Force's highest award for gallantry in combat, the Air Force Cross.—*C. McGrath*

with Laos and Cambodia. With the agreements, came the return of U.S. POWs, the first stop on American soil being Hickam AFB. Released in the order they were captured, Valent 04B, Tom Hanton, would be coming through Hickam at about four in the morning of March 28, 1973.

For an airman appreciative of, but uncomfortable with, the spotlight that had been turned on him—Chuck would receive both the Pitsenbarger Award and the Air Force Cross for doing his job on June 27, 1972—he hadn't forgotten that others had gone down that day. For these men, their combat tour was extended, not by their own consent, but by that of fate. Without knowing exactly what he would say, he felt compelled to be there and reach out to one of the ones that he and the 40th weren't able to get to.

Through a friend working at Hickam, he learned when Hanton would be passing through and arranged to be on the list of people requesting to speak with him. Early that morning a family friend of Hanton's, who was a general officer at Hickam, had arranged to usher the returned WSO through processing, to speed Hanton's eventual reunion with his wife and the young son he had never seen. But in those hurried moments, Hanton had time for a brief conversation that perhaps was much shorter on words than it was in meaning.

Chuck came in and introduced himself, explaining he was the PJ who rescued Hanton's frontseater. "I wish we would have been able to get you," said Chuck. Smiling, Hanton replied, "I wish you would have been able to get me, too."

A certificate from Sikorsky Aircraft, the Winged S Helicopter Rescue Award, honoring Chuck McGrath for his efforts on June 27, 1972.—C. McGrath

CHAPTER NINE

ALL THE WAY HOME

In the early 1980s while assigned to the Pentagon, Lynn Aikman discovered he was working with three of his rescuers. Because Aikman had been flown to the hospital at Udorn shortly after landing at NKP on June 27, 1972, he never had a face-to-face meeting or debrief with his rescuers. Ten years to the day of his rescue, Aikman invited the three to his Northern Virginia home for a cookout. Not too long after that reunion, in 1983, the four posed for this photo as part of a television documentary. From the left, 1st Lt. Chuck McGrath, Colonel Dale Stovall, Lt. Col. Lynn Aikman, and Maj. Rufus Hutchinson.—*P. Reilly*

It's early 1982 in Washington, D.C., nine thousand miles and nearly a decade removed from American military involvement in Southeast Asia. Ground has been broken on a Vietnam war memorial. Perhaps as a fitting, but unintentional, testament to the lengthy war, even the design of the commemorative stirs controversy.

Not far away, in a meeting room of the Pentagon, Major Rufus Hutchinson spies the nameplate of one of his fellow officers. "Aikman" instantly triggers recollection of a harrowing mission Hutchinson flew ten years ago, not even two weeks into his tour with 40th ARRS. As the meeting breaks, he approaches the dark-haired lieutenant colonel.

"Excuse me sir," he says. "You don't have a brother that was shot down near Laos, do you?"

A curious look comes over the officer. "No," answers Lynn Aikman. "But I was shot down near Laos."

Despite the ordeal that the two had shared in the previous decade, Aikman and the copilot of JG 57 had never met face to face. Aikman went straight to Doc Lockridge and the NKP dispensary, and then at 0045 hours on June 28, 1972, Aikman and Reich were flown to Udorn.

Given this chance encounter with one of his rescuers, and the approaching tenth anniversary of the most perilous day of his life, a life he felt he now owed to the men who pulled him off that hillside, Aikman arranged a small get-together with some of his rescuers.

It's not like they would be hard to find. As it turned out, in addition to Hutchinson, two more of Aikman's guardian angels were working at the Pentagon.

The pilot, Dale Stovall, was easy to track down. He was a rising star in rescue and special operations, even if by most accounts, including that of "Ricochet" himself, he was a diamond in the rough. "Stovall," one of his superiors said to the tall red-haired pilot when he first reported to rescue headquarters, "you're 90 percent airspeed and 10 percent direction. We need to change that."

Aikman and the PJ, Chuck McGrath, had struck up a friendship through correspondence. Even if Aikman had lost track of the man who dragged him to safety, finding McGrath might not have been too difficult. After Southeast Asia, Chuck continued in pararescue with an assignment in Hawaii. His wife, Candy, had resigned from the Air Force when she became pregnant with the couple's first child. However, the young airman never left his first Air Force ambition to learn computers. Eventually a job opened up for the PJ as well as an officer's commission. By 1982 he was a data processing officer working in the Pentagon.

Still, the former PJ could occasionally turn military protocol on its head. Particularly when faced with an important meeting or perhaps some other situation where senior officers might be inclined to strut their rank, McGrath made sure not to shortchange his military dress. Stovall, who from time to time would pass McGrath in the halls of the Pentagon, took delight at the sight of senior officers sartorially overwhelmed by this junior data processing officer, whose current assignment belied his remarkable combat record.

"They'd all be there in their uniforms and along would come this guy with a row of ribbons running over his shoulder," recalls Stovall. "They just couldn't figure it out. Who was this guy?"

June 27 fell on a Sunday in 1982, ideal timing for Lynn Aikman to invite three of his fellow Pentagon airmen to his suburban D.C. home to share in a cookout with his family.

The occasion was the first time that McGrath, Stovall, Hutchinson, and Aikman had been together since the rescue. Joining the reunion were Aikman's parents, his wife, Sandy, and their ten-year-old daughter, who had little idea of the ordeal her father had gone through when she was still a baby. As a matter of fact, none of Aikman's family really knew the story, and even Aikman himself only knew the narrow perspective of what he could remember from his semi-conscious state that day.

As afternoon wore into night, led by the effusive storytelling of Stovall, a flood of questions, answers, doubts and laughs came forth. What finally was told was not just THE story, but their stories, the perspectives of each of the men. It was the debrief that Lynn Aikman never had. For ten years he had held onto these questions and feelings for which there was little outlet. While Lynn had returned home and resumed his role as a son, husband and father, something had hung over him. He never spoke to his family about June 27. Now, before their eyes, they saw some of the burden melt away.

Years later, in his home state of Montana, Stovall would initiate "Ten Minutes of Combat," a program within a military officers organization, that would allow veterans and their families to gather so that those who had seen combat could tell their stories, often for the first time. The genesis of the program was the catharsis occurring in this Northern Virginia backyard on June 27, 1982.

Stovall, McGrath, and Hutchinson: they had all been part of the good mission. While they were a decade removed from the frontline of combat search and rescue, the role of a guardian angel perhaps persists even into peacetime. Historians and politicians may call for definitive dates, origins, and conclusions, but for the men and women who serve, there remains a mission above the duty they were assigned, a mission of their own choosing that extends well beyond the confines of a battlefield. To a man, they might suggest their role on June 27, 1972, was simply a matter of assignment, a professional obligation. But as demonstrated by what they did not only under the fire of battle but in the quiet of peacetime later, theirs was more a calling than a job. Catalyzed by factors as random as one blue capsule drawn from a bucket of hundreds, they became the most noble of paradoxes, heroes in denial of their own gallantry.

As such, not even they were fully aware of just how important this informal gathering had become. As Stovall got up to walk into the house, Lynn Aikman's father stopped him with an emotional, heartfelt, acknowledgement. "Thank you for giving me back my son," he said to Stovall.

Stovall was gracious. "Thank you, sir," he said, "but that was just our mission."

The elder Aikman did not move, and his expression deepened. "No," said the father. "Not ten years ago, I meant today."

EPILOGUE

Of those involved in the rescue efforts of Valent 03 and 04, on June 27, 1972, six were or would become recipients the Air Force Cross, the branch's highest award. Other awards—Silver Stars, Distinguished Flying Crosses, and so forth—were also heavily awarded to this cadre of airmen for their service during the Vietnam Conflict. They were and remained professionals of high caliber, with nearly every individual continuing in service to their country for many years after their time in Southeast Asia.

Pararescueman SGT. CHARLES D. MCGRATH would receive the Air Force Cross for his actions in rescuing Aikman on June 27. He would also receive the Air Force Sergeant Association's Pitsenbarger Award in 1973. During his tour with the 40th ARRS, McGrath also received the Silver Star, the Distinguished Flying Cross with an Oak Leaf Cluster, the Purple Heart, and the Air Medal with one silver oak leaf and three bronzes. Later, McGrath would finally obtain the undergraduate degree he had begun while working as a lifeguard. He then attended graduate school and became a commissioned officer, working as systems programmer. McGrath retired from the Air Force in July of 1990.

CAPTAIN DALE STOVALL, the pilot of JG 57, received the Air Force Cross for his daring rescue of Captain Roger Locher (Oyster 01B) on June 2, 1972, requiring him to fly what may have been the deepest SAR into North Vietnam. Stovall would receive his second Silver Star for the Valent 04A

An official U.S. Air Force photo of Chuck McGrath from 1982. After a tour in Hawaii and with a young family, Chuck began to consider transitioning from pararescue into his original Air Force aspiration, computers. Eventually becoming a systems programming officer, he would go on to complete both an undergraduate and graduate degree in addition to receiving an officer's commission. Four decades after being newlyweds in the midst of a war, Chuck and Candy are still in love. "He was my star," she says reflecting her husband as young PJ. "He still is." *–C. McGrath*

After a distinguished rescue and special operations career, Brigadier General Dale Stovall flew for the last time in 1992.*–D. Stovall*

SAR. He was the 1973 recipient of the U.S. Air Force Academy Alumni Association Jabara Award for Airmanship for the Oyster 01B SAR. His other combat decorations include the Distinguished Flying Cross with oak leaf cluster and the Air Medal with five oak leaf clusters. Noncombat decorations include Defense Superior Service Medal, Legion of Merit with oak leaf cluster, Meritorious Service Medal with oak leaf cluster, and Air Force Commendation Medal. Stovall went on to have a distinguished Air Force career serving in both command and staff positions. Stovall was a Council on Foreign Relations fellow and a graduate of the National War College. He served as commander of the 1st Special Operations Wing, Hurlburt Field, Florida, and was the first vice commander of the newly-established Air Force Special Operations Command at

Hurlburt Field. He retired in 1993 as a brigadier general having served as the deputy commanding general of the Joint Special Operations Command at Fort Bragg, North Carolina. After retirement he flew for FedEx for thirteen years.

MAJOR JIM HARDING, the pilot of Sandy 01, received the Air Force Cross for acting as the on-scene commander for the rescue of Major Clyde Smith (Bengal 505A) on April 13, 1972. In addition to his Air Force Cross, Harding also received the Silver Star with two Oak Leaf Clusters, Legion of Merit with one Oak Leaf Cluster, Distinguished Flying Cross with eight Oak Leaf Clusters, Bronze Star with combat V and one Oak Leaf Cluster, Purple Heart with three Oak Leaf Clusters, Meritorious Service Medal, and the Air Medal with thirty-nine Oak Leaf Clusters for his service in Southeast Asia. After returning from Thailand in 1973, he held various command, administrative, and educational positions before retiring as a colonel in 1979.

Jim Harding was never formally presented his Air Force Cross. When scheduled to receive his medal, Harding used the time instead to plead to the general making the presentation for the continuation of the A-1 Skyraider in active service. Forty years later, former president George W. Bush did the honors for the retired Air Force colonel, who, by some measures, is among the twenty most-decorated men in American military history.—*J. Harding*

CAPTAIN STEVE RITCHIE would receive the Air Force Cross after shooting down his fifth MiG fighter on August 28, 1972, making him the U.S. Air Force's only pilot ace of the Vietnam war. Ritchie's weapons systems officer (WSO) CAPT. CHARLES DEBELLEVUE would receive his Air Force Cross after being credited for his fifth and sixth MiG kills on September 9, 1972. In 1974 Ritchie would leave the Air Force to pursue a career in politics and business. He would remain in the Air Force Reserves retiring in 1999 as a brigadier general following thirty-five years of service. DeBellevue would go on to become a pilot, and over a thirty-year career he would hold various staff and command positions before retiring as a colonel in 1999.

CAPTAIN BENNIE ORRELL, the pilot of JG 56, received the Air Force Cross for the rescue of Major Clyde Smith (Bengal 505A) on April 13, 1972. In addition to receiving the Air Force Cross, he also was awarded the Silver Star, the Distinguished Flying Cross with one Oak Leaf Cluster, the Bronze Star, the Meritorious Service Medal with three Oak Leaf Clusters, the Air Medal with nine Oak Leaf Clusters while serving in Southeast Asia. Orrell saw combat serving with the U.S. Air Force's Special Operation Command in Panama during Operation Just Cause, and in Iraq, Kuwait and Saudi Arabia during Desert Storm. In 1998 Bennie Orrell retired as a colonel while serving as the United States Special Operations Command Chairman for the National War College.

LIEUTENANT RUFUS HUTCHINSON received both the Silver Star and the Distinguished Flying Cross while serving with the 40th ARRS. After returning from Southeast Asia he received additional pilot training in both jet and propeller-driven fixed-wing aircraft. He spent a year at Air Training Command Headquarters before being assigned to the Pentagon in 1981 where he worked in the Air Force's Command Operations Center for the next four years. Hutchinson attended the Armed Forces Staff College and later assumed command of the Air Force's Undergraduate Training Program located at Fort Rucker, AL. He retired as a lieutenant colonel in 1991 and later became a captain for United Airlines flying the A320 and A319 Airbus. He retired from United Airlines in 2004.

STAFF SERGEANT CHARLES D. "CHUCK" MORROW, during a five-year span between 1967 and 1972, would serve fifty months in Southeast Asia. During this time he would be awarded three Silver Stars and five Distinguished Flying Crosses for his participation in combat rescues. He would end his career in the Air Force as a master sergeant in 1987. Morrow and McGrath have had an enduring friendship and remain close forty years after their service together in the 40th ARRS. Morrow is the cofounder of the pararescue tradition of getting tattoos of green footprints on one's buttocks.

PJ Chuck Morrow presents Bob Hope with a pair of green combat boots as a souvenir from the 40th ARRS during a USO show at NKP. Morrow served a remarkable fifty months as a PJ in Southeast Asia and is permanently entrenched in pararescue lore for being the cofounder of the tradition of PJs getting a pair of green (Jolly Green) footprints tattooed on their buttocks.—*C. Morrow*

Lynn Aikman and his wife Sandy, a former Air Force nurse, in 2011. The couple met between Aikman's tours in Southeast Asia and had just had their first child when Aikman returned to Southeast Asia. —*L. Aikman*

CAPTAIN LYNN AIKMAN would spend a year in the hospital recovering from his injuries. After additional rehabilitation, Aikman was able to pass a flight physical and returned to flying the F-106. He served in various staff and administrative positions before retiring as a colonel in the mid-1990s. Aikman and McGrath formed a bond during their time while under fire at the bottom of that ravine on the North Vietnam-Laos border. Over the years, they have remained in contact with each other, meeting when time and circumstance allows. They exchange Christmas cards every year. "Chuck McGrath is my friend, I owe him a debt I will never be able to repay," says Aikman.

CAPTAIN ROBERT CRAIG MILLER made a brief stay at the NKP dispensary. The severe bruising he sustained due to the self-inflating one-man dingy on his bailout would cause him to be hospitalized. He eventually returns to the 4th TFS and would serve a total of twenty-two years in the Air Force. In retirement, he worked another twenty years for a military contractor and participated in the program that saw phased-out F-4 Phantoms converted to drones for target use.

TOM HANTON, RICK MCDOW, and TONY MARSHALL, the backseaters (aka Guys In Back), on Valent 04, Valent 03 and Laredo 12, respectively, on June 27, 1972, would all meet as POWs at the Hanoi Hilton in the summer of 1972 (Marshall having been shot down and captured on July 3). McDow, an Alabama native, and Marshall, an African American, would conspire to disturb their captors anyway they could. "We'd get into some kind of discussion or debate, and tell them we were having a race riot," Marshall recalls with a laugh. Hanton also had several methods of getting under the skin of the North Vietnamese. Smacking a mosquito against his cell wall one day, the smeared line gave him inspiration. He proceeded to "paint" an American flag on his wall using nothing but the pulverized remains of mosquitoes. When the guards discovered what he was doing, they whitewashed the wall. And Hanton started again the next day. "There were plenty of mosquitoes," he says.

In late March 1973, all three WSOs were repatriated and all continued their Air Force careers. Partly in recognition of their service as POWs, all received assignments to flight school and eventually moved from the backseat to the frontseat, becoming pilots.

Thomas Hanton retired as a lieutenant colonel in 1992 having participated in Operation Desert Storm and flying missions in AWACS and the EC-130H.

Rick McDow would eventually serve as a squadron commander and wing commander during the late-1980s and early-1990s. He would fly 42 combat missions in 1992 as part of Operation Desert Storm. He retired

F-4 Phantom WSOs Tony Marshall (left) and Tom Hanton (right) join with Marty Cavato (center) at a 2005 "River Rats" reunion in Washington D.C. One week after Hanton and Valent 03B Rick McDow were captured as POWs, Marshall was captured as well. The three eventually met up in North Vietnam's infamous Hanoi Hilton prison camp.—*T. Marshall*

from the Air Force in 1994 as a colonel. After his repatriation, Tony Marshall went to flight school and continued to the fly the F-4. He retired in 1990 as a lieutenant colonel.

In the late 1990s Tom Hanton attended a reunion of "River Rats"—airmen who during the Vietnam war had crossed the Red River, which runs just south of Hanoi. He spoke with a former F-4 pilot, now flying commercial jets. The two have never met but the new acquaintance is certain he recognizes Hanton's name. After going over assignments, recognition suddenly dawns on the man's face, "June 27, 1972," he says. Hanton is amazed but dumbfounded. The former F-4 pilot fills in the gap. "I'm MARTY CAVATO, I saw you get shot down."

STAFF SERGEANT RICK SIMMON would return to the United States in February 1973 after serving with the 40th ARRS for a year. During his time with the squadron Simmon received both the Silver Star and the Distinguished Flying Cross for rescue operations he participated in. Simmon would remain a flight engineer serving in both rescue and special operations squadrons for his entire career. He would serve with Air Force special operations forces in both Panama and in Operation Desert Storm. Simmon retired from the Air Force in 1992 but continued to fly as a flight engineer in special operations MH-53s as a government contractor for the next seventeen years. He would be the flight engineer for the very last flight of an H-53 airframe from Hurlburt Field to Hill Air Force Base on September 18, 2008. Simmon retired shortly after this last flight.

For LT. RANDY SCOTT (LIEUTENANT AMERICA) the A-1 pilot and second on-scene commander (OSC) for the rescue of Valent 04A on June, 27, 1972, this would be a defining point in his life. He had been awaiting the arrival from the States of his fiancée Carol on June 28, and together they would spend his leave in Thailand. Upon landing at NKP from this mission, he was informed that she had called from Bangkok looking for him. The squadron duty officer told her that Scott was out on a mission, and they did not know when he would return. He had gotten the dates mixed up and she was in Bangkok frantic with concern. The next day he took a C-130 to meet up with her in Bangkok. After talking things over, the couple made a call to the U.S. Embassy, scheduled a return flight on Thai Airways to NKP, and two days later were married in NKP's base chapel. In their honor his squadron mates flew a four Skyraider flyby over the chapel after the wedding ceremony. Randy Scott would remain in Air Force flying both the A-7 Corsair II and F-16 Viper. He retired in 1990 as a lieutenant colonel commanding an F-16 squadron. Later he would be a captain for Delta Airlines and after his retirement from the airlines was a corporate jet pilot.

Like the other participants in the June 27, 1972, mission, JOLLY GREEN 57 would continue on with a long and highly decorated military career. Following Southeast Asia, JG 57 continued to serve in the Pacific for ten years, with stops in Hawaii, Okinawa and California. In 1975, the Air Force revisited a night-vision system, code-named Pave Low, for the H-53 airframe. This improved version of devices that had originally been tested during the Vietnam war proved effective. Gradually, the H-53s were modified with this new capability and its successors that featured additional electronics. The HH-53 designation was replaced with MH-53 to identify these new birds that would primarily serve in a special operations capacity.

In 1987, JG 57 went through the transition from a Super Jolly Green Giant to a Pave Low. As such, for the next twenty-one years it served in various corners of the globe. Among the H-53s and their four decades of service, it is believed that thirteen times they participated in missions that resulted in the award of the Air Force Cross. Amazingly, JG-57 was involved in three of those awards. At the time of its retirement in 2008, it was believed that all other Air Force Cross H-53s had been lost in combat. In early spring 2008, JG 57, having flown its final mission, was inducted into the National Museum of the Air Force at Wright-Patterson AFB in Ohio. There it remains on display as fitting tribute to the remarkable airframe and even more remarkable crews that served on it.

Today, Jolly Green 57 resides at the National Museum of the Air Force in Dayton, Ohio. The H-53 airframe had a remarkable forty-year service record. It is believed that thirteen times an H-53 participated in a mission resulting in the award of an Air Force Cross. JG-57 (68-10357) flew on three of those occasions and is believed to be the only surviving Air Force Cross H-53.
—Joel Happeny via National Museum of Air Force

ACKNOWLEDGMENTS

Foremost, recognition must be paid to the men and woman (Candy McGrath) who comprise the heart of this story. We thank them for entrusting us with this piece of their lives and hope that we have treated their recollections with the respect and sincerity they deserve.

Much of the source material for this project has come from audio and video interviews collected over the past three decades. We are greatly indebted to the generous and continual input of the following people: Chuck and Candy McGrath, Lynn Aikman, Dale Stovall, Rufus Hutchinson, Jim Harding, Chuck Morrow, Leo Thacker, Frank Mason, Rick Simmon, Tom Hanton, Rick McDow, Robert Craig Miller, Ben Orrell, Clyde Bennett, J. D. Adams, Tony Marshall, Marty Cavato, Steve Ritchie, Jim Roper, Randy Scott and Byron Hukee.

In addition to these first person accounts, numerous other materials were used in researching the background of June 27, 1972. However, there are some sources that standout as exceptional references, and we note them for those seeking further research. These include Robert LaPointe's *PJs in Nam* Web site (www.pjsinnam.com), which features a comprehensive and unmatched database of SARs in Southeast Asia; Jim Roper's *Quoth the Raven* is an excellent account of Air America Raven FACs flying missions in Laos; Darrel Whitcomb's *The Rescue of Bat 21* remains the definitive account of this controversial SAR at the start of the Easter Offensive; Chris Hobson's *Vietnam Air Losses* is a thorough compendium of U.S. air losses during fighting in Southeast Asia; and Marshall Michel's *Clashes: Air Com-*

bat over North Vietnam, 1965–1972 provides excellent technical insight into Air Force and Navy aerial tactics during the war.

We have endeavored to produce an unembellished narrative of the rescue of Valent 04 Alpha, Captain Lynn Aikman. This rescue represents a remarkable confluence of people and events. As genuine as the recollection of participants may be, each has a distinct perspective, and, as each readily acknowledges, that perspective often was framed by the moments of war. Further, as authors we also accept that to properly convey the events of June 27, 1972, requires a broad context that encompasses not only several other search and rescue missions in Southeast Asia but also the Vietnam War as a whole. We recognize that this specific story, for the most part, has never been told and that even its wider context is something incongruous with the popular representations of the war in American culture. To this end, we have deliberately chosen to write this story for a general audience, opting away from certain military conventions, such as the format of dates.

The authors recognize the personal support of their families in developing this project. Kevin in particular thanks his wife Helen, for her love, patience and unwavering support during this endeavor. The late Donald E. Baruch, the Special Assistant to the Assistant Secretary of Defense for Public Affairs for his early efforts in mentoring me during the very beginning of this project. Also Lt. Col. Paula Kearns of the U.S. Air Force's Public Affairs Office for her guidance and support of this effort. Don Fertman and Sergei Sikorsky of Sikorsky Aircraft for their historical insights. From my undergraduate days at Framingham State University, Jeff Baker and Walter Koroski, two of my instructors for their patience and advise. Staff members Terry Thomas, Mary Salvi, Barbara Bloom who were always willing to help during my research. During my time as a graduate student and professional staff member at the University of Massachusetts Boston, Maria Scoppettuolo, along with my colleague and friend Alan Girelli for their counsel.

Joe recognizes the love and understanding of his wife Courtney, his extended family and numerous friends. While he can never repay their generosity and support over the years, he hopes they recognize that without them he could never have played a role in telling this story. He also expresses his gratitude to his long-since-passed parents, who instilled in him an appreciation for our country, integrity, compassion, and the written word, all of which have been integral to this project.

The authors acknowledge the patience of their business partner William Fleming who allowed his project to take a backseat to *Taking Fire.* We also thank Gail Wurst, for recognizing and marketing the value of this story even when it was in an incomplete form, and Richard Kane of Casemate Publishing for taking a chance on a pair of unknown authors.

For all that must be recognized in the production of this book, it should not be overlooked that this is an incomplete story. At any moment of any day, there is some young man or woman standing in the line of a bullet or a bomb in the name of the United States of America. They are the latest in a litany of men and women that includes the members of Valent flight and those that came to rescue them. The events and heroism of June 27, 1972, remain relevant today for as long as men and women willfully accept the charge of serving in the name of our country.

GLOSSARY

1ST SOS—The 1st Special Operations Squadron was based at Nakhon Phanom RTAFB and was charged with two main missions: interdiction along the Ho Chi Minh Trail and cover for search and rescue operations.

366TH TFW—The 366th Tactical Fighter Wing was the first American wing to be stationed in Vietnam (at Da Nang) and the last to leave the country on June 25, 1972. The 366th adopted the nickname "Gunfighters" after its pilots adopted a gun pod mounted on its F-4Ds.

390TH TFS—A squadron of the 366th TFW. When the wing moved from Da Nang to Takhli RTAFB in June of 1972, the 390th Tactical Fighter Squadron was shut down and its remaining members were rolled in 4th TFS.

4TH TFS—The 4th Tactical Fighter Squadron was home to the members of Valent Flight on June 27, 1972, its first mission from Takhli, RTAFB. It flew the F-4E configured for escort and close-air-support missions.

40TH ARRS—The 40th Air Rescue and Recovery Squadron relocated from Udorn RTAFB to Nakhon Phanom RTAFB in July 1971. Its mission was the rescue and recovery of U.S. personnel and other assets, such as unmanned drones, in Southeast Asia. To accomplish this mission, the 40th relied on its officer pilots and copilots and enlisted crew of flight engineers and highly trained pararescuemen.

555TH TFS—The "Triple Nickel" was based at Udorn RTAFB in June

1972. Throughout the fighting in Southeast Asia, the 555th Tactical Fighter Squadron developed a reputation as MiG Killers, producing two of the Air Force's three aces during the Vietnam Conflict, WSO Charles DeBellevue (six confirmed kills) and pilot Steve Ritchie (five confirmed kills).

AAA—Antiaircraft artillery (also referred to as Triple A). AAA encompasses a broad range of weapons for defense against aerial assaults. Throughout Southeast Asia much of the AAA was comprised of either 57mm or 37mm guns that were part of a very sophisticated air defense network that used modern Soviet technology to improve targeting. Generally, Triple A's effectiveness greatly diminished above 10,000 feet.

A-1—The Douglas A-1 Skyraider was developed toward the end of World War II and saw considerable use during the Korean and Vietnam wars. This propeller-driven attack aircraft featured a large radial engine, fifteen ordnance stations, and a reinforced fuselage around the cockpit. The A-1 developed a reputation for being able to hit back hard even in the midst of fire. The A-1 experienced many iterations. By June 1972 the A-1H was the craft used by the 1st Special Operations Squadron for its interdiction against the Ho Chi Minh Trail and its other main assignment, close air support for search and rescue. In this latter capacity, the 1st SOS flew under the consistent call sign of Sandy, with the term becoming synonymous for describing the hard-hitting aircraft.

ACE—Just as aerial combat has varied with different armed conflicts, the definition of ace has varied, too. However, typically it is recognized as an aviator with five or more confirmed kills and this was the standard applied during the Vietnam Conflict. Weapons systems officers in F-4 Phantoms also received credit for kills and could become aces.

AIR AMERICA—Air America was the name of a passenger and cargo airline covertly operated by the CIA during the fighting in Southeast Asia.

AK-47—Developed in 1947, in the Soviet Union, by Mikhail Kalashnikov, the Avtomat Kalashnikova 47 was a selective fire automatic rifle that could be produced cheaply and quickly. Its design helped the AK-47 develop a reputation for reliability and ease of use and it became dominant assault rifle used by the North Vietnamese military and the Viet Cong rebels looking to overthrow South Vietnam.

ATOLL MISSILE—The Atoll was the Soviet version of an air-to-air heat-seeking missile used by the North Vietnamese Air Force during the Vietnam Conflict.

BAT-21—Bat-21 was the call sign of an EB-66C that was shot down by a surface to air missile in April of 1972. The search and rescue operation for the lone survivor, fifty-three-year-old navigator Iceal "Gene" Hambleton became a massive and costly operation.

BULLSEYE—The nickname given to Hanoi by American aviators.

BENGAL 505—Bengal 505 Alpha was the call sign of Marine Aviator Clyde Smith who was shot down in April 1972 near the Ho Chi Minh Trail. With the rescue effort occurring during North Vietnam's Easter Offensive, Smith's location was surrounded by the well-armed enemy soldiers. Over four days, with intense planning and a well-coordinated aerial attack, 40th ARRS pilot Ben Orrell managed to make the pickup, assisted by the orchestration and aerial marksmanship of A-1 pilot Major Jim Harding.

BOMBING HALT—While the fighting in Southeast Asia featured several halts to the bombing of the North, the most significant of which was the three-and-a-half year hiatus that president Lyndon Johnson ordered on the eve of the 1968 elections in November. Johnson, who had withdrawn from the race, explained the halt by citing progress in peace talks. By late March 1972, however, the North launched a massive offensive.

CAP—Combat air patrol was the term assigned to a broad range of fighter aircraft supporting some other flight. A MiGCAP would be designed to guard against an attacking group of North Vietnamese MiGs. RESCAP would protect rescue forces and the area around a survivor. BARCAP would protect the "barrier" air space between an attacking force and hostile territory.

COIN FLIP—The standard means by which pararescuemen would determine their positions on missions.

COMBAT TREE—Combat Tree was the code name assigned to secret U.S. technology that could identify enemy aircraft by their IFF (identification friend of foe) transponders.

DA NANG—Located almost on the 16th Parallel, Da Nang became the major military base in South Vietnam. Known as "Rocket City" due to the North's frequent attacks on the base, Da Nang was also home to the 366th Tactical Fighter Wing, the first American fighter wing to take up residence in Vietnam. In June 1972 the 366th left Da Nang and relocated to Takhli RTAFB in Thailand.

DMZ (DEMILITARIZED ZONE)—the DMZ was the ten km wide buffer between North and South Vietnam. On March 30 1972, about 30 thousand North Vietnamese troops began to the roll through the DMZ. By most estimates, more than 100 thousand of the enemy would eventually take part in this Easter Offensive.

EASTER OFFENSIVE—On March 30, 1972, North Vietnam launched a massive offensive. While the attack was predicted due to the forthcoming monsoon season, which would hamper an American aerial response, its size caught the United States and South Vietnam by surprise. The U.S. had steadily withdrawn its presence in Vietnam.

ELF (ELECTRONIC LOCATION FINDER)—By the spring of 1972, HH-53C rescue helicopters had an additional Electronic Location Finder package that could assist pilot's in trying to home in on a survivor's location based on his radio signal.

FAC—A Forward Air Controller was a sort of scout aircraft that would identify targets for other aircraft or ground troops and search locations for downed pilots.

FASTFAC—In the mid-1960s, with armaments of North Vietnam and its neighbors, Laos, and Cambodia, becoming more sophisticated thanks to Soviet and Chinese support, the U.S. Air Force introduced the idea of a jet serving as a FAC as opposed to the slower moving prop-driven airplanes.

FAST MOVERS—This was the umbrella term assigned to the jet aircraft used in Southeast Asia, typically F-4 Phantoms. In contrast, the slow movers were broad range of aircraft that included HH-53C helicopters, A-1 Skyraiders, HC-130 tankers, and KC-135 tankers.

FOREST PENETRATOR—a device attached to the hoist line designed to penetrate the heavy jungle canopy of Southeast Asia. The forest penetrator featured three foldable paddles. When unfolded, they formed seats on which a PJ or a survivor could sit. When folded up, the penetrator would resemble something more like a javelin, and could easily break through the canopy.

FRAG—Fragmentary order. Throughout the war, the standing mission of squadrons would be updated daily. These additional "fragmentary" orders detailed the specific assignment. Airmen often refer to their given assignments as the day's "frag" or use the term in an active sense, such as "we were fragged to. . . . "

HANOI—the industrialized capital of North Vietnam. The air defense system surrounding Hanoi is the most sophisticated ever tested by war, with advanced Soviet warning technology, missiles, antiaircraft artillery, and MiG jet fighters all connected via a sophisticated ground control system.

HANOI HILTON—The name given to the Han Loa prison by U.S. aviators held there as prisoners of war.

HAIPHONG—the critical harbor of North Vietnam, it was the country's major supply port during the war.

HC-130—These large prop-driven airplanes were used as refueling tankers by helicopter squadrons.

H-53—The Sikorsky H-53 airframe served the U.S. military for four decades. Of the seventy-two H-53s purchased by the military, the majority were HH-53Cs, Super Jolly Green Giants, used by search and rescue forces. The HH-53, as opposed to some of its other variants, featured a mid-air refueling probe, which permitted to fly extended missions.

HO CHI MINH—the charismatic communist leader who founded the Indochinese Communist Party. Following the creation of North and South Vietnam in 1954, Ho Chi Minh continued to be the political leader of the communist movement in Southeast Asia, which eventually led to open fighting through South Vietnam, Laos, and Cambodia as communist factions attempted to overthrow the governments in these countries.

HO CHI MINH TRAIL—A series of roads and paths that wound from North Vietnam, through Laos, and into Cambodia, to bring supplies to troops and rebels working in the South.

LINEBACKER—Beginning in May 1972 and in response to the North's Easter Offensive, Linebacker I looked to separate the North from its supply routes and infrastructure. In late 1972, Linebacker II commenced after another break down in peace talks. This final bombing campaign had few restrictions and brought the North Vietnam government back to the negotiating table.

NVA—The North Vietnamese Army, as it was known to Americans, is more properly titled the Peoples Army of Vietnam (PAVN). It operated in the northern part of the Republic of Vietnam during most of the war.

ROLLING THUNDER—Operation Rolling Thunder was the name given the U.S. systematic bombing of targets in North Vietnam from 1964 until the bombing halt in 1968.

SAR—Search and rescue: the category of mission to seek out and rescue fellow service men. By the spring of 1972, as the United States withdrew virtually all ground forces from Vietnam, typically the object of a SAR was an Air Force or Navy aviator.

SON TAY—A prison camp just outside of Hanoi that the United States raided in November of 1970. However, a few months before the raid, the North Vietnamese moved the POWs to another location. Still, Son Tay, which featured no casualties, was a major success as the U.S. forces successfully executed the mission, including the unexpected confrontation with a "secondary school" full of soldiers. Also, as POWs eventually discovered news of the raid, it buoyed their spirits and may have contributed to improvement in their treatment.

TOP GUN—The nickname assigned to the Navy's dogfighting school that the branch adopted during the bombing halt of the Vietnam Conflict.